# LIMITED WAR

and

American Defense Policy

# LIMITED WAR

and

# American Defense Policy

*Seymour J. Deitchman*

# THE M.I.T. PRESS

*Massachusetts Institute of Technology*
*Cambridge, Massachusetts*

*To John F. Kennedy,*

who created radical new directions in U.S. defense
policy with respect to limited war

# *Preface*

The limited-war idea expresses a philosophy of the use of military force. It involves an enormous scale of military activity, encompassing virtually the entire American defense structure.

One of the most controversial aspects of that structure is that of "roles and missions"—who is supposed to do what part of any total military task. Any number of serious arguments among the military Services, involving the Executive, the Congress, and the safety of the Nation, have revolved around this core problem. They have included the controversy in the 1940's over the relative merits of long-range bombers and aircraft carriers for strategic deterrence; the "Wilson Directive" limiting the size of Army aircraft; the argument over the use of the Army "Nike" versus the Navy "Talos" missiles for continental air defense; and, most recently, conflict over the proposals to increase substantially the number of aircraft in the Army. All of these conflicts have resulted from attempts of one Service to carry out a military task or use a weapons system to meet its responsibilities, which another claims as its own by right of prior assignment.

My purpose in this book is to clarify some problems of military function and systems, and the application of the systems to tactics and strategy. In short, I am concerned with the job to be done, how it gets done, but not with who does it. I have therefore ignored, to the extent that I could, the "roles and missions" questions, accepting the current Service assignments as satisfactory. Where they do intrude has been indicated, and the potential impact of the intrusion described.

I should like, here, to express my deep gratitude to all those who have, in one way or another, helped make this book possible. Many of them must remain anonymous; virtually every friend and acquaintance of my professional life have contributed in some way, through the continuous interplay of ideas and discussion, to the thoughts expressed here. A few have had a more direct connection with the book. It is a pleasure to thank Dr. Alfred Blumstein, Major General John Cary (Ret), Rear Admiral Robert E. Dixon (Ret), Dr. Jesse Orlansky, Professor Ithiel de Sola Pool, and Mr. Fred Wolcott for the time they spent in reviewing the manuscript and their many helpful suggestions toward improving it; Dr. Joseph E. Barmack for the many hours of discussion and the many ideas without which Part V, on the problems of unconventional warfare, would not have been complete; the library staff of the Institute for Defense Analyses, for their invaluable assistance in tracking down obscure and poorly described references; the management of the Institute, for making available many facilities that eased the task of completing the book; Miss Joyce Sundry, for the endless hours of typing and retyping; Mrs. Joan Culver for compiling the index; and, not least, my family, for getting by without a husband and father for significant periods of time that should have been theirs.

The choice of particular aspects of the limited-war subject area for discussion here was mine; it reflects my own experience and interests. The opinions expressed are mine. Some of these opinions will stir disagreement, for their subjects are controversial. Such a response is to be welcomed. The issues deal with national security; they need thorough, open, and objective discussion.

*I wrote this book while on the staff of the Institute for Defense Analyses. It was not, however, sponsored by the Institute, nor was the work on it performed under the Institute's Government contract. The opinions expressed and positions taken are not necessarily and should not be construed as opinions or policies officially held by the Institute or any branch of the United States Government.*

*Washington, D. C.*          SEYMOUR J. DEITCHMAN
*February 1964*

# Contents

*Preface*    vii

## INTRODUCTION
*The Problem We Face*    1

## PART I
### MILITARY MEANS FOR POLITICAL ENDS

*1*    *Twenty Years of Limited War: Theory and Practice*    13

*2*    *Something New: Unconventional Warfare as a Strategic Weapon*    32

*3*    *Nuclear Weapons, Limited War, and Europe*    43

*4*    *The Future: What Kinds of Limited War?*    53

## PART II
### THE MILITARY BACKGROUND

*5*    *The Forces Available*    67

*6*    *Where They Fight: The Environment*    79

*7*    *How They Fight: The Battlefield*    90

*8*    *The Logic of Multifarious Requirements*    103

## PART III
### THE PROBLEMS OF PLANNING

*9*    *The Planning Process*    111

*10*    *Resource Allocation: Levels of Decision and Constraint*    122

*11*    *The Impact of Technology*    132

# CONTENTS

## PART IV

### THE STRUCTURE OF THE REGULAR FORCES

*Introductory Note*    148

12  *Battlefield Ballistic Missiles*    151

13  *Battlefield Mobility: By Land or by Air?*    158

14  *Tactical Air Warfare: Some Critical Problems*    173

15  *Communications, Command, and Control*    184

16  *Getting There: Strategic Response*    192

## PART V

### UNCONVENTIONAL WARFARE—SOME SPECIAL PROBLEMS

*Introductory Note*    202

17  *Working with Allies*    203

18  *Force Ratios and Organization*    209

19  *Military Assistance and Specialization*    217

20  *The Human Problems of Unconventional War*    222

21  *Who's in Charge?*    230

22  *What About a Turnabout?*    236

23  *Legality and Morality*    242

## CONCLUSION

*Where Do We Stand?*    249

*Notes*    255

*Index*    267

# LIMITED WAR

and

American Defense Policy

# INTRODUCTION
## *The Problem We Face*

DESPITE the nuclear stalemate, the world continues to exist in an almost constant, nibbling state of war. Nuclear weapons have made the citizens of the greatest nations on earth hostage to each other. The leaders of these nations have proclaimed their belief that warfare can no longer be considered a rational tool for settling differences between them. Even so, it has not been discarded.

The United States has, since World War II, tried to use the threat of nuclear warfare to keep our Communist opponents from expanding, from initiating warfare even on a small scale. The Soviet Union has since turned this threat against us. And while both sides have found ways to apply military pressure, by threat, against each other they have also found themselves involved in wars between other, lesser nations. Communist Korea sought to expand by armed attack. The revolutions and civil wars of an earlier time have become "wars of national liberation," captured or instigated, and supported, by the Communists. The United States has become embroiled in these affairs, no longer local but part of a worldwide ideological struggle. Even outside this struggle, we have found small military actions necessary to prevent international violence on a larger, more dangerous scale. Smaller nations, not possessing the means of mass destruction, have gone to war to continue "political intercourse with a mixture of other means" — sometimes as a matter of survival, often not. We have been involved in these wars, in many different ways.

1

The threat of nuclear destruction has not made warfare obsolete,[1] or even reduced its frequency.[2]

For the United States, Korea demonstrated that it is still possible for a major nuclear power to use warfare on less than an all-out national scale, within bounded areas, with application of less than all the means available, to achieve objectives short of complete destruction of the other side. The concept of "limited war" in the nuclear age was born, painfully, and had to be accepted.

The realization of the scope and subtlety with which we would have to use our power in limited military actions has grown slowly. In the evolution of the limited war idea, such warfare was at first conceived as direct, small scale, and localized — the term "brush-fire war" gained currency.[3] It was imagined that a "limited war" could be fought with "fire brigades," as a sort of minor protective action. And yet this view was contradicted by the Korean War itself. It was a "limited war," but it was not a small war. It had a profound effect on our use of national resources and our international position. There were nearly a million casualties on the U.N. side alone, and the armed forces in action totaled about two million men. Other wars, long and hard-fought, also gave the lie to the "brush-fire" idea.

Although large and small wars all over the world influenced the future of the United States, we seemed at first to be aware only of Korea, as a horrible and unique example of limited war. The existence and impact of the others, and their interrelationships, came to the public consciousness much later. Only in retrospect, for example, have the Indonesian War of Independence, the first Arab-Israeli War, and the Greek war against Communist guerrillas, all of which took place before Korea, begun to fit into the pattern we perceive of warfare as a determining factor in the evolution of the world political scene.

The preparation of our military forces for actions short of a massive nuclear exchange has also developed slowly, trailing behind our growing understanding of the problem. The Korean war burst upon us within a few short years of our awakening to the worldwide Communist threat. Our military preparations to meet that threat had been made primarily in terms of intercontinental systems of strategic warfare and the creation of NATO to guard against possible Soviet invasion of Europe. The tactical forces with which we entered Korea were virtually all that could be spared from the reserves needed to defend Europe.[4]

The Korean war saw an increase of defense expenditure, which was never again to sink to prewar levels. But a profound distaste for limited war affected national security policy. Even while the theories of limited war burgeoned, and were espoused especially by the Army and the

2

Marine Corps, the popular revulsion against such war led to the strategy of "massive retaliation." Never again would we be bled by dirty little wars on the enemy's terms; we would, if he started one, punish him at the source.[5] Perhaps this policy worked as a deterrent against attacks similar to the Korean. There were, at any rate, no further Communist aggressions of this kind.

The Communist military advance continued, however, with many gains and few losses. While it was beaten back under favorable circumstances in Malaya and the Philippines, it advanced and succeeded in North Vietnam; it threatened all of Southeast Asia through Laos; it erupted in South Vietnam; it captured the Cuban revolution and threatened Latin America. At the same time, it became obvious in Lebanon and the Taiwan Straits, that, while "massive retaliation" might be the enunciated policy, limited political objectives would require limited application of military force.

But the design of the military forces proceeded largely in the direction of the *stated* objectives for their use. The atomic retaliatory forces absorbed increasing shares of the military budget, while the Army and its supporting branches of the Air Force were relegated to the role of "brush-fire brigades." Much of the development emphasis for new Army weapons was placed on such items as the NIKE ZEUS antimissile missile and the PERSHING nuclear missile for battlefield use. The emphasis looked towards the Soviet-European threat, to the virtual exclusion of possible wars elsewhere. The problem of Communist subversive warfare was largely ignored. While military assistance to the underdeveloped nations continued, it was for the most part devoted to the construction of regular forces designed to resist external aggression.

Awareness of the problems of limited war was, however, growing. Opposition to the course of evolution of our own military establishment was spurred by such events as the retirement of General Maxwell Taylor from his position as Army Chief of Staff, and his protests, in *The Uncertain Trumpet*,[6] against the continuing reduction of the nonnuclear tactical forces. The Draper Committee[7] showed, in its 1959 report, the need for modifications in the military assistance program to meet the problems of limited war as they existed. The problem of subversive war was recognized, if weakly:

. . . the shift in emphasis of the Communist tactics — for the time being at least — from direct military challenges to subversion, propaganda and economic offenses, should . . . be materially credited to the collective security strategy given substance by our Military Assistance Program.[8]

Military and political writing on the problems of limited war continued.[9]
The complete renewal of leadership in the areas of foreign and

defense policy that came with the Kennedy Administration in 1961 brought with it a marked increase of attention to these problems at the highest levels of government. As a result of the continuing ferment in the military-intellectual and foreign policy communities, and of continued violence on the world scene, understanding of the problem matured and entered the realm of practical government.

In his first State of the Union address, President Kennedy declared:

> . . . *we must strengthen our military tools*. . . . In the past, lack of consistent, coherent military strategy . . . [has] made it difficult to assess accurately how adequate — or inadequate — our defenses really are. I have, therefore, instructed the Secretary of Defense to reappraise our entire defense strategy . . .[10]

Later, in a special message to Congress on May 25, 1961, dealing with urgent national needs, the meaning of this reassessment for the limited war forces was spelled out in a general way:

> . . . I have directed a further reinforcement of our own capacity to deter or resist non-nuclear aggression. In the conventional field, with one exception, I find no present need for large new levies of men. What is needed is rather a change of position to give us still further increases in flexibility.
>
> Therefore, I am directing the Secretary of Defense to undertake a reorganization and modernization of the Army's divisional structure, to increase its non-nuclear firepower, to improve its tactical mobility in any environment, to insure its flexibility to meet any direct or indirect threat, to facilitate its coordination with our major allies, and to provide more modern mechanized divisions in Europe and bring their equipment up to date, and new airborne brigades in both the Pacific and Europe.
>
> And secondly, I am asking the Congress for an additional $100 million to begin the procurement task necessary to re-equip this new Army structure with the most modern material. New helicopters, new armored personnel carriers, and new howitzers, for example, must be obtained now.
>
> Third, I am directing the Secretary of Defense to expand rapidly and substantially, in cooperation with our Allies, the orientation of existing forces for the conduct of non-nuclear war, para-military operations and sub-limited or unconventional wars.
>
> In addition, our special forces and unconventional warfare units will be increased and reoriented. Throughout the services new emphasis must be placed on the special skills and languages which are required to work with local populations.
>
> Fourth, the Army is developing plans to make possible a much more rapid deployment of a major portion of its highly trained reserve forces. When these plans are completed and the reserve is strengthened, two combat-equipped divisions, plus their supporting forces, a total of 89,000 men, could be ready in an emergency for operations with but three weeks' notice —

two more divisions with but five weeks' notice — and six additional divisions and their supporting forces, making a total of ten divisions, could be deployable with less than eight weeks' notice. In short, these new plans will allow us to almost double the combat power of the Army in less than two months, compared to the nearly nine months heretofore required.

Fifth, to enhance the already formidable ability of the Marine Corps to respond to limited war emergencies, I am asking the Congress for $60 million to increase the Marine Corps' strength to 190,000 men. This will increase the initial impact and staying power of our three Marine divisions and three air wings, and provide a trained nucleus for further expansion, if necessary for self-defense.[11]

These steps, as outlined, seem straightforward enough. The implementation of the directives began with the Berlin Crisis of 1961, and it continues. But this implementation can, within the scope of the late President's words, take many forms. A modern military force has many components; among its hundreds of subsidiary units are distributed thousands of different pieces of equipment and many kinds of weapons systems. These determine how, and how well, the military forces will be able to "respond, with discrimination and speed, to any problem at any spot on the globe at any moment's notice."[12]

Since the limited-war forces had been allowed to shrink and the modernity of their components to deteriorate, the weapons and equipment of the newer, larger forces will, to a great extent, have to be new ones, in concept as well as manufacture. Many weapon developments were initiated but not fully incorporated in the armed forces during the lean years. They will call for changes in military organization and modes of operation to a degree not yet fully comprehended.

Furthermore, this revolution will take time. It takes years to develop, prove, and manufacture new military equipment — whether an improved rifle or a new kind of airplane. The men who use it have to be regrouped and trained in its use and in the new methods of warfare it makes possible.

We are, then, at a crossroads. Military policies of 10 and sometimes 20 years' standing are being turned over. A host of decisions, large and small, for a missile or the whole shape of an Army Division, is being or is about to be made. The decisions will affect for 10 or 20 additional years the structure and adequacy of our armed forces for limited war.

For two primary reasons the directions for these decisions are not obvious: there are many different kinds of limited war in which we may have to engage, each making its own demands on the military structure; and we are presented by modern technology with an enormous array of possible tools, from which must be selected those needed to help

5

solve our urgent military problems. These facets of the planning problem interact. If we had unlimited material and human resources, if we were willing to spend them, and if we knew what we wanted to do with them, then it would be a relatively simple matter to meet our needs. But resources are finite, and the defense budget has always reached a point of pain. We must therefore select from the many possible means to meet the most necessary ends, and compromise where importance decreases or cost becomes excessive.

The many kinds of limited war can be categorized roughly. Basically, there are three: war in the NATO context of Western Europe; "formal" war between organized military forces in the more remote or less developed parts of the world; and the internal wars of subversion which have loomed so large in current events.

The European and non-European wars can be differentiated by many factors, military and political, that affect force structure. In Europe:

- We face the full military power of our most formidable enemy.

- A substantial fraction of our forces is already in the area — they must and can be heavy and powerful.

- Forces, tactics, and strategy can be based upon many fixed defenses.

- Whether it occurs or not, the nuclear outbreak is imminent, so that the forces and their operating modes must never fail to be prepared for it.

- Most of our NATO allies are fully as capable as we in much of military technology and can develop and operate their own military systems.

- Any military action has severe political implications, both for relations between the opponents and within their own alliances.

Outside Europe:

- Fixed defenses will be relatively few, and American forces, when they are needed, probably must be deployed to the conflict area from afar.

- Speed of response to aggression is usually more telling than massive military power, requiring the deploying forces to be light and highly mobile.

- There is an enormous variety of geography, from hard, flat desert to impenetrable mountainous jungle, presenting military problems not easily encompassed *in toto* by forces of a single type.

- The nuclear problem recedes into the background, except in extraordinary circumstances.

- The United States almost wholly equips and trains its allies, for most of whom sophisticated military technology is new and alien.

- The political problems are vastly different from, and sometimes in conflict with, those we face in Europe.

Finally, the internal wars face us with a host of still different problems, because

- The United States finds itself in a supporting rather than an active military role in someone else's very intimate war.

- Even when the active war has begun, long-term political, social, and economic problems are far less easily separated from the immediate military pressures.

- There is no easily identified war zone and civilian or logistics rear area — war is everywhere.

We shall not, for the moment, try to identify any of these types of war as more likely or more important for our defense planning than others. Assuming that we must meet the threat where and as it exists, we must provide the military tools of policy implementation. Once we have set our objectives and developed the policies, our industrial machine and the military technology it gives us make it possible to undertake worldwide commitments with some hope of meeting them.

Here lie the seeds of many of our problems in building armed forces. Certainly, not all of the problems are technological; but today technology has become one of the dominant factors affecting defense planning.

If to prepare an Army and a Navy depended still on the acquisition of a few military items such as muskets, cannons, horses, wagons, and feed, and ships based on a centuries-old technology, the planning needs would be largely those of size and deployment of the armed forces. There would, of course, still exist the problems of training, organization, generalship, and political decision. The latter are still with us.

But even in the days when these were the main problems of raising and using armed forces, technology had an uncomfortable way of intruding. The advent of the musket, the rifle, the artillery shell, the steamship, all had an impact on military operations. These improvements came slowly, however, and there was time to digest them; those who did not ignored them at their peril. The pace increased after the Civil War, and has accelerated since World War II to the point where now a single generation of military officers may see several generations of equipment and tactics come and go.

As science has allowed us to reach to ever greater distances in ever shorter times with ever increasing destructive power, the tasks military forces can accomplish have multiplied and diversified. The scope of military actions now includes the ability to deliver total destruction to the other side of the world; the ability to apply, with great restraint and sensitive control by a central command, nondestructive military pressure in a small area at almost any point on earth; and an infinitude of steps in between.

If the diversity of the equipment and weapons systems permitting these actions is enormous, so, too, is their cost. Even the last few years have seen a tremendous growth in our military expenditures. The defense budget increased from about $10 billion in 1949[13] to $53 billion in 1964,[14] far exceeding the inflation of the dollar in that time. This growth occurred in part because of increases in force size, but also because of the increased cost of research, development, and procurement of the new or improved military equipment that the evolution of technology has continued to make available at an accelerating pace. To take a single example: a cargo aircraft might have cost $100,000 to purchase and $100 per flying hour to operate at the time of World War II; today, a much more modern and capable cargo aircraft can be expected to cost $3½ million or more, and its operating cost might exceed $1,000 per flying hour. Not only has the cost of achieving better-performing versions of the familiar weapons and equipment — artillery, ships, airplanes — increased, but scientific research and technology have given us new capabilities which we wish to incorporate into the military machine — which, in fact, the arms race demands that we acquire. The long-range, nuclear-tipped missile is one example; helicopters and vertical-takeoff aircraft, supersonic fighter aircraft, radars, and communications systems with which we can talk halfway around the world without interference by the enemy or weather are others.

As the cost of the defense establishment and its activities has grown, the strain on national resources has become great enough that we no longer believe we can afford to obtain all of the military capability that may appear desirable. Let it be accepted that we must give first priority to the strategic offensive and defensive units that most directly guard our survival — the long-range nuclear forces and the continental defense. As the defense budget is shaped today, we will, in doing so, have committed some 18 to 30 per cent of the military budget to this purpose.[15] About half of what is left must be allocated to the "General Purpose Forces" — those which would be used in limited war — and to the research and development that creates the most modern weapons and equipment for them.[16] The remainder provides for various kinds of support of the entire defense establishment. Yet all of the current military budget, and more, might be devoted to the General Purpose Forces alone if all the requests by various responsible sections of defense management were to be met.

It is necessary, therefore, to assign priorities for resource allocation among various military capabilities and the possible situations we want them to meet. But the choices among military systems are not simple or obvious. They can be made for a variety of reasons, not all associated with military strategy or international policy, or even with efficient management of the military-industrial complex. In making them, we choose, often implicitly, among various kinds of armed force that can be used for various purposes, and this has a direct impact on our ability to meet military commitments in support of foreign policy in various parts of the world.

From these interactions will be forged the military-political facts of our future national and international life. This is why, in this period of rebuilding our armed forces for limited war, we find ourselves at a crossroads. It is not easy to determine where we go from here.

Some of the alternatives available and their possible consequences will be the subject of this book.

PART I

MILITARY MEANS
FOR
POLITICAL ENDS

# 1

## Twenty Years of Limited War: Theory and Practice

### Limited War in Theory

WE have an intuitive understanding, given reality by the recent memory of World War II and the overbearing pressure of the massive nuclear threat, of the meaning of total war. The idea of limited war is much more elusive.

When one has boiled the essence out of the many existing definitions, he finds that they refer to almost any military action that does not threaten the *immediate* destruction of the United States and the NATO powers, on the one hand, and the Soviet Union (including its Eastern European empire) and Communist China, on the other. Limited war, as all war in the past, is but an extreme distortion of an infinitely variable economic, political, social, and ideological activity. Much of it has arisen from "the revolution of rising expectations" in the underdeveloped world; from the formation and conflicts of new centers of power, large and small, out of the old colonial empires; and from the thrust of Communism into this political maelstrom.

In the long run the issues for the major powers in any limited war center on their relative positions in the world political structure. Each of those powers therefore has a strong interest in encouraging an outcome favorable to itself and its own policies. Yet the immediate points of contention do not always warrant a response that would absolutely assure such success.

The ensuing process of accommodation can favor neither side abso-

13

lutely, nor one side all the time. Both the United States and the Soviet Union are capable of adding relatively infinite resources to support one party or another in a military confrontation. But if the conflict is to be kept within bounds, each must stop short of this degree of support. The limitations either is willing to impose or accept are, however, obvious to neither at the time of action, but must be assessed in terms of objectives, risk, and potential gain. The whole operates, always, in an atmosphere of uncertainty and only partial decision.

This has caused some difficult adjustments in our own policies. Acceptance of something less than "victory" in military conflict runs counter to all American military training and to the American view of its history and aspirations in the world. Since the issue is, ultimately, survival, the goal is clear while the obstacles to achieving it are but dimly perceived. The pressure to neglect these obstacles can therefore be great.

Nevertheless we have allowed constraint to govern our actions. Because of the enormous risk of all-out war between them, the major Western and Communist powers have consistently tried since Korea to avoid a direct clash. The dangers of Berlin in 1961 or Cuba in 1962 were not the imminence of thermonuclear war (since options for many minor military actions were open to both sides) but uncertainty regarding the ability of either to control events in an open military confrontation between the giants themselves.

Since the international contest between the two unavoidably involves and is involved in the interests and actions of many other nations, strong and weak, the major nuclear powers have been able to act in their own interests by indirection, through a framework of international responsibility and maneuver. Both sides have taken advantage of the existence of the United Nations to lend sanction to their policies, to control the level of conflict, and to save face through mediation and termination of military conflict when it no longer serves the purposes of either side. Both sides have also found their alliances useful as a shield against direct confrontation.

While these policies have had the positive advantages of safety and collective strength, they have also fostered inhibition and constraint. For the United States in particular, the implications of alliances and participation in the United Nations are those of responsibility. Since our own involvement in a limited war usually represents action in common interest with a third party, we can rarely act alone. The luxury of a surprise military strike to resolve an international problem swiftly and successfully, such as that of the Israelis in Sinai, would jeopardize all of our foreign policy unless a threat were clear, serious, and imminent.

14

In the philosophy of the free world, moreover, we cannot, except in those extraordinary circumstances, command others — we must somehow persuade or induce our allies to follow us. Thus we have found, that as a leader we can become virtually captives of our following.

The domestic uncertainty and conflict over limited war arise from this interplay of pressure and constraint. The political question becomes one of clarity of objectives; of knowing precisely what we want to achieve in each limited engagement; and of knowing how to use the results of each, good or bad, to prepare for the next.

The military forces are one of the tools of foreign policy. They must be fashioned to meet the objectives of that policy. Pursuit of certain objectives can affect profoundly the military force structure and the defense policies for building it. The issues concerning the use of nuclear weapons, the practice of subversive war, and the preparation for military conflict in one part of the world or another are of this kind. Underlying these issues is the need for certain qualities, which we shall explore in detail, that the military forces must have regardless of our objectives in using them.

The political theory of limited war can provide a certain amount of guidance for defense policy. For the rest, that policy must be forged by resolution of its own internal issues and conflicts.

## Limited War in Practice

Depending on what is judged to be military conflict, we can count over thirty military engagements that have taken place since the end of World War II. Some of them are still in progress. A number have been described in detail and documented copiously; others have been meagerly recorded; still others are known to us only from current newspaper accounts. All have something to teach us that can be useful in understanding the problems of preparing a military capability for limited war.

In Table 1.1 these military engagements are listed together with the years of their duration, the identity of the belligerents, and the numbers of men involved on each side.[1] Although lists of numbers can look very definite, the reader should not be misled by the force figures given. Information on force sizes is particularly difficult to come by, except for major wars that are carefully documented by historians. Furthermore, strengths vary during an engagement of any substantial duration. The numbers of troops listed here should properly be considered as rough estimates made at a single point in time rather than as valid statistical data. Nor is it always certain when a war or military encounter

## TABLE 1.1

### SOME ACTIVE OR INCIPIENT MILITARY ENGAGEMENTS SINCE WORLD WAR II

| Engagement | Date | Belligerents | Approximate Number of Men on Each Side |
|---|---|---|---|
| Indonesian Independence | 1945–1947 | Netherlands | 140,000 |
| | | Indonesian Rebels | 140,000 |
| Chinese Civil War* | 1945–1949 | Chinese Nationalists | 1,600,000 |
| | | Chinese Communists | 1,600,000 |
| Greek Civil War | 1946–1949 | Greek Government | 210,000 |
| | | ELAS Rebels | 25,000 |
| Kashmir Dispute | 1947–1949 | India | 97,000 |
| | | Pakistan | 56,000 |
| Arab-Israel War | 1948–1949 | Israel | 100,000 |
| | | Egypt, Syria, Jordan, Iraq, Lebanon | 100,000 |
| Philippine Civil War | 1948–1952 | Philippine Government | 25,000 |
| | | Hukbalahap Rebels | 5,000 |
| Indochinese War | 1945–1954 | French Colonial Government | 500,000 |
| | | Viet Minh Rebels | 300,000 |
| Malayan War | 1945–1954 | British Colonial Government | 175,000 |
| | | Communist Terrorists | 10,000 |
| Korean War | 1950–1953 | United Nations– Republic of Korea | 1,000,000 |
| | | North Korea/ Chinese Communists | 1,000,000 |
| Taiwan Interposition | 1950–Current | United States China | Uncertain |
| Kenya Terrorism | –1953 | British Colonial Government | 50,000 (?) |
| | | Mau Mau Terrorists | (?) |
| Sinai Campaign | 1956 | Israel | 45,000 |
| | | Egypt | 45,000 |
| Suez Intervention | 1956 | Britain/France | 100,000 |
| | | Egypt | 35,000 |
| Hungarian Rebellion | 1956 | Soviet Union | 40,000 (?) |
| | | Hungarian Rebels | 80,000 (?) |
| Quemoy/Matsu Bombardment | 1954–1958 | Chinese Nationalists | 200,000 |
| | | Chinese Communists | 200,000 |

* The Chinese Civil War is included here as a "limited war" with great reservation, mainly because it was listed as one by General Taylor. It was, however, only one phase of a vast struggle over a quarter of a century which included also the multisided actions of the Japanese invasion and World War II. Even the post-World War II phase of this war was characterized by maneuver of large armies over an area that, if it were not in Asia, would be virtually continental in extent. The sovereignty of a major world power was involved. If it was "limited," this was so from our own and the Soviet points of view only.

16

## TABLE 1.1 (*continued*)

| Engagement | Date | Belligerents | Approximate Number of Men on Each Side |
|---|---|---|---|
| Lebanon Landing | 1958 | United States/Lebanon<br>Lebanese Rebels | 18,000<br>11,000 |
| Tibetan Rebellion | 1959 | Chinese Communist<br>  Government<br>Tibetan Rebels | Uncertain |
| Cyprus Terrorism | 1955–1959 | British Colonial<br>  Government<br>EOKA Terrorists | Uncertain |
| Algerian Rebellion | 1956–1962 | French Government<br>FLN Rebels | 500,000<br>35,000 |
| Cuban Rebellion | 1958–1959 | Cuban Government<br>Castro Rebels | 43,000<br>7,000 |
| Laotian Civil War | 1959–1962 | Laotian Government<br>Pathet Lao | 80,000 (?)<br>20,000 (?) |
| Kuwait Intervention | 1961 | Great Britain<br>Iraq | (few hundred)<br>(?) |
| Occupation of Goa | 1961 | Portuguese Government<br>India | Uncertain |
| Yemen Civil War | 1962 | Royal Government Forces<br>Revolutionary Government<br>  Forces | Uncertain |
| U.N. Congo Pacification | 1960–1962 | Congo Government/<br>  United Nations<br>Rebelling troops/<br>  seceding states | 40,000<br><br>(?) |
| Cuban Invasion,<br>  Bay of Pigs | 1961 | Cuban Government<br>Refugee Force | 50,000 (?)<br>1,200 |
| South Vietnam Rebellion | 1959–Current | South Vietnam<br>  Government<br>Viet Cong Rebels | 200,000<br>25,000 |
| India/China Border War | 1959–1962 | India<br>Chinese Communists | Order of 50,000–<br>100,000 each |
| Angolan Rebellion | 1960–Current | Portuguese Government<br>Angolan Rebels | Uncertain |
| West New Guinea Invasion | 1962 | Netherlands Colonial<br>  Government<br>Indonesia | Less than<br>10,000 each |
| Colombia Rebellions | 1960(?)–Current | Colombian Government<br>Guerrillas | Uncertain |
| Cuban Quarantine | 1962 | Cuban Government/<br>  Soviet Union<br>United States | 10,000 Soviet<br>plus Cuban<br>armed forces<br>200,000 (?) |

begins or ends. The data given are included simply to give a rough idea of the magnitudes and durations of the military engagements listed.[2]

Table 1.2 summarizes, for each of these engagements, the major issues, extent of geographical area covered, and the outcome. In Table 1.3, the kind and extent of involvement by "nonbelligerent" powers is listed for each engagement, with special notes on limitations, other than the most obvious, which appear to have been in effect.

Despite the length of this list of limited wars, we should hasten to add that many military encounters or engagements have occurred since World War II that are not listed in the tables. These may have been internal revolts such as have occurred in Argentina, Guatemala, and the Dominican Republic, or such confrontations as occurred in October, 1961, beween American and Soviet tanks in Berlin. (The purpose of the latter was stated to be the elicitation of an admission by the Russians that they control East Berlin, rather than a threat of armed clash.)[3] It is a moot point whether these fall within the scope of any limited war definition. The criterion for inclusion here has been the possibility of drawing lessons for long-term planning purposes rather than completeness of the historical account. The engagements that have been included are sufficient in number to permit exploration of the nature of limited war as it influences the defense planning problem.

There appear from the tables to have been three major classes of military engagement; each one listed can, if somewhat arbitrarily in some instances, be put into one of them:

1. *Conventional wars:* organized, conventional military forces are overtly involved on both sides.
2. *Unconventional wars:* unconventional military forces, in the form of paramilitary, irregular, or guerrilla forces, are involved on one side, and conventional military forces as well as police and civil guards are used on the other side in the attempt to suppress or defeat the former.
3. *Deterred wars:* conventional or unconventional military forces face each other in a threat of war, but there is no active armed conflict between the two sides.

Table 1.4 shows how the wars listed fall into the three classes. We can see that the greatest number of these engagements fall in the second class. A few other facts of interest about these wars are emphasized by Table 1.5, which highlights some of their major characteristics. The Communists have attempted but four times to expand their suzerainty by conventional war. Far more often, they have taken the more subtle road of subversion and unconventional warfare. Three times they have

18

been on the defensive in this type of war: in Hungary, Tibet, and Cuba. The record shows that they have dealt with the threat expeditiously. Where they have been on the offensive this way, the wars have seldom been small or easy to win by either side. This has been true for the unconventional wars in which Communists were not involved, as well. Only two of the conventional wars have lasted over two years, while most of the unconventional wars have been of longer duration.

The "deterred wars" deserve some brief attention. They illustrate well the "lower end of the scale" of military action. They were, of course, really not wars at all, but military actions taken in anticipation of the outbreak of war, which appear to have deterred it. One of the main factors which operated for deterrence was the rapid buildup of a significant military force in the area where the threat existed. While these forces, in all but the Cuban Quarantine, were much smaller than those that would probably have had to be committed if active warfare had broken out, they were significant to the extent that they would, at the very least, have been able to act effectively in a delaying action pending the arrival of reinforcements. Thus their commitment constituted a clear promise to establish new, higher thresholds of force limitation (that is, to "escalate") if deterrence was unsuccessful.

The important factor in such deterrence is that the deterring forces must obviously be able to follow through with the threat of war. The Seventh Fleet and our tactical air forces on Taiwan were, and are, ready for action should an attack on Taiwan be made. The Sixth Fleet and alerted reserves backed up the Lebanon landing. British expeditionary forces were readied to augment the few hundred men in Kuwait. Sufficient strength was massed in Florida and the waters off Cuba to stage an invasion if necessary.

There have been arguments about the difference between strategic nuclear forces designed to deter war by holding cities hostage and those designed to "win" by destroying the enemy counterparts in a first or second strike. These distinctions do not act in limited war, unless we intend to threaten total war as an immediate consequence of failure in "showing the flag." Short of such an incredible and suicidal policy, there is no way to build a limited war force solely for displays of American presence. These displays are, rather, made by appropriate elements of the fighting forces. It is with their ability to fight that we shall have to be concerned.

As for the conventional limited wars of the last 20 years, they differ from those of prenuclear days only in the varying cast of characters

TABLE 1.2

LIMITED WARS: SCOPE, ISSUES AND RESOLUTIONS

| Engagement | Geographical | Major Issues | Resolution |
|---|---|---|---|
| Indonesian Independence | Netherlands East Indian Islands | Indonesian guerrilla war for independence from Dutch after World War II. | Independence granted. |
| Chinese Civil War* | All of China | Chinese Communist war to gain control of China from Nationalists; continuation of pre-World War II effort. | Communists defeated Nationalists and control mainland China. |
| Greek Civil War | Greece | Attempt of Greek Communists to seize government by guerrilla warfare after fighting Nazi occupation. | Communist guerrillas defeated after premature attempt to operate as organized field force. |
| Kashmir dispute | State of Kashmir | Control of Kashmir after partition and independence of British India. | U.N.-arranged cease-fire left divided control along cease-fire line. |
| Arab-Israel War | Palestine | Arab attempt to destroy State of Israel, created by United Nations, after British withdrawal. | U.N.-arranged armistice after Arab defeat left Israel with more territory than allotted in U.N. Palestine partition plan. |
| Philippine Civil War | Philippine Islands | Attempt of Communists to seize government by guerrilla war. | Communists were defeated when Magsaysay rallied people and used guerrillas' tactics against them. |
| Indochinese War | All of French Indochina | Post-World War II attempt of Communist anti-Japanese guerrillas to control Indochina, prevent French from re-establishing French-supported government. | French military defeat; agreement at Geneva in 1954 to divide Vietnam into Communist-controlled area north of 17th parallel, and independent South Vietnam, Laos, and Cambodia; Communist troop withdrawal into North Vietnam and guarantees of neutrality for remainder of area. |
| Malayan War | British Malayan Peninsula | Attempt of "Communist Terrorists" (guerrillas), largely Chinese, to seize control of British Malay States. | Communists defeated by British offensives combined with massive population shifts into protected villages; independence granted to Malaya. |
| Korean War | Korean Peninsula | U.S.-led U.N. forces entered to help ROK forces repel North Korean Invasion; later attempt to unify Korea frustrated by Chinese Communist intervention. | Armistice agreement leaving Korea divided roughly along 38th parallel, as before. |

| | | | |
|---|---|---|---|
| Taiwan Interposition | Taiwan Straits | U.S. 7th Fleet patrols to prevent either side from attacking the other. | Still in force (officially applied to Communists only, since 1953). |
| Kenya Terrorism | Kenya Colony | Kikuyu tribe terrorism to drive white settlers off desirable farm land and out of Kenya. | Uprising suppressed and leaders jailed. |
| Sinai Campaign | Sinai Peninsula of Egypt | Israeli preemptive strike in response to Arab raids, threats, and arming. | Virtual destruction of Egyptian armed forces, destruction of raiding bases, opening of Aqaba Gulf to Israeli shipping, interposition of U.N. police force on Gaza border following Israeli withdrawal. |
| Suez Intervention | Suez Canal Zone | British-French attempt to reoccupy Canal Zone to protect it and prevent other Arab countries from entering war between Egypt and Israel. | British-French withdrawal in response to U.N., U.S. and U.S.S.R. pressure, after bombardment of Egyptian airfields and occupation of Port Said; canal blocked by Egyptians for six months. |
| Hungarian Rebellion | Area around Budapest | Hungarian attempt to drive out Russian occupation, greatly dilute Communist rule by establishing more liberal government. | Suppressed by Red Army; stronger Communist government installed. |
| Quemoy/Matsu Bombardment | Quemoy & Matsu | Chinese Communist attempt to harass and dislodge reinforced Nationalist garrisons by heavy artillery bombardment. | Gradual lifting of bombardment when Nationalists, supported by United States, stood fast. |
| Lebanon Landing | Beirut Area | American landing of Marine and airborne troops on request of Government of Lebanon, after rebellion when Christian President Chamoun tried to succeed himself. | United States withdrew after peaceful change of government led to Mohammedan president acceptable to both sides. |
| Tibetan Rebellion | Southern Tibet | Lamaist rebellion against Chinese Communist attempt to integrate Tibet with China. | Rebellion suppressed, Dalai Lama and some followers fled to India; Tibet annexed to China. |
| Cyprus Terrorism | Cyprus | Attempt of Greek population to oust British rule and join Cyprus to Greece, over opposition of Britain, Turkey, and Turkish minority on Cyprus. | Island made independent after agreement for coalition government, guaranteed rights for Turkish minority, and retention of British military base on lease. |

21

TABLE 1.2 (*continued*)

LIMITED WARS: SCOPE, ISSUES AND RESOLUTIONS

| Engagement | Geographical | Major Issues | Resolution |
|---|---|---|---|
| Algerian Rebellion | Algeria | Attempts of Algerian Mohammedan leaders and guerrillas to gain independence for Algeria over opposition of France and French-Algerian population. | Independent Algeria with guarantees for rights of European population and economic ties with France; almost destroyed by terroristic Secret Army Organization and later struggle for power among Algerian leaders. |
| Cuban Rebellion | Cuba | Guerrilla war by Castro followers against Batista dictatorship. | Batista government deposed when rebels attacked in open; followed by expropriation, breaking of relations with United States, and declaration of Marxist state by Castro government. |
| Laotian Civil War | Laos | Reopening of Pathet Lao guerrilla attacks against government when the United States supported rightist government which deposed neutralist regime. | Pathet Lao given a role in coalition government including the three factions under neutralist premier; peace and neutrality underwritten by the United States and the Soviet Union at Geneva Conference; armed forces and three factions remain to be integrated. |
| Kuwait Intervention | Kuwait | British troops landed when Iraq threatened to annex Kuwait. | British withdrew when threat subsided. |
| Occupation of Goa | Goa and two other Portuguese enclaves in India | Indian occupation of colonies on its territory, at time of election and Chinese pressure on northern border. | Action successful, supported by Communists and Neutralists in the United Nations. |
| Yemen Civil War | Yemen | Army rebellion and assumption of government after death of old Imam, or ruler. | U.S. recognition of revolutionary regime as new Republic of Yemen. |

22

| | | | |
|---|---|---|---|
| U.N. Congo Pacification | Congo Republic | U.N. attempts to restore order after Belgian departure, on request of Congo government; assistance to that government in protecting mineral wealth in Katanga state by military pressure on secessionist government. | Disciplining of rebellious army; end of secessionist moves. |
| Cuban Invasion | Bay of Pigs, Cuba | Attempt of U.S.-trained refugee group to establish a beachhead in Cuba and ultimately overthrow Castro. | Attempt defeated by Castro forces; possible internal revolt suppressed by mass arrests; invaders captured. |
| South Vietnam Rebellion | South Vietnam | Guerrilla "War of Liberation" against South Vietnam government essentially a continuation of Indochina and Laos. | In progress. |
| India/China Border War | Eastern and Western Indian-Tibetan Borders | Chinese claim to 45,000 square miles of territory previously under Indian rule. | Sporadic skirmishing; brief Chinese attack overwhelmed Indian border forces and Chinese withdrew to original positions. |
| Angolan Rebellion | Portuguese Angola | African attempt to throw off Portuguese rule by guerrilla attacks. | In progress; dormant after Portuguese suppression. |
| West New Guinea Invasion | Few coastal settlement areas of West New Guinea, and surrounding seas | Attempt of Indonesia to annex Netherlands West New Guinea. | U.N. assumed control after U.S. mediation; Indonesia to take over, with referendum on independence to follow in some years. |
| Colombia Rebellions | Colombia hinterlands | Attacks against government by various guerrilla groups, some Castroist. | In progress. |
| Cuban Quarantine | Seas around and airspace over Cuba | U.S. partial blockade to force withdrawal and prevent new influx of Soviet offensive atomic weapons; included U.S. aerial reconnaissnace over Cuba. | Soviet withdrew weapons; attempts to establish on-site inspection by U.N. and obtain U.S. no-invasion pledge failed. |

* See footnote to Table 1.1.

## TABLE 1.3

### INVOLVEMENT OF "THIRD POWERS" IN LIMITED WARS

| Engagement | Involvement of "Nonbelligerents" | Special Notes on Limitation |
| --- | --- | --- |
| Indonesian Independence | U.S. pressure on Netherlands to grant independence. | |
| Chinese Civil War* | U.S. arms aid to Nationalists; U.S. attempts to form coalition government; U.S.S.R. support for Communists. | |
| Greek Civil War | Yugoslav and Bulgarian aid and refuge for Communist guerrillas, ended by closing of Yugoslav border after Tito broke with Stalin; U.S. arms aid and military advice for Greece under Truman Doctrine. | Soviet political support for guerrillas, but no overt arms or military support. |
| Kashmir Dispute Arab-Israel War | Good offices of United Nations to arrange cease-fire. U.N.-arranged armistice and Armistice Commission. | No combat or border attacks outside Kashmir. |
| Philippine Civil War Indochinese War | U.S. arms aid, military mission, and political support. Communist Chinese arms aid and training of Vietminh; Soviet participation in Geneva Conference; U.S. military assistance to French forces in Indochina. | The United States and Britain considered, and declined, active intervention at Dienbienphu. |
| Malayan War | Communist support and some arms aid for terrorists. | Treated by British as police action against "bandits"; Communists encouraged to surrender. |
| Korean War | Prior Soviet training of North Koreans and Chinese; Soviet arms aid to North Koreans and Chinese; India's good offices to aid in arranging truce and control of prisoner exchange; U.N. branding of Communist China as aggressor. | No attacks against supply lines outside Korea; no U.S. use of atomic weapons; no Communist air attacks against U.N. ground forces; no U.N. attacks against China; no U.S. use of Chinese Nationalist troops. |
| Taiwan Interposition | | Intended to prevent *both* Chinese forces from attacking across Formosa Straits. |
| Kenya Terrorism | | |
| Sinai Campaign | U.N. pressure for Israeli withdrawal after Egyptian defeat; British request that Israel not attack Jordan because of military alliance; U.N. border guards at Gaza strip. | No air action against enemy forces outside Sinai Peninsula; Israeli forces withdrew from Suez Canal on British/French request. |
| Suez Intervention | U.N. pressure for cease-fire, supported by United States and the Soviet Union; Soviet threat to use rockets if necessary against Britain, France; U.S. aid in subsequent clearing of canal. | Action limited to canal zone; air strikes against Egyptian airfields and canal block-ships only. |

24

|  | | |
|---|---|---|
| Hungarian Rebellion | Austrian and Yugoslav assistance to refugees, former aided by the United States; U.N. condemnation of the Soviet Union. | The United States took no action; misunderstanding abroad of "liberation" statements. |
| Quemoy/Matsu Bombardment | U.S. convoys of Chinese Nationalist supply ships to Islands; U.S. arming of Nationalist Air Force with Sidewinder missile; U.S. deployment of composite Air Strike Force to Taiwan. | Ambiguous warning by the United States that attempted invasion of Islands would lead to U.S. intervention; Chinese Communist bombardment on alternate days in measured use of force. |
| Lebanon Landing | Soviet protests, limited to political action. | No shots fired by the United States. |
| Tibetan Rebellion | Indian refuge for Dalai Lama and followers. | |
| Cyprus Terrorism | Greek inflammatory radio broadcasts; Turkish threats. | Minimum use of force by British against rioters and guerrillas. |
| Algerian Rebellion | Egyptian supplies and arms (originally Soviet) to rebels; Moroccan and Tunisian refuge for rebel guerrillas. | Violence increased and both sides used torture as they became desperate; Secret Army Organization resorted to uncontrolled terrorism in effort to stimulate Moslems to new attacks, but failed. |
| Cuban Rebellion | U.S. arms aid for Castro guerrillas reported; the United States immediately recognized Castro Government. | |
| Laotian Civil War | U.S. military assistance for Laotian Government; Soviet flew supplies, arms and North Vietnamese troops into Laos for Pathet Lao; North Vietnamese troops entered Laos clandestinely; the United States sent troops into Thailand when Pathet Lao attack on Nam Tha made border crossing appear imminent; Communist China attended Geneva Conference. | The United States threatened but did not send combat troops into area. |
| Kuwait Intervention | | No shots fired. |
| Occupation of Goa | Neutralist political support, Western condemnation in the United Nations. | |
| Yemen Civil War | The United Arab Republic sent troops into Yemen to support and assist revolutionary government; Saudi Arabia and Jordan gave refuge to deposed Imam, reportedly used troops in attempt to regain throne. | Action limited to territory of Yemen despite intervention of other Arab powers. |
| U.N. Congo Pacification | Neutralist contributions of troops to U.N. force; rumors of Soviet arms aid for leftists through Sudan; U.S. political support for central government, airlift of troops and materials for U.N. force; British and Belgian political support for Katanga. | U.N. action limited to protection of facilities and self-defense until military occupation of key points in Katanga after political and economic pressure to end secession failed. |

## TABLE 1.3 (continued)

### INVOLVEMENT OF "THIRD POWERS" IN LIMITED WARS

| Engagement | Involvement of "Nonbelligerents" | Special Notes on Limitation |
|---|---|---|
| Cuban Invasion, Bay of Pigs | The United States trained and supplied invasion force in various locations, probably Central America. | The United States declined use of air support by U.S. forces at critical moment in invasion. |
| South Vietnam Rebellion | North Vietnamese supplies and training for Viet Cong guerrillas; use of Laos as supply route for Viet Cong; U.S. military assistance, including materials, training, transport into combat for South Vietnamese troops, and participation in battles as military advisors; U.S. pressures for political reform of South Vietnam Government. | The United States states no combat formations have entered South Vietnam; all troops are logistics and support. |
| India/China Border War | The Soviet Union expressed support for "ally," China, despite "friendship" with India; the Soviet Union reported to have pressured China secretly to halt operations; the United States and Britain shipped arms to India after Chinese attack in October 1962; took advantage of situation to pressure India and Pakistan to settle Kashmir dispute; Pakistan announced Kashmir border agreement with China at critical time; small group of neutralist nations interceded to arrange terms. | Neither side used air attacks against troops or installations; Chinese halted Fall 1962 attack voluntarily after driving Indian troops from disputed border area. |
| Angolan Rebellion | Congo said to be the training and supply area for rebels. | |
| West New Guinea Invasion | The Soviet Union gave Indonesia armaments, including ships, submarines, aircraft and weapons, and encouraged territorial claims; the United States permitted, then denied, permission for Dutch airlift to refuel in the United States; the United States offered compromise plan for transfer of West New Guinea control temporarily to Indonesia via the United Nations. | |
| Colombia Rebellions | Suspicion of arms passing to guerrilla groups from Cuba. | |
| Cuban Quarantine | The United Nations provided vehicle for mediation of dispute. | No U.S. armed attacks; Soviets cooperated in close visual inspection of ships removing missiles and aircraft from Cuba; the United States carried out low-altitude aerial reconnaissance over Cuba unimpeded after warning that force would be used to protect aircraft from interference. |

* See footnote to Table 1.1.

26

## TABLE 1.4

CLASSIFICATION OF LIMITED WARS

| Conventional Wars | Unconventional Wars | Deterred Wars |
|---|---|---|
| Chinese Civil War | Indonesian Independence | Taiwan |
| Arab-Israel War | Greece | Lebanon |
| Kashmir Dispute | Philippines | Kuwait |
| Korea | Indochina | Cuban Quarantine |
| Sinai Campaign | Malaya | |
| Suez Intervention | Hungary | |
| Quemoy/Matsu | Tibet | |
| Congo | Kenya | |
| India/China Border | Cuban Revolution | |
| Goa | Algeria | |
| West New Guinea | Cyprus | |
| Yemen | Cuba: Bay of Pigs | |
| | Laos | |
| | South Vietnam | |
| | Angola | |
| | Colombia | |

and their setting in time. Most of them have been played out among the new nations establishing their places in the scheme of post-World War II international politics. It will be worth examining a few of them in some small detail, to illustrate the patterns of conventional limited war. The reader can flesh out these patterns more fully by examination of the tables.

The Arab-Israel War of 1947–1949 approached closely the deadly seriousness of total war. In the immediate area, the very survival of a state (newly formed as it was) was at issue. For the Arabs, too, there were questions of survival. Having archaic economic systems, they believed that this new state could, by its example of modernization, stimulate an internal threat to their existence as national entities.[4]

The war ended when the United Nations was able to negotiate armistice agreements between the two sides. The Israelis had achieved their objectives; they had established their state, and defeated the attempt of the Arabs to wipe it out. The Arabs were faced with accepting its existence. The stigma of defeat was one of the factors leading to the Egyptian revolution of army officers and the accession of Nasser to power. Later events, embroiling many of the major nations of East and West and keeping the Near East in continuing ferment, were to flow from this Egyptian revolution.

By 1956, the Israeli armed forces had grown into a large and effective fighting machine. The Egyptian armed forces had been regrouped and retrained with greatly augmented military equipment resulting from

27

TABLE 1.5

MAJOR CHARACTERISTICS OF LIMITED WARS

| | Major Wars (over 100,000 men on at least one side in combat area) | Free World— Communist Conflict Directly Involved | Wars Between "Third Powers" (not Bloc vs. U.S. and/or allies) | Number Lasting over Two Years |
|---|---|---|---|---|
| Conventional Wars | Chinese Civil War<br>Korean War | Chinese Civil War<br>Korean War<br>Quemoy/Matsu<br>India/China border | Arab-Israel War<br>Kashmir Dispute<br>Sinai Campaign<br>Suez Intervention<br>Congo<br>Goa<br>West New Guinea<br>Yemen | 2 |
| Unconventional Wars | Indonesian Independence<br>Greece<br>Indochina<br>Malaya<br>Algeria<br>South Vietnam* | Greece<br>Philippines<br>Malaya<br>Hungary<br>Tibet<br>Cuba: Bay of Pigs<br>Laos<br>South Vietnam*<br>Colombia* | Indonesian Independence<br>Kenya<br>Cuban Revolution<br>Algeria<br>Cyprus<br>Angola* | 13 |
| Deterred Wars | | Taiwan*<br>Cuban Quarantine | Lebanon<br>Kuwait | |

* Still in progress.

28

Egypt's arms agreements with the Soviet Union and Czechoslovakia. There had been a period of Arab paramilitary activity in Israel on the part of infiltrators (Egyptian *fedayeen* and Jordanian Arabs) who made attacks on border villages and towns at night and generally carried out acts of terrorism against the Israeli population. There had been a number of reprisal attacks against Arab villages by the Israelis.[5] The immediate threat to the Israelis appeared to them to be increasing in severity with the augmented armaments of the Egyptian Army, with broadcast promises to attack and destroy Israel, and with an agreement on the part of Egypt, Jordan, and Syria to establish a common military command. All of this led to Israel's attack on Egypt in 1956.

The Israeli campaign in the Sinai peninsula is probably a unique example, a "classic" model, of what we might imagine when the term "limited war" is used. Even from the point of view of the participants it was not (immediately) a war for survival; the objectives were limited and, as they emerged after the war, quite precisely defined. The war was planned by Israel in such a way that only the first objective (elimination of the *fedayeen* raids) was announced and obvious; the war could be halted or continued according to its success at various levels of achievement, and according to reaction by the Arabs and other nations.

Undoubtedly, ultimate and indirect benefits could be foreseen. If all of the immediate Israeli objectives were achieved, this could very well lead to the downfall of Nasser and the establishment of a government in Egypt that might be influenced to make peace and break the solid Arab front arrayed against Israel. Conversely, if the war led to an Israeli defeat and a successful Arab counterattack, the Arabs' objectives of the previous war — destruction of Israel — might have been within reach.

The sudden and very aggressive Israeli attack and the relatively poor training of the Egyptian forces resulted, within 5 days, in a total defeat for the Egyptians. The only one of the Israeli objectives not achieved was the opening of the Suez Canal to Israeli shipping. The Gulf of Aqaba was opened. The guarantee that it would be kept open, and also that a U.N. force would be interposed between Israel and Egypt along the Gaza strip to stop Egyptian raids into Israeli territory, were the conditions on which the Israeli forces withdrew from the Sinai peninsula. The Egyptian armed forces in the Sinai peninsula were humiliated and destroyed as effective fighting units. Many thousands of them were captured, and all of the equipment which the Egyptians had obtained from the Soviet bloc and had stored in the peninsula was taken by the Israelis.

Probably, the Israeli drive could have taken control of the Suez

Canal, since it reached the canal and was then withdrawn for 10 miles on request of the British and French. The stated reasons for the British-French intervention were the reoccupation and protection of the canal zone and the prevention of the Sinai War's spread.[6] Their attack was, however, quite different from that of the Israelis. They opened it in conventional style with an air bombardment to neutralize the Egyptian air force and other targets, while a seaborne attack was brought up from Malta, 6 days away.

The difference in timing and boldness of the military action is significant. The outside world hardly had time to react before the Israeli campaign was over. By the time the British landed at Port Said, however, 10 days had gone by. There had been time for the Egyptians to offer some resistance on the ground, and to block the Canal so effectively that it would take 6 months to clear it. The Soviets implied the threat of a rocket attack against England and France. Massive diplomatic pressure on the part of the United Nations, made potent by lack of American support for the British and French action, presented an insurmountable obstacle to the pursuit of all their objectives. Although their intervention may have kept the Israel-Egypt war from spreading, further success was largely frustrated. In large part this was due to the lack of military forces able to respond adequately to the emergency.[7]

If the Sinai Campaign was short, decisive, with clear-cut objectives and a plan for discontinuing the attack when the best achievable results had been reached, the Korean War was, as we know, none of these. Clearly, it was intended to be so at its outset: a rapid drive south through the peninsula by the North Koreans, defeat of the Republic of Korea Army, destruction of a pro-Western presence on Communist borders, and a vastly improved Communist position for domination of the Far East. The American response, also, was intended to be decisive: the North Korean move was to be stopped quickly. Within 3 days of the time the North Korean army crossed the border, United States tactical aircraft were attacking it, and in 10 days United States troops were engaged together with the South Korean Army in trying to stem the invasion. However, given the American military posture at that time, the response was not and could not be strong enough to end the war quickly. American and South Korean troops were almost driven off the peninsula, but were finally able to mount a major military effort to break the strength of the North Korean forces. This effort had to be increased still further with the intervention of Communist China, which could not tolerate a strong American presence on its borders. Thus the war started with clear objectives and the anticipation of rapid decision, but events acted to plunge it into a morass of indecision and ambiguity for both sides.

The idea of limitation of objective and scope was brought to the national consciousness during the Korean War, and like most ideas this one was not born fullblown and perfectly developed. Rather, it emerged slowly and painfully through a series of adjustments between desires and the pressures of reality. Our objectives, themselves, were not clear-cut after the initial reaction, and changed several times with the course of events. During the retreat to Pusan and the subsequent assumption of the offensive by the U.N. forces, it appeared that the objective was the restoration of the 38th-parallel boundary between the two Korean states. When the North Korean army was defeated and we saw an opportunity to unify the country under a government friendly to us, that became the objective. When the Chinese Communist intervention and subsequent military stalemate faced us with the choice between expanding the war — by using nuclear weapons, increasing our forces, or crossing the boundaries of Korea — or settling for the 38th parallel, we chose the latter.

This vacillation from one objective to the next typifies the uncertainty attending delay of a decision of arms. It has been argued, for example, that the Korean War could have been won by the United Nations with a modestly increased force on the Korean peninsula,[8] if we had not ceased our offensive drives at the time the truce negotiations began. But since both sides included the major powers (with the Soviet Union giving major assistance to the Communist Chinese), it was clear that at any point if either side were willing to change the accepted limitations the nature of the war and its scope could be expanded. The choice open to both sides appeared to be to settle for virtually no gains or a much larger war, which neither side wanted.

It would appear from the data on conventional limited wars that for the successful side objectives must be clearly understood and achieved with extreme rapidity. The other alternatives, resulting from inconclusive military action, appear to be escalation or an agreement, probably tacit, to settle by negotiation for limited gains. And the best that can be achieved may be little better than the *status quo ante,* with the added material and political costs of the war, for both sides.

# 2

## *Something New: Unconventional Warfare as a Strategic Weapon*

CONVENTIONAL wars have occupied the center of our attention and our defense planning during most of the years since World War II. But the tables of the previous chapter show that unconventional wars have been the most frequent and persistent since that time. Not all of them have involved Communist powers, although they represent an important instrument by which the Communists hope to extend their influence and control over the areas that previously were within the Western colonial empires. In the words of Raymond Aron,

> In our time [guerrilla war] is due either to the collapse of a social order, to popular reactions provoked by an invasion, to patriotic uprisings, or finally, to a deliberate decision taken by the leaders of a state or a counter-state. . . . [It is] the refusal to allow the regular armies a monopoly on war . . . Guerrilla warfare, as such, is a military technique, not a political action. But this military technique . . . is admirably suited to revolutionary action. It is pre-eminently the instrument of 'the war of liberation.' . . . Guerrilla warfare is not a return to anarchy. It is a form of organized combat. . . .[1]

For any nationalist group seeking independence, with few resources but their bodies and ideals, unconventional warfare is usually the only means available to take strong action when political pressure fails. For the Soviets and Communist Chinese, this kind of warfare is the embodiment of the teachings of Lenin and Mao on the means for the weak to overcome the strong. It is an instrument of indirection, permitting them to spread the Communist revolution by using the hands of others, often with little more than the means the others have available.[2] It removes them several steps from overt warfare with the West, and from the risk of nuclear war.

Khrushchev stated in his now famous speech of January 6, 1961, that

There will be liberation wars as long as imperialism exists, as long as colonialism exists. Wars of this kind are revolutionary wars. Such wars are not only justified, they are inevitable. . . . The peoples win freedom and independence only through struggle, including armed struggle. . . . We recognize such wars. We have helped and shall continue to help people fighting for their freedom.[3]

He reiterated the Soviet intention to support such wars in his December 12, 1962, speech, *after* the Cuban crisis.

In the December 31, 1962, editorial in the *Peking People's Daily* the spokesman for the Chinese Communist Party indicated their belief that in the event of nuclear war, which would be started by the "imperialists," Communism would win. Most Western comment on the Sino-Soviet dispute has dealt with this issue. More significantly for the probable course of events, however, it was stated that

The Chinese Communist Party holds that the struggle for the defense of world peace supports, is supported by, and indeed is inseparable from the national liberation movements and the people's revolutionary struggles in various countries. . . . The Communists of all countries . . . must resolutely support the national liberation movements and all the revolutionary struggles of the peoples, and *must resolutely support wars of national liberation and people's revolutionary wars* [author's italics]. . . . at the same time taking full advantage of the contradictions among our enemies . . . for utilizing the method of negotiation as well as other forms of struggle.

.   .   .   .   .   .   .   .   .   .   .   .

The aim of this stand is *precisely the effective prevention of a world war and the preservation of world peace* [author's italics]. . . . The allegations that the Chinese Communist Party underestimates the destructiveness of nuclear weapons and wants to drag the world into a nuclear war are absurd slanders . . . the history of the 17 postwar years shows that local wars of one kind or another have never ceased. . . . When imperialism and the reactionaries employ armed force to suppress revolution, it is inevitable that civil wars and national liberation wars will occur.[4]

It is clear that the Chinese view total war involving nuclear weapons is to be avoided, and the main thrust of the "revolutionary struggle" is to be via "national liberation movements" and "wars of national liberation."

Only recently have we recognized such wars as definable military engagements of legitimate concern to our defense establishment.[5] In contrast to the wars we have been used to think about, in which organized armies representing identifiable political entities engage in formal battles according to well-understood tactical and strategic doctrines, the unconventional wars face us with ever-changing military aspects and confusing political convolutions. Starting in a variety of ways; representing at one time and in one place a facet of Communist expansion and elsewhere a legitimate nationalistic impulse; assuming from one time to another the military qualities of a war against bandits, a full dress military exchange, or a purely political action with the military hidden from view — the recurring patterns of these wars are hard to discern and harder to deal with.

Usually, we become fully aware of the existence of these wars late in the dynamics of their evolution. We are not even certain how to characterize them. They have been called guerrilla wars. When the French fought the Communist Vietminh in the jungles of Indochina, the Vietminh acted like guerrillas. They struck suddenly but disappeared into the terrain when attacked. They used few of the advanced weapons and techniques of a modern army. They did not accept any challenge to fight a war of maneuver in the open field. Yet by the time the French were heavily engaged, from 1950 onwards, the Vietminh had armed forces organized in battalions, regiments, and divisions. At Dienbienphu, the French found themselves faced by an organized military force which had artillery and well-established lines of supply, and which, in fact, they could not defeat. It was at this point that the United States weighed active intervention. But this was guerrilla war no longer, and we would have deceived ourselves had we believed it to be.

Often it is difficult to identify the belligerents. One can always expect the military and police forces of the government under attack to be involved. But the other side in the war can have any of a number of components. There may be a guerrilla force arising from and made up of the people of the country. The Communist terrorists in Malaya and the Hukbalahap in the Philippines were internal revolutionaries, who appeared to have little or no assistance, overt or covert, from the outside. In Southeast Asia, however, the North Vietnamese have assisted the Communist Pathet Lao and Viet Cong by sending troops to work with them, either merged with their units or in separate combat organizations of their own.[6] Yet, to use South Vietnam as an example, over two years of war went by before we could officially identify the North Vietnamese as participants.[7]

Why are these affairs so difficult for Western man to cope with? Why are they so often successful for the revolutionary or the Communist subversive? To answer, we shall have to examine the course of their development in all its subtle diversity.

34

Typically, such wars begin with an initial phase in which there is no military action at all. Depending on the circumstances, this phase can take many forms; perhaps three have occurred most often.

In one, there will be an urge towards freedom from colonial domination. A substantial political and economic grouping will support this movement and it will be broadly based on the sympathy and encouragement of a large segment of the population. The opening phase of the war becomes one of organizing the support, pressing political demands, and preparing for the use of force if they are not met. The dissolution of the great colonial empires after World War II included many such instances, in various forms. If possible, Communist parties would play a part in these actions, hoping to be in a position to exert bargaining power with the newly formed independent government, or even to capture control of it. But often they have had little or no role—they did not in Cyprus, Kenya, or Algeria. In the Philippines and Malaya they did; and the Communist role in Indonesia was a strong one even though their position was not dominant. It is uncertain to this day whether the Cuban revolution against Batista was Communist-dominated from the start.

In a second form of the opening phase of an unconventional war, most notably in Greece and Indochina, the Communists found themselves at the end of World War II in a position of power in the country, and sought by political means to consolidate their strength. Failure of the political maneuvers then led to the use of military action.

Probably the most dangerous beginning to such war, because it is so difficult to detect before armed conflict breaks out, appears when the Communists set out deliberately to capture a country that may or may not be under colonial rule. As in Laos or South Vietnam, from recent reports in Thailand,[8] and in actions beginning in Latin America, this becomes a deliberate form of conquest.

The preparation for it is long and patient. Young men from various areas in the target country are selected for advanced education in Communist countries, or by Communist activists in their own countries. They become literate, and they learn political doctrines, methods of political organization and propaganda, methods or organizing and carrying out guerrilla warfare, and strict Communist discipline. They then return to their homes, where they begin to organize a "resistance movement" and transmit their knowledge to others.

These cadres, spread out over an area with which they are familiar and where they are known, at first simply foment unrest and dissatisfaction with the existing government. Their attack is not Communist-oriented; it has a base in reality. It is not necessary to create a false

35

image of the existing government. They need only attack that government's weaknesses, which, in a colonial regime, a newly formed independent government, or in an area such as Latin America where political and economic development have lagged, are bound to be many and obvious. The cadres lay the foundations for later popular support of military activities and for establishment of a government in an area under their military domination, which will be accepted by the population at the appropriate time.

All such acceptance is not gained by verbal persuasion alone, of course. When the dissidents are ready to assume a more openly militant role, they resort to violence and terror to subdue or eliminate the elements of the population who are not sympathetic to their aims. Assassination of local leaders friendly to the existing order, landowners, the middle class, and any others who might oppose them is part of the campaign to build, ultimately, a base of support in that major part of the population which has the least to lose and (in their view) the most to gain from political and economic revolution. If the support given is due for the most part to fear and passive acceptance, rather than to active commitment, this is in the last analysis of little consequence to the result (although it can be a crucial factor in counteraction).

Guerrilla activity will begin on a relatively small scale at first, when the cadres feel they have a sufficient base of support and trained men to raid government, military, and police bases for armaments. They will also heighten their terroristic activities to shake the confidence of the population in the existing government and to gain further support for themselves. Destruction of order is always easier than its maintenance, and this activity can be rather loosely directed; raids in any local area can be suited to the special circumstances of geography and organization in that area.

As they gain experience and skill, and increase their armaments, the small terrorist groups will consolidate into larger paramilitary units who can make more tightly directed attacks on the government forces and, especially, the facilities by which the government maintains order and economic activity in the country. Police and local guard stations, power plants, transportation facilities, warehouses, centers of local government, all will come under attack to make it more difficult for the government to run its affairs in an orderly way. Any existing disorder, corruption, or unresolvable factionalism simply makes the attack easier.

The defeat of the government's army is not the main objective of this attack. Its purpose is rather to so disorganize the orderly processes of government control that the demonstration of government weakness will gain further popular support (by default if not by active sympathy) for

36

the guerrilla force. At the same time, the dissolving power of established authority permits the guerrillas to institute military control over substantial segments of the population and the land on which it lives. Taxes can be collected and a new "revolutionary" governmental authority can be substituted for that destroyed in these areas.

Meanwhile the guerrilla forces will have gained in military experience. Their store of arms and military supplies will have been substantially augmented by the gains of its raids as well as through external assistance by sympathetic foreign powers. As their assumption of ruling authority demands better organization of their activity and more centralization of control, their continuing military success creates the capability for such organization and control. The military operation then enters a third phase, in which the guerrilla bands coalesce into battalions, and perhaps regiments and divisions. They cease to be a collection of more or less independently operating paramilitary units and become an army.[9]

This army may retain many of the aspects of discipline, equipment, and tactics of guerrillas — the ability to live austerely, to move rapidly on foot, to keep the enemy scattered by choosing his weak points for attack. Most likely it will not be equipped as well as its opponents. It may or may not be able to defeat them, but it does not have to, even then.

The last is a crucial point — the function of this army is to be the military arm of a newly constituted governing authority in the territory it occupies. It provides for internal security and backs up the plans and orders of the political directors with force. It may engage the forces of the original government, but all it really has to do is keep from being defeated by them while it retains and expands its territorial and popular control. The most important military objective at this stage of the "war of liberation" is to support a credible image of a government that is the choice of the people, that has an armed force than cannot be defeated, and that must be dealt with as an equal.

In North Vietnam and in Laos the defending forces were defeated militarily. But in Algeria the French forces were able to operate with great military success against the Moslem Army of National Liberation (ALN). The French were never defeated in a large battle. The main work of the ALN was done in attacking the economic base of government support and the population which sustained that base. These attacks continued even though the ALN suffered military defeats. As they lost men, new groups arose from the population and took up arms. In the ultimate settlement the parent political body, FLN (Federation of National Liberation), achieved the independence it was fighting for while half a million French troops remained in the country, militarily secure and strong, but able to defeat the rebels only by completely terrorizing and suppressing an Arab population of 10 million.

The war now reaches the final stage, that of resolution of the conflict. This can also take a number of different paths.

Quite possibly the government that was attacked simply collapses because it has lost all popular support and ability to govern. The "revolutionary" government replaces it, as happened in Cuba and Indonesia.

More frequently, as in Algeria and particularly in the wars of the Communists, an impasse will be reached. Neither side can completely defeat the other, and the prosecution of the war becomes a difficult burden for the original defender. In a Communist war the prospect of a complete Communist victory may create a dangerous situation for them. They face, for example, possible American intervention and enlargement of the area and scope of the conflict (as was threatened in Laos in 1962). Conversely, the insurrectionists may, unknown to the defenders, have reached the limit of their resources unless there is more open intervention from the outside; they may need a pause to consolidate their gains and prepare new action.

In any case, the impasse is resolved by mutual consent in political action at the conference table. The "weapon" of negotiation can now be used. The role of the external supporter of the revolutionary is vital in arranging this resolution. And his need to appear honestly in support of an ostensibly free revolutionary government, arisen within the embattled country, is one of the main reasons why military aid must remain in the shadows.

The conflict can be settled in many ways. In Laos the Communists became part of a newly constituted government. In Indochina they retained control of the part of the country they had substantially conquered, and there was a partition agreement. In either case, they had made substantial gains and were in a position to renew their pressure at a later date, by political and limited military action in Laos, by renewal of the "war of liberation" in South Vietnam. In Algeria the insurgents obtained the independence they were fighting for, subject only to the tenuous promise, which was later jeopardized by the Secret Army Organization of European terrorists, to cooperate economically with France and protect the rights of the European population of Algeria.

We can now see why it has been so difficult to recognize and meet the threat of unconventional wars. The aspect they present to us depends very much on where in their evolution our awareness and interest are heightened. When they are in the first, or political action stage, we may sense only a degree of disturbance in a country, a conflict among competing political parties (including Communists) for political power. There is no obvious military activity; all is below the surface.

Our aid programs cannot easily have a direct effect at this point. They have been designed to increase the general level of welfare, most often in cooperation with the existing government. They cover a very broad base and are not focused on the possibility of internal war. Military aid has in general been designed to build conventional armed forces against the threat of invasion. Neither economic nor military aid deals directly with the incipient subversion.

If guerrilla activity begins, it is, at first, of low intensity, sporadic, perhaps confused with banditry, and seemingly controllable through normal military and police channels. A convulsive military response is clearly inappropriate, and would in any case fail — first, because there are insufficient targets for it, and second, because any major inconvenience or injury it brings upon the population due to suppression of their free activity will ultimately engender more support for the guerrillas. Hungary was clearly an exception. But here an extremely powerful political-military force intervened to destroy an essentially undeveloped, un-organized, impromptu revolt taking place virtually in the center of Soviet power, and with little possibility of outside support.

It is just at this point that the future course of the war is in great measure determined. By its actions the government may create a still more difficult situation for itself. Or it may never react strongly or intelligently enough to turn the tide. If the United States tries to help the defender and does so ineptly, it could very easily be dragged into ultimate political defeat before the world, with the loser. And if we fail to recognize the guerrilla activity for what it is, we may find that by the time we do enter the fray the war has entered its third stage and is not unconventional war in the military sense at all. This was precisely the situation we faced when we weighed intervention at Dienbienphu. The same situation was impending when we sent large numbers of troops to South Vietnam in 1961.

None of the wars of this kind that have taken place since World War II has ever been won by the government originally in power after the war entered the third stage. The dynamics of the war make it an extraordinarily difficult proposition even if it enters the second stage, that of guerrilla and terrorist action.

The idea of "win" or "lose," itself, cannot be accepted in the conventional sense. Suppose we think of "winning" on the part of the defender as the suppression of subversive or guerrilla activity to the point where it is more or less controlled at a low or "safe" level. It should have no chance of renewed growth; on the contrary, the expectation should exist that it will ultimately be destroyed by the growth of an orderly and healthy economy and political structure.

To succeed in this, experience has shown, three types of counterattack are necessary:

- There must be a determined effort to gain the support of the population through political, cultural, and economic activity that, in the end, results in the transformation of the entire society in a way that brings general benefits and satisfactions more attractive than the gains offered by the original insurgents. Quite possibly new and different groups will rise to power. The people who represent the insurgents' source of support must feel a quickening of progress, which they want, and which the insurgents suddenly seem to be threatening.

- The people and the machinery of law and order must be defended against the guerrillas' necessary campaign of combined persuasion, terror, and violence; the guerrillas must be separated from their base of popular support.

- The government must take the offensive against the guerrillas in their territory. It must mount military attacks; it must send men to live and fight like guerrillas against the guerrillas; it must persuade the doubtful guerrilla to return to the fold.

These steps are interdependent. The government cannot attack the guerrillas without the assistance of the mass of people in providing intelligence, at least; the people will not actively withhold support from the guerrillas unless they feel some measure of sympathy and friendliness toward the government. This attitude must be brought about through the economic, social, and political actions that make the people's lives better and gain their sympathy for the government. And the government cannot take any steps unless the people, the railroads, the police stations, and all the rest can be protected. The three aspects of counterattack must be undertaken simultaneously in what is very much a "bootstrap operation."

The wars in the Philippines, in Malaya, and in Greece were won in this way. The Malayan war and those in Algeria and on Cyprus illustrate the depth of the changes that may be necessary to take even the first step. For the "defender" may never be able to offer the population satisfactory changes in their situation short of ceasing to be a defender. The British in Malaya gave the colony its independence even though they had to continue the defense against the Communist onslaught. The only way the French and the British could satisfy the revolutionary

40

urge in the other two, where the Communists were not involved, was by withdrawing. And once this step is taken in such cases, the military steps are hardly necessary.

It is important, obviously, to distinguish between true independence movements and attempts of the Communist world to encroach upon and take control of those movements or of already independent countries. The revolutionaries will generally have our sympathy and support if they are genuine; we are committed to beating back the Communists. And when the Communists enter, it may be found, as the British learned in Malaya, that even if the only way to gain the support of the population against the Communists is for the original government to relinquish control, that government or its allies may have to stay on to continue the fight. But then they face the problem of convincing the local populace of their motives, because their very presence and their recent actions appear to belie sincerity.

In this kind of war, military, political, economic, sociological, and ideological activities are inextricably intertwined. They all operate together, even though at any particular time conflict in one of these areas may appear to be in the forefront. It is this complex interaction of many factors, as well as the time it takes to reach objectives in each area of endeavor, that causes unconventional wars to be so lengthy. This is also what has made it so difficult for us, until recently, to comprehend the nature of this form of limited war and to take effective steps to defeat it as a Communist instrument of aggression.

The issues of participation and escalation are relatively easy to see in conventional war. For example, there was little doubt about whether we would intercede in Korea. While there may have been great uncertainty about the *consequences* of escalation, the choices were clear. In the Cuban quarantine, American interference with Soviet shipping might have led to submarine attacks on our naval ships, a limited sea war in the Caribbean or an American attack on Cuba. The Soviets could have responded to that militarily in Cuba or elsewhere. These are all relatively unambiguous military alternatives with easily comprehended, if unpredictable, consequences.

In South Vietnam, on the other hand, these issues have existed on a much lower and more ambiguous level. The critical question for some time was whether American armed forces (other than the military assistance mission) should enter the area at all. To decide this, we had first to determine the extent of the danger to South Vietnam; we had to find whether the Communists themselves had entered the area from outside; we had to estimate, from observations over a period of time, whether the South Vietnamese civil and military forces could handle the situation

41

themselves; we had to decide the extent to which we were willing to risk American lives and prestige in the area; and we had to assess what could be accomplished by various actions short of open warfare. The next stage of escalation in Southeast Asia, beyond our current participation, could be the overt engagement of United States troops in offensive combat, or perhaps extension of military operations to Laos to disrupt the flow of reinforcements and supplies to the Viet Cong.[10]

Consideration of these and the previous steps is tempered by concern over the impact of American moves on the North Vietnamese and Communist Chinese view of the threat to their vital interests, which could cause their overt intervention and escalation into conventional war in all Southeast Asia. We have had to judge, also, whether the assumption of such risks in Southeast Asia might jeopardize our other commitments, such as those in Berlin.

Thus by use of the technique of unconventional warfare the Communists have succeeded in reducing their own risks to a much lower level. In presenting us with a military situation at a relatively low level of violence, entangled with political problems of great complexity, they have increased the number of alternatives for our choice. Many steps can be taken before we reach the points of decision that we and they faced in the Korean War. Each of these can be accompanied by controversy and debate equivalent to that which characterized the escalation problem in Korea. The Communists have therefore bought time as well. Although their "war of liberation" contains the same ultimate dangers as conventional war, they are on much safer ground, with much greater opportunity to influence our decisions by their own political and military actions.

# 3

# *Nuclear Weapons, Limited War, and Europe*

THE most important single factor in determining the shape of the armed forces since World War II has been the nuclear weapon. The need for nuclear weapons systems was posed originally by the threat of Soviet expansion, especially in Europe. Because they absorbed most of the resources we wished to make available for defense, our armed forces, their tactics and the strategy of their use, came to be built around these weapons. If it appeared necessary to plan for the use of these weapons in limited war, this probably happened to a great extent because we did not believe we could make much else available.

Now a large body of strategic and tactical doctrine exists for the use of nuclear weapons in local engagements. Even though there has, lately, been much greater stress placed on strengthening the armed forces to fight without them, tactical nuclear weapons remain part of the arsenal available for limited war. We are ready to use them as local situations and the threat to our national safety and that of our allies demand. The advisability of planning for their use in limited war poses questions crucial to the design of the future weapons, equipment, organization, and tactics of the armed forces.

If the choice is not forfeited because we have nothing else available, then the use of nuclear weapons might be contemplated in the following circumstances:

- Against an enemy who is overwhelmingly superior in manpower.

- Against an enemy who has them.

• If their use appears to offer a means to defeat any enemy with great economy of force.

The problem of overwhelming numbers on the enemy side has forced us to rely on the potential use of nuclear weapons against Soviet or Chinese Communist forces, if no others. In the past, the assumption that we would inevitably face manpower superiority in a war against them was a foundation of military policy.[1] The argument for using nuclear weapons under such conditions was, however, weakened after the Soviets obtained a nuclear capability, by the reasoning that a large army with nuclear weapons could defeat a small one so armed.[2] Nor is the Soviet advantage in manpower as great as it might appear, if the potential NATO strength is viewed against it. More significantly, it has recently been claimed[3] that a Russian manpower advantage on the ground would not be important relative to the defensive mission of NATO in Europe; that, because of the 3 to 1 superiority supposedly needed by an aggressor (based on a strategic analysis of Liddel-Hart)[4] the NATO powers can, without undue strain on their resources, build their ground forces to the point where the Soviets would not be able to accomplish aggressive designs against them.

We must still face the problem of Communist Chinese manpower, based on a population approaching a billion. These numbers would be difficult for the West to match, especially should the circumstance of involvement on the Chinese mainland be forced upon us by external events. Outside the Chinese mainland it is probable that the logistics problems posed by distance, terrain, and in some cases the need for the Communist armies to cross an expanse of water would act against the building of manpower superiority by the Chinese. The condition of their economy must also limit the size of the armies they can send outside their borders. In Korea, for example, the gross size of the opposing forces was nearly equal, despite the vast population differential behind them.

There are, of course, some special cases. Conceivably a direct attack might be made on Taiwan, so strong an attack that it could only be met by nuclear weapons. Although our current policies give no indication that we would contemplate it, events that could lead to an engagement on the Chinese mainland certainly cannot be dismissed for all time. We might feel impelled to use nuclear weapons there in disregard of the need, and probable objective, of inducing the general population to be friendly to us. But this would most likely happen if there were no other hope or opportunity of defeating serious Chinese Communist aggression and deposing a Communist government with which the population might be disaffected, that is, if it appeared to us that a threat overriding all other considerations existed. This could, however, only be a strategic problem of vital importance. In these circumstances, the intercontinental, strategic forces would certainly come into play. The nuclear weapon problem would be beyond the realm of limited war.

If the pressure of manpower superiority would not necessarily force us to use nuclear weapons in limited war, the enemy can make the decision for us by using them first. At present, only the Soviet Union is able to do this. At some future time, this may become true of the Chinese Communists as well. But the problems of using nuclear weapons in limited war are as difficult for the Communists as for us. If they do, indeed, have a superiority in nonnuclear ground forces for limited war, it appears unlikely that they would compound the problems of military operation needlessly.

The problems of limited nuclear war against the Russians and the Chinese must remain different in many respects, however, and certainly require separate assessment in detailed force structure planning. But many of the more general considerations apply to both. Although we shall concentrate on the problem of limited nuclear war against the Russians, certain extensions to the Chinese problem will be obvious.

What about the problems of using nuclear weapons as a viable instrument of limited war when *we* have the choice? Much has been written on these problems.[5] It is not necessary to cover the arguments completely here, but it will be useful to review the general lines of reasoning. In the main, they revolve around questions of military and political utility, and escalation.

Whatever the anticipated advantages of using nuclear weapons in a limited war, it is obvious that we shall not initiate their use if we believe we have more to lose than to gain by doing so. The potential losses may take two forms. If both sides use nuclear weapons, our forces may be hurt more than the enemy's, due to purely military factors in force structure and size. If we use such weapons unilaterally when the war is being fought for limited objectives, the possible political losses may outweigh potential military gains. It is obvious, for example, that if the enemy armies mix closely with the civilian population whose support would be one of the major political objectives of the war, the population would probably be resentful of a nuclear liberation that would decimate it along with the enemy.

Suppose it is argued that nuclear weapons would be used only against obvious military targets, and that these weapons would be of a small tactical type having only local effects on the military forces and installations hit. Can we be sure of maintaining such limitations? We can set aside the arguments that military and civilian targets cannot necessarily be separated from each other by assuming that nuclear weapons will be used only against military forces or installations that are separated from the civilian population by far more than the lethal radius of the largest weapon used. Use of nuclear weapons at sea against naval forces might be an unambiguous example of such application. And we might also assume the development of "clean" weapons with no secondary fallout effects.

There would still be difficulties. Limitations in war are in general tacit, not known precisely to either side during its ongoing military and political operations. Neither side can be sure of the future actions the enemy will take; both must attempt to predict intentions from past and current observations. This has led the Soviets to make clear their belief that nuclear war cannot be kept limited. They have stated that American planning for *tactical* nuclear weapons is merely a strategem to hobble the Soviets in case of war; if we use *any* nuclear weapons, they will feel free to use any size weapon in their arsenal that will bring a military advantage.[6] While such statements obviously have deterrent and propaganda value, they have some clear logic as well.

If tactical losses, potentially translatable into vital strategic losses, are suffered through nuclear weapons, it is most likely that the military setback will be much more obvious and sudden than would be a defeat inflicted by nonnuclear weapons. In such a situation intangible factors, such as loss of prestige and emotional commitment to winning regardless of the consequences, are likely to dispel objective consideration of the wisdom of expanding the military conflict and its objectives. Commanders, from those in the field to the topmost levels of government, might in such a climate try to recoup their losses or regain the tactical and strategic initiative by using more effective weapons, rather than acceding to the consequences of defeat.

In other words, this is a question of stability of limited conflict in the face of unlimited power of weapons. The Soviets say that the use of any weapons of this kind *must* make an unstable situation. Is this necessarily true? It may not be. But we certainly cannot know for sure, because such "truth" depends on human conception of the alternatives and imminent consequences rather than on any objective measures.

We are faced, then, with a problem of delineating clear boundaries between stable and unstable situations. It is undoubtedly true that, even if there were no nuclear weapons in existence, as long as neither side applied the maximum force available there would be a danger of escalation to higher levels of force. But the difference between nuclear and nonnuclear weapons in such a situation is one of kind rather than degree. Escalation to higher levels of force within a nonnuclear conflict is inherently limited by the ultimate level, however high, of resources that can be applied. Such limits clearly were reached by both sides in World War II. If nuclear weapons are used, however, it is possible that no limits of force application will be reached until the entire population of both sides is exterminated by a series of blows and counterblows.

The only clear boundary, without shades of difference between small steps of escalation, is that between nonnuclear and nuclear weapons. While the tacit limitation of nuclear weapon use is certainly possible and may occur, since the enemy would be no more desirous of being wiped out that we would, there can be no certainty. Therefore, before crossing the threshold we must assess the risks we would undertake by making an incorrect estimate of possible enemy response, and the stability of the ensuing situation.

Aside from the possibility of uncontrolled escalation, a very large element of risk exists in the military uncertainty of tactical nuclear exchange. We will elaborate, in Chapter 7, on a number of contradictions in tactical conceptions of a nuclear battlefield. These contradictions have not been resolved in tactical and strategic military theory. It could therefore not be said *a priori* that, on initiation of nuclear attacks, the military situation could be controlled. There is simply no experience on which to base such a conclusion. Introduction of nuclear weapons would thus throw the tactical situation into a realm where military commanders could have no clear idea of the possible denouement, or even of whether they can win at all. As in preatomic wars, an audacious commander may be willing to risk the uncertainty, believing he can improvise well and rapidly enough to win. But in view of the attending risks of escalation into major strategic war, the question is whether the *nation* can afford to let any military commander undertake such risks to win a limited war which must have limited immediate objectives.

Where will the potential need for nuclear weapons on the battlefield be so great that there is a strong probability they will be used? We have seen that outside Western Europe the major Communist threat is one of unconventional warfare; that conventional limited war is more likely to result from miscalculation or escalation than from deliberate initiation. Certainly nuclear weapons have no place in unconventional war. It is difficult to imagine an enemy, other than the Soviets or the Communist Chinese, against whom we would feel we must use nuclear weapons to win at all. And in Korea we found it politic not to use them, even though we had a virtual monopoly.

In the current situation, we are faced, if engaged with either major Communist power, by a strong probability that nuclear initiation will elicit a like response. Outside Europe our vital strategic interests, that is, our *immediate* survival, would not be involved in a conventional-weapons limited war, while the danger of escalation after nuclear initiation would immediately involve those interests. By using nuclear weapons, we might needlessly create a situation of maximum danger out of keeping with limited, local objectives. Nor can we forget the constraints of working with allies whose own survival would be at stake in such a war. All of these factors make it appear highly unlikely that such weapons would be used in areas outside the most vital.

The question of using nuclear weapons in limited war then resolves primarily to war in Europe. The possibility of nuclear limited war in Europe is intimately related to the question of whether limited war in Europe is possible at all.

President Kennedy and Defense Secretary McNamara stated that we will use nuclear weapons if necessary to defend Europe.[7] This has, in fact, been a cornerstone of U.S. and NATO military policy since World War II. We are not, however, committed to their use in all circumstances. The Kennedy Administration made it clear, and the policy has not been reversed, that greater flexibility of response is sought in a buildup of nonnuclear forces in the NATO alliance.[8] "Options" are desired to enable lesser military engagements that do not warrant risking the very existence of Western Europe, and also to face the Soviets with a nonnuclear force that can withstand an attack long enough for the main nuclear deterrent to be brought into play. That is, substantial nonnuclear forces are desired in Europe as an added increment of deterrence and to raise the threshold of nuclear response above small military actions.

A number of military situations apparently fitting the conception of limited war can be visualized in the European area:

• Conflict over Berlin and its access routes might be limited to a local air battle or engagement on the ground in the region of the Wall or the supply routes; only East German forces might be involved on the Communist side.

• As indicated by the Yugoslav support of Communist guerrilla war against Greece in the late 1940's, such wars in NATO are possible; they could escalate into border engagements between the Soviet satellites and the nations on the underdeveloped eastern fringes of the NATO area.

48

• NATO intervention of a limited character, such as securing border-crossing areas for refugees, may be contemplated in the event of a revolt in a satellite area like East Germany.

• If we let our imagination run farther afield, it is possible to visualize a limited Soviet attack on West Germany in response to severe NATO economic and political pressures against East Germany, related in turn to extreme Soviet pressure on Berlin.

• Soviet military pressure on Austria, in connection with the latter's potential association with the European Common Market, is also remotely conceivable.

In any of these situations, one can foresee that objectives might be limited and related to the immediate situation. Such limited objectives might act in turn to keep the scope of military engagement limited, and they would probably lead to political and military stalemate, as did Korea, because neither side could afford to allow the other complete victory nor yet to press for complete victory itself. If engagements such as these are possible, then we must plan our forces to meet them, and greater stress on nonnuclear forces for the NATO area is both logical and desirable.

There are reasons, however, against planning to engage in limited war in Europe. The most obvious is that the Soviets might have a clear military and political advantage. Given the magnitude of their armored ground forces,[9] it is inconceivable that an attack westward could be halted on the West German boundary. Every land battle in World War II indicated that no line, however strongly defended, was impregnable; regardless of which side won ultimately in a test of armored strength, the attacker made initial penetrations into enemy-held territory. More often than not these penetrations took place in a matter of hours or days, even though in some cases the attacker may have been stalled for weeks. If such an attack is made, and if it is assumed to be much more likely that it would be initiated by the Soviets than by the West, then the threat to bring the strategic forces into play might become clear enough to halt the fighting at a time, after only a few days or even hours, when the attacker may in fact have penetrated moderate or even substantial distances into NATO territory.

Given the Communist skill in the use of negotiation as a strategic weapon, it is easy to anticipate that negotiations for a return to some acceptable preattack condition could take place without shifting the line of contact; that as negotiations stretched out occupation of cease-fire positions could harden; and that as a result of this inconclusive resolution the Soviets could remain in indefinite possession of territory captured in a few days of fighting. The threat might be made to bring the strategic nuclear forces into play in order to force a withdrawal. It would appear, however, that such a threat would lose force as fighting stopped and negotiation continued. An ultimatum threatening immediate use could be given even if there were virtually no opposition to the military action. And in that case it might be even more credible.

If the conventional engagement threatens to penetrate Communist territory, it becomes important to consider the Soviet view of its Eastern European empire as an essential buffer between its own homeland and the West.[10] Just as the possible loss of NATO territory to Communist control would be viewed in this light by the Western powers, the possible loss of the satellite nations of Eastern Europe would be considered by the Soviets to represent a severe threat to their own survival. Penetration and holding of even a small amount of territory by either side would shake the political foundations of either the NATO alliance or the Warsaw Pact. An attack on West Germany which ended inconclusively with Communists holding West German territory could break that nation's ties to NATO, thereby shattering the European Economic Community and the NATO alliance. Conversely, a Western penetration into Communist territory could, by stimulating revolt, destroy the security of the Soviet western boundary and the essential economic ties between the Soviet Union and the satellite nations. In such circumstances neither side could afford to allow a limited war to end unfavorably for itself. The penalty of even a moderate lack of success would appear to be very close to threatening ultimate survival. It would be extraordinarily difficult to limit a war that went beyond a skirmish.

The sensitivity to these issues in NATO is indicated by European reaction to the American policy statements regarding the need for stronger nonnuclear forces in Europe,[11] and also by the flurry of apprehension that major policy changes had occasioned the appointments of General Taylor to the Chairmanship of the Joint Chiefs of Staff and General Lemnitzer to replace General Norstad in the NATO command. The possibility that nuclear weapons would not be called into play immediately, and perhaps in a strategic sense, in the event of Soviet military action in Western Europe raises fears of serious potential losses and disadvantages to Western policy in important European government circles. American writers, notably Kissinger and Brodie, sensitive to both the European viewpoint and the logical difficulties, have taken issue with the plans for a conventional buildup in Europe.

But if we insist that we will use nuclear weapons from the start of any military engagement in Europe, other difficulties arise. Here more than anywhere, military action revolves around transportation, communication, and industrial facilities deeply embedded in the industrial matrix of the civilian population. Since according to policy we are much more likely to use nuclear weapons defensively after a Soviet attack, these weapons will almost unavoidably be used in a way that must endanger the NATO civilian population and economic structure. Moreover, with the stakes in even a small war so great that issues of survival for both sides are introduced almost immediately, the situation must be considered extremely unstable if nuclear weapons are introduced, and the risk of uncontrolled escalation extraordinarily high. The obvious character of this risk has led an important body of opinion in Europe to believe that the United States is trying to avoid the use of nuclear weapons for the defense of Europe, on the assumption that we would not wish to risk the survival of the American homeland for that defense.[12] In opposition to this fear has been the earlier apprehension that any Communist move would automatically lead to a strategic war involving the total destruction of Europe.[13]

If at first it was believed that we would be too quick on the trigger, it is now feared that we do not want to pull it at all. This dilemma has been behind much of the pressure on the part of the European nations to have control of nuclear weapons, and has led to much of the political difficulty with President de Gaulle. It has also brought about changes in NATO force deployments, such as the reported removal of United States nuclear-armed tactical air squadrons from France.[14]

The most logical resolution of the dilemma is no war; that is, deterrence must act. Practically, this could well mean that we should not admit the possibility of limited war in Europe, that we should make it clear that Communist military moves against the non-Communist powers of Europe would mean an immediate attack on the Soviet homeland and Soviet bases in the satellites.

Even if this strategy should work, however, the weapons-systems planning problems arising from nuclear weapons would not be resolved. For we do not know how decisive nuclear weapons will be in settling the military issues early. The American view is that a massive nuclear exchange will be decisive in a short war, one lasting a few hours or days. The Soviet view is that, despite the importance of the initial massive nuclear blows, a relatively long war, perhaps lasting months, will have to be played out by the combined air, land, and sea forces before the war is ended in favor of one side or the other.[15] If the latter view is a correct one, then all the nuclear weapons systems, rather than the B-52, Polaris and Minuteman alone, will be important in our military strategy.

But this will be true only if the idea of a nuclear battlefield in land war is tenable. It may not be, as we shall see in Chapter 7.

From all this the following questions may be posed:

- If limited war using conventional weapons is not a viable instrument of policy for Europe, why allocate resources to it?

- Should we allocate resources to expensive *tactical* systems based on the use of nuclear weapons for land war in Europe?

- If strategic deterrence must be the primary instrument of policy in Europe, to what extent should the tactical problems of European war dominate the planning of the force structure for limited war?

Partly, some answers to these questions lie in the very uncertainty surrounding them. Since they have no definite answers, we would assume substantial risks if we did not prepare for the eventualities of limited war in Europe or tactical nuclear warfare anywhere (whether the latter is part of limited war or general war), if only for insurance against the possibility that we may judge wrongly. In addition, some of the tactical forces, such as the tactical air wings in Europe, are very much a part of the major strategic deterrent as well. Finally, whether or not a long war of strategic character is deemed possible in Europe, as long as the Soviets *believe* that it is possible, the appropriate forces are necessary as a deterrent against Soviet military action.

We must, apparently, allocate resources to nuclear tactical forces. The question of how much to allocate depends on the interaction between the need and the resources demanded, for these forces and the nonnuclear forces designed for use outside of Europe in various other kinds of war.

# 4

# The Future: What Kinds of Limited War?

IN what ways, and in what kinds of war, will we have to employ the Army, the Navy, the Tactical Air Forces in the coming years? No one can be prescient enough to answer these questions positively. Yet some kind of prophesy, a judgment based on anticipation of American strategy and world conditions, must be made by our highest policy makers before they can shape the armed forces of the future.

This judgment must be based, at the very least, on the foreign policy commitments the military forces may be called upon to support. Estimates must be made of the likelihood that we shall have to take military action with respect to any of these commitments in one part of the world or another. And before a commitment is made to stress preparation for one kind of war, in one place, over others, it is necessary to consider the penalties for failure if we have made an incorrect judgment — if the unanticipated war happens. None of these factors can, *a priori,* be paramount in the planning. All must be weighed carefully and balanced against each other.

## Commitments Implying Military Action

There are many reasons for which our armed forces may be called into action: to keep the peace in quarrels between other nations; to protect or evacuate U.S. citizens in danger in foreign lands; to take part in the defense of the free world against the Communist threat of expansion.

If the last has been the primary source of our involvement in war or the threat of war in the past, it promises to continue so in the foreseeable future.

We are firmly committed to resist Communist aggression. It is common to think of this as a uniform commitment, equally strong anywhere in the world. Critics of our foreign policy on the domestic scene become vociferous if the Administration — of whatever Party — appears to waver.

The truth is, however, that the depth of our commitments and the depth of our interests vary in many subtle ways in different parts of the world. Treaties for mutual defense differ in their words, and they imply different kinds of response to particular enemy acts, depending on the area of the world the treaty covers and on the extent to which the security of the United States can be threatened there.

Even the same words can have a different meaning in the context of actual events. The North Atlantic Treaty commits us to consider an attack on any NATO country as an attack on the United States. In his October 22, 1962, speech, President Kennedy stated that a nuclear missile attack from Cuba on any Latin American nation would be considered an attack on us, and the Soviets would be held responsible. In the NATO case, Soviet missiles are trained on our European allies. The words of the treaty must mean precisely what they say. But in the Cuban case, the Soviet missiles were clearly meant to threaten us, not the other Latin American countries. Could the same words have had the same meaning as for NATO? Or were they, perhaps, but a veiled warning to the Soviets to keep the missiles out of Castro's hands?

The NATO alliance is, in fact, the only one that automatically commits us to war if another nation is attacked. Other treaties are qualified to say that we will help if in our judgment an attack on a foreign country is a threat to our security. Or they may be based on the need for a request for assistance, not requiring any action on our part if the request is not forthcoming.

Regardless of the strength of a commitment, it can be given unilaterally or it can be undertaken as an obligation, with one set of allies, to protect third nations; then any action we would undertake requires the allies' consent as well. We may agree to military action as a part of the United Nations, or agree to refrain from it through international agreement to respect neutrality and sovereignty. The degree of obligation can also differ, for the same country, if aggression against it is overt and comes obviously from external sources, or appears as internal subversion that may not be easily identified as aggression or ascribed to another nation. The former represents, of course, a much stronger

54

promise to undertake military action, because the threat is obvious. The latter is weaker because of the frequent uncertainty whether an internal disturbance is Communist-inspired or may truly be an internal revolution.

The treaty obligations and other commitments of the United States in various parts of the world have been presented piecemeal to the public, in the newspapers, as they were made. Their scope and the range of their variability becomes evident when they are viewed comprehensively. Table 4.1 presents a listing of the most important international military agreements the United States has entered into and the obligations it has undertaken. The table shows, also, whether the obligation is unilateral or confirmed in a treaty. Without going into the fine shadings of detail, some indication of the presence of qualifications in the commitments is also given.

In general all of the obligations are strongest with respect to external attack, and weakest in those areas where we have formed no alliances but have simply indicated that we would act to impede the spread of Communism. The latter is exemplified by our determination to oppose Communist or Communist-inspired military actions in Africa south of the Sahara, despite the absence of specific defense agreements with most nations in that area.

The threat of subversion has received ever increasing recognition, nevertheless. The impact of this awareness is evident in the treaties and unilateral declarations with respect to the underdeveloped nations, as shown in the table. The kinds of commitments shown, in any case, reflect our view of the threat as it has developed over the years, and they forebode the future. They are not immutable; new ones are added, and old ones may lose force even though they remain on the books.

## The Likelihood of War

Faced with the huge and diverse array of commitments, the defense planner must anticipate where we are likely to be involved in conventional or unconventional limited war. Which of the agreements are we most likely to be called upon to honor? Certainly it is impossible to assign a quantitative probability to each. There are serious problems in much of the world that could lead to any kind of warfare anywhere at almost any time. Each area is different from the others.

Over the long run, however, and relatively independently of *today's* crises, we can look for factors making limited war of different kinds more or less likely in different parts of the world. (Recognizing that many of the "crises" have been with us since World War II and are, in

MILITARY MEANS FOR POLITICAL ENDS

## TABLE 4.1*

### U.S. COMMITMENTS AGAINST COMMUNIST AGGRESSION

| Region | Treaty, Automatic Commitment | | Treaty, Qualified Commitment | | Unilateral Declaration | |
|---|---|---|---|---|---|---|
| | Ext.** | Subv.** | Ext. | Subv. | Ext. | Subv. |
| **NATO** | X | | | | | |
| Turkey | | | | | | |
|   Pact of Cooperation[1] | | | X | X | | |
|   CENTO[2] | | | | | | X |
| **Rio Pact** | | | X | | | |
|   Bolivia ⎫ | | | | X | | |
|   Costa Rica ⎪ Bilaterals: military | | | | X | | |
|   El Salvador ⎬ assistance to | | | | X | | |
|   Guatemala ⎪ maintain internal | | | | X | | |
|   Panama ⎪ security[3] | | | | X | | |
|   Honduras ⎭ | | | | X | | |
| **SEATO** | | | X | X | | |
|   Thailand (Rusk Statement)[4] | | | | | X | X |
|   Pakistan | | | | | | |
|     Pact of Cooperation | | | X | X | | |
|     CENTO | | ι | | | | X |
|   Vietnam | | | | | X | X |
|   Laos[5] | | | | | X | X |
| **ANZUS** | | | X | | | |
| **FAR EAST** | | | | | | |
|   Japan ⎫ | | | | X | | |
|   China ⎪ Mutual Security | | | | X | | X[6] |
|   Korea ⎬ Bilateral | | | | X | | |
|   Philippines ⎭ Treaty | | | | X | | |
| **MIDDLE EAST** (CENTO excluded) | | | | | X | X[7] |
|   Lebanon ⎫ | | | | | X | X |
|   Jordan ⎪ Eisenhower | | | | | X | X |
|   Israel ⎱ Doctrine | | | | | X | X |
|   Saudi Arabia ⎭ | | | | | X | X |
|   Morocco | | | | | | |
|   Tripartite Declaration[8] | | | X | | | |
|   Iran | | | | | | |
|     Pact of Cooperation | | | X | X | | |
|     CENTO | | | | | | X |
|     Eisenhower Doctrine[9] | | | | | X | X |
| **AFRICA** | | | | | | |
|   Dahomey ⎫ Bilaterals: military | | | | X | | |
|   Niger ⎬ assistance to assure | | | | X | | |
|   Senegal ⎭ security and inde- | | | | X | | |
|      pendence[10] | | | | | | |

\* The author is indebted to Miss Elizabeth C. Roy, Institute for Defense Analyses, for compiling the information presented in this table and its footnotes.
\*\* Ext. — External: Commitment against external threat.
Subv. — Subversion: Commitment to assist against subversion.

[1] Bilateral Treaty between Turkey and the United States entered into force 1959. Identical Treaties with Iran and Pakistan.
". . . Recalling that, in the abovementioned Declaration (Multilateral Declaration Respecting the Baghdad Pact, London, July 28, 1958), the members of the Pact of Mutual Cooperation making that Declaration affirmed their determination to maintain their collective security and to resist aggression, direct or indirect; . . . In case of aggression against Turkey, The Government of the United States of America, in accordance with the constitution of the USA, will take such appropriate action including the use of armed forces, as may be mutually agreed

upon and as is envisaged in the Joint Resolution to Promote Peace and Stability in the Middle East, in order to assist the Government of Turkey at its request."

[2] The United States, although not a signatory member of CENTO, is a member of its Anti-Subversion Committee and the military and economic committees as well.

[3] ". . . concerning the furnishing of defense articles and defense services to the Government of Bolivia for the purpose of contributing to its internal security capabilities . . . The defense articles and defense services referred to above shall be used for internal security purposes and for the defense of the Western Hemisphere in accordance with the Charter of the United Nations and the Inter-American Treaty of Reciprocal Assistance." (Example of this type of agreement; quote from bilateral with Bolivia called *Defense: Furnishing of Articles and Services*)

[4] State Department Press Release 145, March 6, 1962.
"The Secretary of State reaffirmed that the United States regards the preservation of the independence and integrity of Thailand as vital to the national interest of the United States and to world peace. He expressed the firm intention of the United States to aid Thailand, its ally and historic friend, in resisting Communist aggression and subversion . . . agreed that such association (SEATO) is an effective deterrent to direct Communist aggression against Thailand. They agreed that the Treaty provides the basis for the signatories collectively to assist Thailand in case of Communist attack against that country. The Secretary of State assured . . . that in the event of such aggression, the United States intends to give full effect to its obligations under the Treaty to act to meet the common danger in accordance with its constitutional process. The Secretary of State reaffirmed that this obligation of the United States does not depend upon the prior agreement of all other parties to the Treaty, since this Treaty obligation is individual as well as collective.
"In reviewing measures to meet indirect aggression, the Secretary of State stated that the United States regards its commitments to Thailand under SEATO and under its bilateral economic and military assistance agreements with Thailand as providing an important basis for US actions to help Thailand meet indirect aggression. In this connection the Secretary reviewed with the Foreign Minister the actions being taken by the United States to assist the Republic of Vietnam to meet the threat of indirect aggression. . ."

[5] Laos, declared neutral as of 1962, has asked to be no longer a beneficiary of formal SEATO assistance.

[6] The SEATO treaty and the bilateral treaty with China mention subversive activity "directed from without."

[7] The Middle East Resolution was construed to apply to indirect aggression in the 1958 crises in Lebanon.

[8] An agreement with England and France to preserve the peace in Israel in the event of an Arab attack.

[9] The Eisenhower Doctrine is applicable to the general Middle East area. Joint Resolution to Promote Peace and Stability in the Middle East, 1957. "The President is authorized to undertake, in the general area of the Middle East, military assistance programs with any nation or group of nations of that area desiring such assistance. Furthermore, the United States regards as vital to the national interest and world peace the preservation of the independence and integrity of the nations of the Middle East. To this end, if the President determines the necessity thereof, the United States is prepared to use armed forces to assist any nation or group of such nations requesting assistance against armed aggression from any country controlled by international communism. . ."

[10] "The Government of the Republic of Senegal requires and shall use the military equipment, materials and services furnished by the Government of the United States of America solely to maintain its internal security and legitimate self-defense." (Example from agreement with Senegal)

## THE UNITED NATIONS

All of the regional defense arrangements are recognized under Article 52 of the Charter of the UN:

"Nothing in the present Charter precludes the existence of regional arrangements or agencies for dealing with such matters relating to the maintenance of international peace and security as are appropriate to regional action, provided that such arrangements or agencies and their activities are consistent with the Purposes and Principles of the United Nations." (Article 52, Para 1)

Additionally, Article 51 states the following:

"Nothing in the present Charter shall impair the inherent right of individual or collective self-defense if an armed attack occurs against a member of the United Nations, until the Security Council has taken the measures necessary to maintain international security. . ." (Article 51)

Action by the United Nations with respect to threats to peace, breaches of the peace, and acts of aggression is provided for in Chapter VII of the Charter:

"The Security Council shall determine the existence of any threat to the peace, breach of the peace, or act of aggression and shall make recommendations, or decide what

57

fact, "long term" rather than "today's.") This assessment need not depend on our ability to predict where or when specific, unforeseen events (for example, Soviet missiles in Cuba or the Chinese invasion of India) will trigger warfare; where deterrence by the limited-war forces will work and where it will not; and where the specific effects of local conditions and economic-political policies will act to encourage or repress unconventional warfare. The problem can be dissected and each of its elements examined individually.

*Proximity to Communist powers and the direct pressures they can exert endangers small nations, in direct relation to the inaccessibility of an area to the United States.* Such facts of geography in combination with the relative aggressiveness of various Communist powers, their relative fear of escalation, and their needs and desires to expand for economic or other gains can make overt aggression more or less likely. For example, the Soviet Union has long sought an outlet to the Mediterranean; North Vietnam needs the rice of the South. The ideological debate between the Soviet Union and Communist China appears to have shown the Chinese to be far less afraid of escalation. If we have better access to the Middle East than to the northern reaches of Southeast Asia, and if the Soviets are more wary of escalation than the Chinese Communists, then the danger of open aggression by the latter may be greater. But this must depend also on the interplay between their strategy of unconventional warfare and our strategy for meeting it.

*Communist logistic problems in areas not contiguous with their borders must affect the strategy of their aggressive thrusts.* Since the Communists are not major sea powers in the same sense as the United States and Great Britain, they would have difficulty supporting major overseas expeditionary forces in the face of active opposition. They are almost forced to infiltrate and take control by internal coup or revolution unless friendly governments invite their presence. This makes un-

---

Note to Table 4.1 (*continued*)

measures shall be taken in accordance with Articles 41 and 42, to maintain or restore international peace and security." (Article 39)

"Should the Security Council consider that measures provided for in Article 41 (not involving armed force) would be inadequate or have proved to be inadequate, it may take such action by air, sea, or land forces as may be necessary to maintain or restore international peace and security." (Article 42)

"1. All Members of the United Nations, in order to contribute the maintenance of international peace and security, undertake to make available to the Security Council, on its call and in accordance with a special agreement or agreements, armed forces, assistance, and facilities, including rights of passage. . . ." (Article 43)

Except for the Mutual Defense Treaty with Korea, all other agreements specify their relationship with the United Nations:

"Any such armed attack and all measures taken as a result thereof shall immediately be reported to the Security Council. Such measures shall be terminated when the Security Council has taken the measures necessary to restore and maintain international peace and security." (Article 5, NATO)

conventional warfare more likely. It is also very desirable for them to
work through third parties — proxies — to lay the foundations for and
support the unconventional warfare. For example, if Cuba undertakes
this task in Latin America, the major Communist powers would, by
working through Cuba, be a step removed from actual operations in
other countries. We would face not Soviet or Chinese aggression but
Cuban.

*The internal stability of an area or lack of it, can affect Soviet and
Chinese strategy indirectly, inviting their expansion or hindering it.* The
susceptibility of an area to revolutionary pressures is determined in part
by its economic state and the progress that is being made toward modernization. The division among industrial and agricultural, urban and
rural elements of a society can determine the ease with which it is
penetrated by Marxist ideology. Dissatisfaction attends separation
between rich and poor, population pressures, and the country's inability
to feed its population. Psychological attitudes, stemming from recent
contacts with colonial rule, and the lingering effects of ancient traditions
on the current outlook toward democracy, autocracy, oligarchy, or
religious rule can work against economic growth.

All of these factors are sources of instability in the newly emerging
nations because the traditional societies offer few guiding principles
with respect to the needs of the modern world. The process of transition cannot be firmly directed or controlled, so the entire process of
change is unstable. In such situations the Communists can be active and
their approach to modernization attractive. The areas are in many cases
ripe for Communist penetration by unconventional warfare or for
Communist capture of revolutionary and nationalistic movements.

There are other kinds of instability, making war likely among governments that have reasonably firm control over their populations. This is
most obvious in the Middle East, where rival groups are always vying
for power. The continual push and pull among Egypt, Iraq, pro-Western
Tunisia and the Arabian kings; the Algerian war; the coup in Yemen;
the revolts in Syria and Iraq; the creation, dissolution, and attempted
reformation of the United Arab Republic have kept the area in turmoil.
The major powers often appear to be trying to avoid direct involvement
in these affairs at the same time that they attempt to exert influence behind the scenes. Alliances in this area, such as the Arab League, cannot
hold together even against the common enemy, Israel. The Arab-Israel
rivalry itself threatens to flare up at any moment as Israel goes about
the business of building its economy and its international influence in
Africa and Asia, while the Arab states sense an ever-increasing threat
from this vigorous and growing state.

For the major powers who have interests in the area — oil and trade routes on the part of the West, a Mediterranean outlet, and a pressure source for the Soviets against NATO's southeastern flank — this region offers excellent opportunities to play one side against the other. By trying to engineer coups or encouraging various factions to do so, applying economic pressures against one nation or another, or offering economic- and military-aid enticements, they can keep the area in ferment and take advantage of this ferment for their own purposes. Such a background would appear to make conventional limited war the most likely kind to expect here. Yet in adjacent regions there is a substantial probability that unconventional warfare may break out. Iran, for example, is beset by the same revolutionary pressures under the shadow of the Soviet Union that the Southeast Asian nations face under the shadow of Communist China.

There is, too, a risk of unstable degeneration of events in areas of direct confrontation between the Communist and Western centers of power. Those that come to mind immediately are Berlin, Taiwan, and Korea. The situation in these areas may actually be quite stable beneath the umbrella of U.S. and Soviet mutual nuclear deterrence. There are, however, the continual shocks of the Communist maneuvers to dislodge us, which may cause conventional war, nuclear or not, by accident more than by design.

The threat of open warfare arises from still other causes. We have already become involved, in a small way, in the war between India and China by sending arms to India. It is likely that we will undertake, with Britain, to guarantee the air defense of India.[1] Successful resistance to the Communists in South Vietnam and Laos can lead to an invasion from the North. It certainly seems possible that the threat to India and the remainder of Southeast Asia can reach the point where the United States must become involved in conventional limited war there, as a belligerent.

The pattern that emerges from all of these international rivalries, Communist and Western competition, and revolutionary pressures is something like that shown on the map in Figure 4.1. A map like this can have some utility. It might show, for example, that if we were to put first things first we might plan for conventional limited warfare in Europe and the Middle East and unconventional warfare almost everywhere else. The resulting conventional forces might then be used with whatever compromises in capability were necessary, if they were needed elsewhere. But they might then fall far short of being adequate in the mountains of Assam or the jungles of Laos. The map can show what might be needed *first,* perhaps, but it cannot show all that is needed.

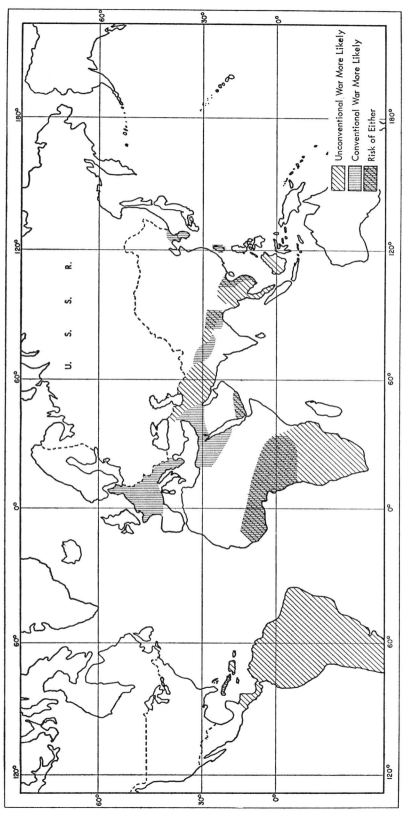

Legend:
- Unconventional War More Likely
- Conventional War More Likely
- Risk of Either

U. S. S. R.

FIGURE 4.1  POSSIBLE DISTRIBUTION OF LIMITED-WAR THREAT

Concurrently with assessing the likelihood of an outbreak of warfare, we must also have some idea of how important it is to us to anticipate war of one or another kind in various places.

We like to think that our policies must be successful everywhere. But without discounting the importance and desirability of success, we must in truth recognize that the impact of gain or loss in a limited war on our world position varies with the area of the world in which the war takes place and the nature of our commitment there. Subtle shadings of value do exist.

We might measure the impact qualitatively by the effect on our foreign relations and influence abroad, and by the portent it seems to have for our survival in the struggle with Communism. The importance of success in limited war might be tempered if, after a lost engagement, there is time and opportunity to influence international policy and position by new moves; if there is a chance to recoup the losses. The need to win becomes much greater if the chance to recoup is lost with the war.

We must decide explicitly the relative importance of preparing for subversive war in Southeast Asia, conventional war in the Near East, or nuclear war in Europe. We must re-examine our commitments in light of the dynamics of international political developments. Should Chinese Communist aggressiveness and willingness to risk nuclear war cause the Soviet Union to drift closer to the United States, the danger of war in Europe might appear to decrease relative to the risk of continued Chinese Communist expansion. We may be forced to conclude that to risk a war with the Chinese Communists in Asia would no longer be to risk "the wrong war, at the wrong place, at the wrong time, and with the wrong enemy."

## Toward a Balanced Judgment

Faced with all of the considerations previously sketched, the defense planner must consider how each of the factors of commitment, likelihood, and importance should influence his decisions toward the future evolution of the limited war forces. Until now, the strength of our commitment and its importance have led us to emphasize planning for war in Europe, almost to the exclusion of other considerations. Yet the likelihood of war in that area may be quite low, for all the reasons discussed in the previous chapter. Commitments may be somewhat less powerful in other areas, but they exist, and the likelihood of war is much higher. While it may be possible, there, to take a greater risk of losing, there is no reason why this risk should be taken if it can be avoided with a reasonable investment. We must try to build the most effective forces most economically, as far as that can be done. Where compromises are necessary, we shall have to decide what stress we wish to give to each of the factors affecting the decision.

We are, in this situation, in much the same position as a man who has to insure himself against various contingencies of theft, illness, accident, or death, within the confines of a limited budget. The conditions of his way of life and the costs of various types of insurance have all to be balanced against each other so that he will be able to distribute his resources in a reasonably satisfactory way. While the individual in his early years might be considered unwise to spend most of his money on the least likely contingency, the fact remains that life insurance usually takes precedence over others — the consequences of death are more severe than those of nonfatal accident or theft. But if he lives in a neighborhood where burglaries are rife, he may feel that burglary insurance is a necessity. He cannot afford not to have it, perhaps, even though it means cutting down on his life insurance.

For the individual, the decision is a personal one, depending to a great extent on his subjective values. In the defense problem, the judgments are often just as subjective. But they are made for the nation.

PART II

THE MILITARY
BACKGROUND

# 5

## The Forces Available

OUR purpose in this chapter will be to sketch in rough outline the organization, modes of operation, and equipment of the forces available for limited war. The outline can show only the forces that exist at a moment in time. It represents, as it were, a still picture taken from a slow-motion movie. Within the basic triad of air, land, and sea forces new subsidiary fighting and auxiliary units arise to replace old ones in a continuing process of evolution as new products of scientific research and weapons or equipment development appear on the scene.

### The Regular Forces

The main units of the ground, sea, and air forces, and the major equipment they use, are illustrated in Table 5.1.[1] The major tools of warfare listed determine the basic strength and character of the armed forces, and their over-all fighting ability. There are, in addition, thousands of smaller items, including weapons such as pistols and bayonets, radios, cargo-handling machines, electronic computers, and such mundane items as shovels, field kitchens, and mess kits. All of these represent the workaday tools of continuous military activity.

When these forces are committed to action, their mission is usually stated as the destruction or neutralization of enemy forces and their ability to wage war.[2] In carrying out this assignment, the elements of the separate military Services must work together as an integrated military

## TABLE 5.1

OUTLINE OF REGULAR ARMED FORCES STRUCTURE FOR
LIMITED WAR

### *GROUND FORCES*

| Main Units | Subunits | Major Equipment |
|---|---|---|
| *Field Army,* including any of<br>Infantry<br>Mechanized<br>Armored<br>divisions, differentiated by numbers and kinds of armored combat vehicles, and<br>Airborne divisions<br>Independent battlegroups and various specialized units such as missile commands | Brigades making up combat arms of divisions, and divided into battalions and companies specialized for<br>Artillery<br>Infantry or armored infantry<br>Tank<br>Aviation<br>Signal<br>Logistic Support and Administration functions. Also separate missile battalions | Rifles, machine guns, etc.<br>Various towed and self-propelled artillery, from recoilless rifles to 280 mm. atomic-capable gun<br>Logistic vehicles — trucks, trains, ships, etc.<br>Armored combat vehicles — tanks, etc.<br>Army aircraft including<br>Observation and liaison<br>Attack and transport helicopters<br>Light transport aircraft<br>Battlefield unguided rockets in various sizes<br>Guided surface-to-surface missiles from small Davy Crockett to Pershing, all atomic-capable<br>Air defense guided missiles<br>Antitank guided missiles<br>Automatic data processing systems for command, control, and inventory management<br>Various communications systems<br>Engineering and construction equipment |

### *AIR FORCES*

| Main Units | Major Equipment |
|---|---|
| *Tactical Air Force,* including tactical fighter, bomber, reconnaissance, and transport or troop-carrier wings; wings are composed of squadrons<br>*Composite Air Strike Force,* including combat aircraft, reconnaissance, and transport squadrons; organized for rapid deployment to area of actual or incipient outbreak of war | Various aircraft including<br>Air superiority fighters<br>Tactical fighter-bombers<br>Tactical bombers<br>Fighters or bombers used for reconnaissance<br>Transport aircraft of various sizes, for airborne operations in support of Army, and general logistics support<br>Nonnuclear weapons for ground attack, including machine guns and cannons, bombs, rockets, guided missiles<br>Nuclear bombs and missiles for ground attack<br>Guided missiles for attacking other aircraft<br>Air search and tracking radars |

## AIR FORCES (continued)

| Main Units | Major Equipment |
|---|---|
| | Air base support equipment, including fuel trucks, electric power supplies, instrument landing systems, etc. |
| | Various communications systems |
| | Automatic data processing systems for command, control, and inventory management |

## SEA FORCES

| Main Units | Subunits | Major Equipment |
|---|---|---|
| *Fleets,* including Attack-Carrier Antisubmarine warfare Amphibious task forces | Task forces, including carrier or cruiser divisions, destroyer squadrons, etc. | Ships of the Fleet, including |
| | | Attack carriers |
| *Marine* Division/Air Wing teams | Naval air squadrons for attack, air defense, etc. | Antisubmarine warfare carriers |
| | Marine divisions with associated air wings, organized much as combination of Army and Tactical Air Force; also organized into battalion or regimental landing teams for amphibious operations | Helicopter-assault carriers |
| | | Cruisers, destroyers, frigates |
| | | Mine sweepers and other small ships |
| | | Amphibious command ships |
| | | Amphibious assault transports |
| | | Specialized ships for beach landing |
| | | Fleet support transports and tankers |
| | | Amphibious landing craft |
| | | Aircraft, including Air superiority fighters Long-range attack bombers Troop support attack bombers Antisubmarine search and attack aircraft Assault and transport helicopters Liaison and utility helicopters Long-range land and sea-based patrol aircraft |
| | | Shipborne naval artillery |
| | | Air and sea search and tracking radars |
| | | Air defense guided missile systems |
| | | Automatic data processing systems for command and control |
| | | Various communications systems |

*(continued)*

### SEA FORCES (continued)

| Main Units | Subunits | Major Equipment |
|---|---|---|
| | | Air-base support equipment, as for Air Force, aboard carriers, and for Marines ashore |
| | | Marine weapons and equipment as for Army, except for surface-to-surface long-range guided missiles |

### STRATEGIC (LONG-RANGE) SEA AND AIRLIFT

*Military Air Transport Service*, with mixture of piston-engine, turboprop, and turbojet transport aircraft, and base facilities.

*Military Sea Transport Service*

*Civil Reserve Air Fleet*, drawing on civil airline aircraft in emergency.

*Reserve Merchant Marine*

### RESERVE FORCES

*U.S. Strike Command* — Combination of eight Army divisions (including two airborne) and a Tactical Air Force to form a combat-ready reserve for overseas deployment in emergency.

*Army, Navy, Air Force reserve units in United States* — subject to call to active duty and deployment after training.

*National Guard Units*

force. Each can perform unique tasks, and the task of each is essential for the success of the others and of the entire military endeavor.

In the process of engaging enemy ground forces to defeat them, the Army must take and control territory for many purposes. They range from specific, local needs for high ground to emplace artillery or observe enemy activity to the broad objective of controlling major strategic areas to deny resources and popular support to the enemy.

When the Army occupies land it also provides essential base areas for the tactical air forces. In the absence of enemy air power the missions of the latter are twofold. They must attack deep into enemy territory to destroy his major sources of supply, military reserves, and the transportation net by which he moves them forward to the combat zone or front; and they must attack the enemy forces at the front to prevent them from concentrating their strength against our own troops in the immediate ground battle. A necessary corollary to these missions is the destruction of enemy air power when it exists, in the air or at its airfields on the ground, to prevent its carrying out identical missions against our own forces. Air Force planes must also observe enemy deployments and activities by air reconnaissance, so that both the ground and air forces can plan their future actions according to up-to-date knowledge of where the enemy is and what he is doing.

When the Army takes and holds the land on which the Air Force's bases are built, it also helps to support these bases by providing surface transportation of supplies, Army Engineers to construct the bases, and troops and weapons to protect them against ground and air attack. The Air Force, at the same time, helps by using its transport aircraft to bring materials into the bases, for use at the bases, and also for transfer by land or smaller Army aircraft to the Army fighting forces.

The Army and Air Force work most closely together during airborne attacks. Tactical aircraft attack and destroy local enemy defenses in the landing zone, if necessary, and help to protect the troops once they are landed. Paratroops of the Army airborne divisions drop from Air Force assault transports. More troops and supplies are flown in by air as the airhead builds up; they are usually unloaded after landing, or *airlanded,* after the initial assault has secured a landing area.

Since all limited wars that we contemplate are far from the United States homeland, the troops and materials of war must cross the sea. While some of the materials, and the fighting men especially, are transported by Air Force aircraft, most of them are transported on the sea, especially in a war of any length. It is then a primary mission of the Navy to see that sea transport is protected, that the sea lanes are kept open and free for our use without disruption by enemy attack. Since many kinds of attack on the sea lanes are possible — by submarines, surface fleets, or aircraft — the Navy engages in combat against surface and undersea naval forces and also against land-based air forces and their supporting resources. Obviously, too, it will protect itself from enemy attacks aimed at destroying its power to protect the sea-lanes, and will attack any sea lines of supply the enemy may have. It may also strike the enemy's troops and facilities on land, as it did in Korea.

The combination of Navy and Marine Corps also has some of the responsibility for injecting our military strength into the area of conflict from outside. There has grown for this purpose the highly specialized amphibious task force. Fighting ships, troop transports, large landing ships that can discharge their cargo directly onto the beach, small craft for landing troops, aircraft carriers, and helicopter carriers are all part of this force. It must clear the defenses from the beach with air power and fire from the sea, transport the troops ashore, supply them, protect them, and preserve itself from enemy attack while the beachhead is taken and expanded.

Once ashore, the mission of the Marine Corps, with its associated tactical air wings, is much the same as that of the Army. It must defeat enemy forces and at the same time gain and hold ground to be taken over by the Army and Air Force. The latter will then continue the attack inland against enemy forces.

When forces are deployed to the field, their separate elements are drawn from the various major components of the force structure listed in Table 5.1. There is here a clear need to establish a command structure which can carry control and direction of these forces all the way from the President to the smallest unit in the field. The command structure reflects the needs of modern warfare, which have forced the separate branches of the armed forces to work together for success in battle. Separate air, land, and sea commands, each able to take independent action within a broad design of war plans, are a thing of the past. If the elements of the Armed Forces must be integrated, so must their command chain.

This has led to the Joint Chiefs of Staff at the top level, to joint or "unified" commanders in a theatre of warfare, and to "joint task forces" composed of Field Armies, Tactical Air Forces, and Fleets to undertake military missions. Moreover, the task force idea does not stop at that level; the trend for the future is toward joint task forces that may include only a brigade and a few squadrons of aircraft. While a task force commander may be drawn from any one of the Services, his ultimate responsibility is to the Joint Chiefs, and his immediate responsibility includes all the forces under his command, as equals.

This structure is illustrated in the organizational diagram of Figure 5.1.[3] It is even more complex than the illustration implies, for the command links do not always operate in the orderly progression shown. During active warfare, orders may pass from level to level in chain of command, with each unit commander at each echelon carrying out his assigned tasks in direct response to *his* immediate superior. But in incipient military engagements, the President himself may wish to exert direct control down to the lowest force levels. Experience has shown that he may, for example, want to be in direct contact with the military command at the Berlin Wall when a few U.S. and Soviet tanks face each other there, or in direct contact with the captain of a destroyer intercepting a Soviet ship near Cuba.

It would obviously not be possible, for political reasons as well as the sheer enormity of the resources required, to have enough troops for all possible contingencies stationed in every area where the United States has military commitments or anticipates the possibility of war. Nor, on the other hand, do the political situations in some areas (for example, NATO) or the reaction times of airlift and sealift — which, after all, can only respond to orders in a finite time interval — permit a policy of initiating all force movements from the United States itself. Therefore the mixture of mobile naval units, reserves at home, and some ground and

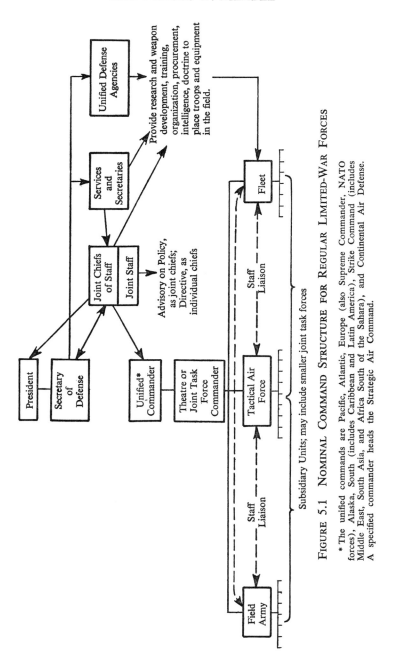

Subsidiary Units; may include smaller joint task forces

FIGURE 5.1 NOMINAL COMMAND STRUCTURE FOR REGULAR LIMITED-WAR FORCES

* The unified commands are Pacific, Atlantic, Europe (also Supreme Commander, NATO forces), Alaska, South (includes Caribbean and Latin America), Strike Command (includes Middle East, South Asia, and Africa South of the Sahara), and Continental Air Defense. A specified commander heads the Strategic Air Command.

air forces at a number of forward bases is designed to effect the best compromise between the undesirable extremes.

The overseas bases (other than those of the Strategic Air Command) serve to launch military actions by deployed forces more rapidly than would be possible from the United States. They serve also as staging areas for force movements from the United States; as forward stockpiling areas for military supplies and equipment needed prior to the establishment of the supply line from the United States in case of war; and as primary logistic support centers for a theatre of operations during war.

Some idea of this far-flung distribution of U.S. military power can be gained from the map in Figure 5.2.[4]

## Forces for Unconventional Warfare and Military Assistance

Components of the regular forces may take part in unconventional as well as conventional war, as they have in South Vietnam. There are, furthermore, two separate but related parts of the national military structure that have a major role in limited wars of all kinds, but especially in unconventional warfare. These are the special forces and the Military Assistance Advisory Groups.

Each of the military Services has units designed specifically for the military tasks of unconventional warfare. The largest of these is the Army "Special Forces."[5] Special Forces personnel are carefully selected for maturity, intelligence, and ability. They are trained to be able to operate largely independently in the field, in very small units. Teams of a dozen people will have skills in communications, demolitions, improvisation and use of simple weapons, treatment of wounds and certain diseases, and training of other soldiers. Some, if not all, members of the team may be skilled in the local language of their operating area, or another usable one (for example, French in Southeast Asia). Their training will have stressed the ability to "live off the country" and to make do with materials at hand. While they do have to receive supplies periodically in the field, the nature of the supplies they need is such that, given basic food and materials, infrequent contacts with the base of supply will suffice. With the stress in their own training on the skills necessary to train others in at least the rudimentary arts of warfare, a Special Forces team of twelve men is intended to train an irregular or paramilitary force that may number several hundred. They can also train regular military forces for ranger- or commando-type raids against the rear areas of enemy-occupied territory.

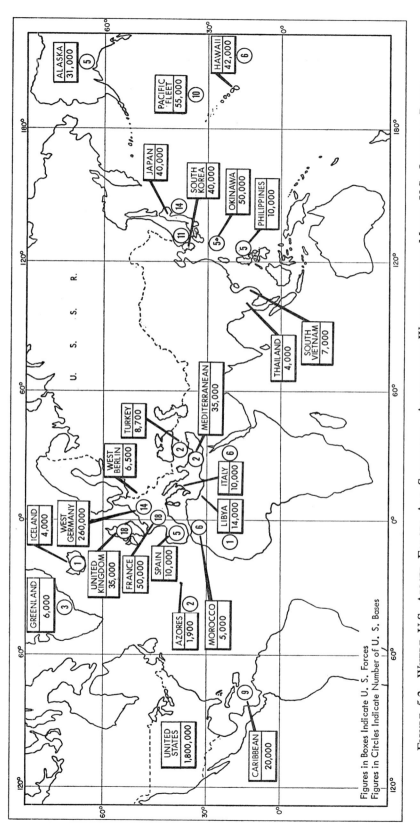

FIGURE 5.2  WHERE U.S. ARMED FORCES ARE STATIONED AROUND THE WORLD AND THE MAJOR U.S. OVERSEAS BASES

The mission of the Special Forces is twofold. In time of declared war, they are intended to operate deep in enemy territory, seeking out and organizing dissident groups within the population as guerrillas. They will then lead the guerrilla troops in attacks against the organized enemy to harass his lines of supply, hamper his logistic and reserve buildups, and force him to divert forces to their protection.

In situations other than declared war, in "cold war" or in Communist-inspired unconventional warfare, the Special Forces' mission is the training of indigenous forces in counterguerrilla warfare. While their primary task is oriented towards building the local military strength for this type of warfare, they may very often become involved in civil activities that are not ordinarily within the province of the military, such as medical treatment of the villagers in remote rural areas.

In both of their roles the Special Forces teams operate in a manner completely different from that of organized Army battalions or divisions. But they remain uniformed soldiers, carrying out their military tasks openly. Covert operations — that is, those in which their identity is not known and in which every attempt is made to prevent the attribution of their activity to the United States — are not within the scope of their mission.

The other Services have corresponding organizations on a smaller scale. In the Navy, they are tailored to the particular needs and scope of war on and near the water, such as underwater demolition of off-shore defenses prior to a beach landing. The Air Force, in trying to define a role for itself in limited war, implemented a counterguerrilla force known as "air commandos." In his announcement of this Air Force effort,[6] Air Force Chief of Staff General LeMay described guerrilla and counterguerrilla activities using aircraft suitable for operations under austere conditions, but obsolete for organized warfare, such as the old C-47 (Dakota) transport and trainers adapted for attack against targets on the ground.

The armed forces are, in addition to their fighting duties, responsible for the management of military assistance to foreign countries. In all nations with whom we have military assistance agreements, there are Military Assistance Advisory Groups (MAAGs) or equivalent military missions whose task is to assist in training and organizing the allied forces, and integrating American military equipment into their structures. These groups can take a number of forms, depending on the nature of their activities and their size. In general they are organized along joint task force lines, including ground, air, and naval warfare experts who work with their counterparts in the allied armed forces. The MAAG operates under a chief who reports to the Joint Chiefs of

Staff through the unified commanders, and also to the Ambassador in the latter's capacity as head of the "Country Team." (The Country Team includes the chiefs of all the agencies of the U.S. Government in a foreign country: State, Defense, AID, USIA, and so on.)

The MAAG chief is in command of all U.S. peacetime military activity in a country, except for those of regular units under independent command (as in NATO). This includes the Special Forces, even while they are assisting actively in counterguerrilla warfare. If the magnitude of the task becomes big enough, however, the pattern may change. A precedent was set in South Vietnam, where a Joint U.S. Military Assistance Command, reporting to Commander in Chief, Pacific, was established to direct the activities of over 10,000 American military men in that country.

## The Fruits of Technology

New weapons systems beget new military organizations to use them. The Armed Forces have their present form as a direct consequence of the advance of technology, which allows them to carry out military tasks today in a manner and with speed and power that would have been unheard of a generation ago. These improvements have paralleled those of our civilian industrial economy and are of a piece with them. They are pretty much taken for granted.

At the same time that the advantages of technological improvement are gained there are penalties that must be paid. These are too often overlooked. But the advantages and penalties, together, have had a profound impact on the military structure, creating new limitations along with new capabilities. No description of the armed forces would be complete without some attention to this fact.

The higher mobility that is perpetually sought for all ground units has led to increases in the number and variety of vehicles, and to the acquisition of large quantities of aircraft other than the tactical fighters and bombers which made up the bulk of military aviation in World War II. There is also much greater and more diverse firepower than was characteristic of combat forces 20 years ago. The current Army divisions include as new weapons not only those capable of delivering nuclear firepower against the enemy, but also many more kinds of conventional firepower with more efficient warheads than ever existed. The air forces include aircraft and weapons with capabilities, such as supersonic speeds and missile guidance systems, that could hardly have been imagined during World War II. Naval ships have changed in design, in their modes of propulsion, and have in great measure changed their weapons from guns to guided missiles. Advances in the science of electronics, starting with radio before World War I and radar before World War II, have made possible many of the other changes in military technology; they have, in fact, paced the over-all advance in recent years.

The trend to more complex equipment has, despite all efforts to the contrary, increased the logistics burden over the years. Even aside from the impact of nuclear weapons systems, the added conventional firepower with its growing ammunition requirement; the increased maintenance and fuel needs of diverse vehicles, aircraft, and electronic equipment; and the longer and more difficult task of training men to use complex and unfamiliar equipment, all have worked to increase the effort necessary to maintain the armed forces in the field.

The enormous complexity characterizing the major weapons systems of the armed forces cannot be emphasized too strongly, because it conditions all planning for their composition and use. It can best be illustrated by the modern tactical fighter-bomber and some of its auxiliary systems.[7]

The development of such aircraft has pressed the application of scientific and engineering ingenuity to military problems as much as any other military need. To fly at supersonic speeds for significant distances, the aircraft must be large. They are inordinate consumers of the precious commodity, fuel; a single combat sortie may use enough fuel to drive the ordinary family car for three years. They need complex "power steering" systems to overcome large aerodynamic forces. The pilot must live in a carefully, automatically controlled cockpit environment with special provision for escape from a disabled aircraft. Radio communications, automatic navigation, flight, missile fire control, and bombing systems add complication and maintenance problems in the form of hundreds of electronic components.

The aircraft must be equipped for delivery of a wide variety of weapons including many variations on the old-fashioned "iron bombs," nuclear weapons, and guided missiles. Its missions occur at such high speeds that coordination of the activities of many aircraft engaged in attack and defense is beyond the capacity of unaided human control. Automatic data-processing systems with farflung semiautomatic radar and communication networks are necessary to insure efficient use of this tremendously expensive weapon system.

And this is but one of many systems, equally sophisticated and complex, in use by all the Armed Forces. It is no wonder that the number of troops engaged in "support" tasks can outnumber by far those engaged in combat.

# 6

## Where They Fight:
## The Environment

THE possible environments in which American troops may have to fight limited wars are as varied as the geography of the world itself. One of the major problems in military planning is to search for some underlying order in this apparently infinite variability, to introduce thereby a logical basis for matching force structure and equipment to area of operation. It is possible to codify the environmental features, isolating those that would lead to common requirements for general-purpose military forces. From this, also, we can identify the unique characteristics of particular areas which, presenting special problems, make a substantial degree of specialization in military organizations and equipment inescapable.

### The Natural Environment

Leaving aside for the moment man-made features, and excepting of course the high seas, the most important characteristics of any environment that affect the duration and character of a war are those favoring or obstructing the movement of military forces. If rapid movement is easy, clashes between maneuvering forces become possible, the war covers large areas, and there are opportunities to end it rapidly by a decisive *coup de grâce* against a critical strategic point.

If lightning maneuvers are not possible, however, then military action can easily stabilize along a front or around points of static defense. In rough terrain military maneuver is generally constrained to follow terrain contours. Roads and railroads follow valley floors. A small force can defend itself well against a large one. If large forces must traverse long distances over a long period of time to attack and occupy major strategic areas or destroy enemy reserves, there is much opportunity to frustrate them by frontal defense and harassment along the flanks and in the rear. A war can then be long and indecisive.

A functional description of this symbiosis of tactics and terrain can be based on the structure of the earth's surface and the climate over it.

Terrain can be flat or mountainous. There is, of course, no hard-and-fast boundary between the two. In a general way, they can be distinguished by the degree to which mass military movements on the ground are free of major terrain contour variations. Hilly terrain can be considered essentially flat if the slopes are gradual and low enough that major military maneuvers can take place without being unduly inhibited by the terrain contours. On the other hand, in some areas which might be considered essentially flat, there may very well be zones of surface roughness that are broken and have very steep, if relatively short, slopes and obstacles such as large boulders or waterways that cannot be easily negotiated by vehicles. But the two basic geoforms are qualitatively separable.

Landforms and surface roughness do not alone obstruct surface movement. Other natural barriers can occur in the form of vegetation; soil softness or stickiness that prevents or inhibits the building of roads, cross-country movement of vehicles, or the landing of aircraft; drainage paths in the form of rivers, streams, or dry washes; and inundated areas such as swamps. Most of these are influenced by local climate as it interacts with geological structures. Even though local conditions vary with latitude, average annual rainfall can be taken as a rough indicator of weather, vegetation, and drainage volume.

In areas of very light rainfall, say, less than 15 inches per year, there will be few vegetation barriers to movement. Although movement across desert surfaces is difficult for military vehicles, the problem has been solved with specialized designs. For our purposes, therefore, we can consider that the obstacles to maneuver in dry or arid regions are presented primarily by landforms rather than by vegetation or soft, sticky soils.

Areas of moderate rainfall, perhaps from 15 to 40 or 50 inches per year, present a great variety of vegetation barriers to military movement. Flat regions in such climates have by and large been the areas of greatest industrial and agricultural development. Although there may be some regions of dense forest in these areas, they are, in the main, given over to cultivation; the vegetation is low and rarely obstructs movement. (The hedgerows of Normandy were a notable exception.) Very often, however, much of the rainfall occurs in particular seasons of the year, and at these times soils will be soft. In addition, since flat areas of moderate annual precipitation are most often encountered in temperate climates, substantial areas will be covered by snow in winter. While temperate vegetation may not overly restrict the mobility of mechanized forces, mud and snow most certainly will.

Mountainous areas with moderate rainfall tend to be covered by heavy forests, while the valleys are devoted to agricultural and industrial development. In such areas (for example, Italy or Yugoslavia) the landforms and climate combine to channelize military movement and seriously reduce freedom of maneuver.

In the regions of heavy rainfall, greater than 50 inches per year on the average, terrain and vegetation combine to restrict military operations most severely. Whether the land is mountainous or flat, vegetation can become extremely heavy. In tropical rain forests and jungles almost all surface movement without prior road construction, except by men on foot with machetes, is impossible. Here, too, are encountered the extensive coastal mangrove swamps, associated with vast river deltas, that make access to the inner reaches of tropical regions so difficult. (To be sure, coastal swamps are not a unique feature of wet tropical areas. The head of the Persian Gulf is inundated by coastal waters for many miles, and military landings through the resulting marshes would be virtually impossible. The northern temperate zones also have large regions of coastal swamp which would have similar effects on military operations.)

Large portions of the wet, flat areas, although not covered by heavy wild vegetation, are given over to rice cultivation. For large periods of the year this creates soft and flooded areas that are impassable to mechanized units. Thus, in almost all of the tropical regions, military movement on land must be carried out on foot, on water, or it must be confined to roads and railroads. It is worth noting as well that some of the major rivers of the world exist in these areas. Much of the economic and cultural activity is centered on the rivers and adjacent canal systems; they are thus major focuses for military action in addition to being avenues of approach to the hinterlands.

What is the distribution of flat and mountainous terrain, and of rainfall, in areas where limited wars are likely? If the two factors are considered together, then the combinations can be taken to describe six "generic" geographical environments, in which, insofar as the features critical to military operations are concerned, variations *within* a given type are small relative to differences *between* types:

81

| | |
|---|---|
| Flat-Dry | Mountainous-Dry |
| Flat-Moderate | Mountainous-Moderate |
| Flat-Wet | Mountainous-Wet |

These environment classes are independent of national boundaries. Any country can include areas of more than one generic environmental type, and each generic geographic region can encompass parts of several countries.

The apparently infinite variation of physical geography can thus, for purposes of comprehensive planning, be reduced to six basic types (excluding the arctic and subarctic regions). They can be defined with reasonable precision in terms of terrain heights, slopes, and average annual rainfall. Their distribution over the portion of the world that is of concern for limited-war force structure is typified by the 4⅓ million square miles in the southern Eurasian periphery. The map of Figure 6.1 shows what this distribution is.[1] Let us consider this map an intermediate step towards a description of the basic environmental demands on a limited-war force; we shall return to it shortly.

## Man-Made Features in the Environment

Without extensive roads, railroads, ports, airfields, and communication centers, a campaign by present-day ground armies must either build up slowly or be undertaken by small forces, simply because the supply tonnages required cannot be delivered without those facilities. If they are few, their destruction can cripple a force that depends on them. If they are few, therefore, not only must the force be smaller because of its supply problem, but a larger fraction of it must be given over to protection of the roads, railroads, or ports available. Still further effort is required for construction as the campaign builds up, if large forces are needed. The existence of transportation and communications facilities is thus of great interest to the military planner.

These factors can be correlated with the six generic types of geographical region described in the previous section. Let the number of miles of railroads and roads and the number of major ports and airfields per square mile of the Northeast United States* each be represented by an index of 100. Then comparable indices for each of the generic geographical regions can be determined. These indices are shown in Table 6.1 for the same region covered by the map of Figure 6.1 in the previous section.

It becomes immediately evident that only in the flat-moderate regions,

* Including New York, Vermont, New Hampshire, Massachusetts, Connecticut, Pennsylvania, Maryland, Virginia, West Virginia, Kentucky, Ohio, Indiana, Illinois, Michigan.

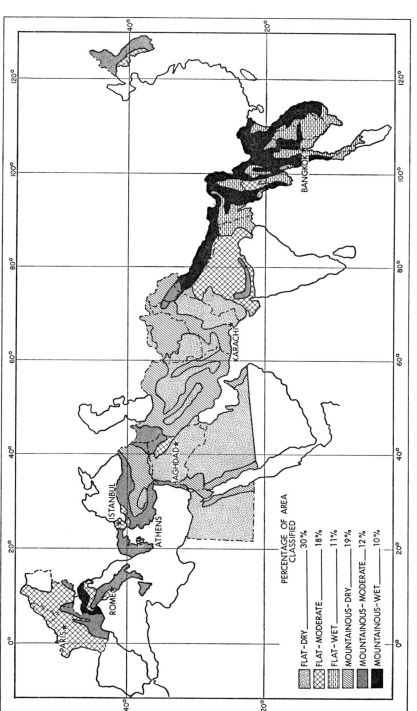

PERCENTAGE OF AREA
CLASSIFIED

| | |
|---|---|
| FLAT-DRY | 30% |
| FLAT-MODERATE | 18% |
| FLAT-WET | 11% |
| MOUNTAINOUS-DRY | 19% |
| MOUNTAINOUS-MODERATE | 12% |
| MOUNTAINOUS-WET | 10% |

FIGURE 6.1  DISTRIBUTION OF "GENERIC" ENVIRONMENTS IN THE SOUTHERN EURASIAN PERIPHERY

and to some extent in the mountainous-moderate, have such facilities reached any substantial state of development. These developments are thus associated with the industrial European economy, and with the derivative development of communication facilities by the British during their lengthy occupation of India.*

## Combination of Natural and Man-Made Factors

The natural and man-made geographical factors affecting the operation of military forces can now be viewed in combination. The result is

TABLE 6.1

RELATIVE AVAILABILITY OF DEVELOPED SUPPORT
FACILITIES IN VARIOUS "GENERIC" GEOGRAPHICAL
REGIONS

| Generic Classification of Region | Road* Index | Rail* Index | Major Port* Index | Major Airfield* Index |
|---|---|---|---|---|
| Flat-Dry | 0.02 | 5 | 12 | 8 |
| Flat-Moderate | 30–100† | 30–100† | 90** | 100** |
| Flat-Wet | 0.02 | 15 | 30 | 10 |
| Mountainous-Dry | 0.005 | 3 | †† | 5 |
| Mountainous-Moderate‡ | 0.03 | 25 | 50 | 25 |
| Mountainous-Wet | 0.005 | 3 | †† | 5 |

* Indices give the linear miles of roads and railroads, or number of ports and airfields, per square mile of area in the generic region as an approximate percentage of corresponding quantities in the Northeast United States.
† Includes Northwestern Europe as well as North Central India.
‡ Includes Southern Europe, primarily.
** Northwestern Europe, only.
†† These are primarily inland areas where no ports are expected.

a comprehensive picture of the types of military force that are suited to the demands of various regions where limited war might occur. This picture is shown in Figure 6.2, again for the southern Eurasian periphery.

The map shows clearly that Northwestern Europe is virtually the only part of the entire region in which the kind of confrontation of huge armies that characterized the defeat of Germany in World War II is possible. Elsewhere there must be extraordinary effort to build roads,

* This is not to imply that, even though the two fall in the same generic category, North-Central India is exactly comparable to Northwestern Europe in terms of military operations. However, as geographers and historians elsewhere have pointed out, major industrial developments have tended to take place where terrain and climate are favorable for the growth of closely integrated communications and easy transfer of resources and commercial goods among different parts of an area. The result is that all such areas have, in some degree, certain essential similarities relative to the operational capabilities of modern military forces.

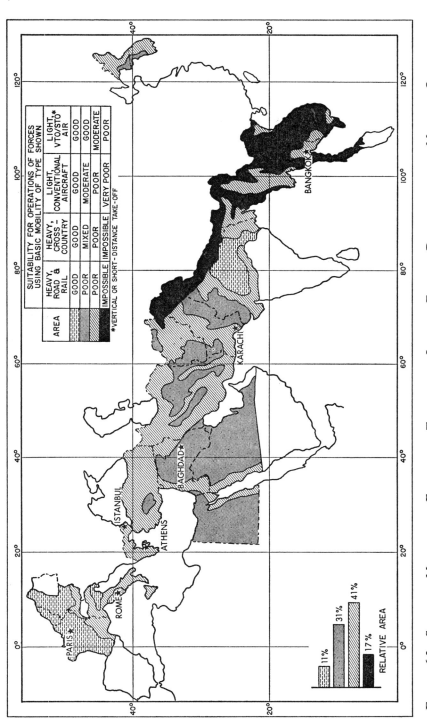

| AREA | SUITABILITY FOR OPERATIONS OF FORCES USING BASIC MOBILITY OF TYPE SHOWN | | | |
|---|---|---|---|---|
| | HEAVY, ROAD & RAIL | HEAVY, CROSS-COUNTRY | LIGHT, CONVENTIONAL AIRCRAFT | LIGHT, VTO/STO* AIR |
| | GOOD | GOOD | GOOD | GOOD |
| | POOR | MIXED | MODERATE | GOOD |
| | POOR | POOR | POOR | MODERATE |
| | IMPOSSIBLE | IMPOSSIBLE | VERY POOR | POOR |

*VERTICAL OR SHORT-DISTANCE TAKE-OFF

FIGURE 6.2  SUMMARY MAP OF THE EFFECTS OF TERRAIN AND LOGISTIC FACILITY DEVELOPMENT ON MILITARY OPERATIONS IN THE SOUTHERN EURASIAN PERIPHERY

railroads, bridges, and supply centers, or the military buildup must be relatively small. Supplies must enter the area through a few ports or airfields, potentially serious bottlenecks, highly vulnerable to enemy action.

The implications for a limited war force structure are clear. If we base that structure on the needs of a European war on the plains of France and Germany, the forces will be limited in their capability elsewhere. We shall then have to hope that conventional limited wars outside Europe remain small, or else we shall pay the price of lengthy and massive military buildups and long, possibly inconclusive wars. If we wish to avoid this penalty, the military forces intended for use outside Europe will have to be reconstituted. There are ways to do this, as we shall see later.

The analysis of the military geography of the South Eurasian periphery can be extended to other areas of the world. It is possible, on the basis of their physical and economic geography, to divide Africa, South America, Indonesia, and so on, into elements assignable individually to one of the six generic types of physical geography. Much the same development of man-made facilities will exist in each of the generic types anywhere. There will be areas of the flat-moderate type which are rather more developed than the remainder; the Sao Paulo–Rio de Janiero region of Brazil is an example.* But outside of the developed parts of the Western world such areas are small and are imbedded in much larger undeveloped regions.

## Human Factors in the Environment

A discussion of the geography of potential limited war areas would not be complete without attention to the impact of the populations of those areas on the military problems.

The reader is familiar with the highly developed civilization of Western Europe. A number of factors could act to inhibit military operations in a limited war there. For one thing, it is not unreasonable to expect that the first requirement of any limited conflict will be the preservation of industrial and cultural centers. While destruction is obviously difficult to control when armies clash, the desire to limit it may well condition the tactics of attack and defense and the use of certain weapons. (In World War II, for example, Paris was declared an open city.)

Another factor, and one with a much more immediate impact on

---

* Since division into generic types is a useful device for analysis and not a law of nature, it need not be interpreted rigidly. Portions of Africa or South America may be flat-moderate but meagerly developed, for example. In such cases, the requirements for military operations will be much the same as those of the flat-dry regions.

military operations, made itself felt during the invasion of France by the Germans in World War II. In the panic created by the German onslaught, the French and the Benelux populations took to the roads, with whatever belongings and vehicles they could muster, in a blind attempt to escape from the German armies. The consequent clogging of transport and communication facilities in France, in the Allied rear areas, contributed in no small measure to the inability of Allied forces to maneuver against the German armies, and so to their inability to stop them. A recurrence of uncontrolled mass movement of the population at a time when speed of movement of the military forces and efficient logistic support is crucial to their success could well have a similar impact on the outcome of a future limited war in the European area. Design of forces, even for Europe, must take this possibility into account by stressing independence of fixed facilities.

Outside Europe and a few other areas such as Japan and Israel, the meager state of economic development poses a number of additional human problems that effect modern military operations. Most individuals in those areas have not been exposed from birth to the material and mechanical accouterments of Western civilization. They have not, as we have, been educated to understand them so intimately that they cannot conceive of living and working without them. While these derivatives of Western culture have influenced other cultures the world over, they are not integral parts of these cultures. Although we assume this integration in speaking of the "inherent mechanical ability of American youth," we cannot make such assumptions about people in the underdeveloped areas.

But the indigenous populations, and especially their governments and armies, are fundamental components of any American action in limited war. The indigenous military forces generally use equipment we have given them. They must learn to maintain and operate this equipment if they are to be effective. Most likely these forces will be organized according to American military doctrines, which have developed around the availability and use of particular weapons and equipment.

Our inescapable problem in limited war in the underdeveloped areas is therefore to instill both technical and tactical competence through extensive prior effort in training and education. We might, ourselves, assume a substantial part of the maintenance and other logistic problems. We cannot, however, evade the problem of developing combat capability based on the limited technical capacity that is potentially available. American forces must rely on their allies to carry part of the combat load; they become a critical link in the military chain. The lack of technological sophistication in underdeveloped areas therefore affects our own military operations and force structure planning profoundly.

The strictly technical aspects of working with foreign soldiers during limited war are only part of the problem. The military and political leaders of our war effort must be able to work effectively with those who control the local social, political, and economic life. Although such activities in the European environment are difficult enough, we may claim to have some familiarity with the important population characteristics, born of long experience. This is not true in the underdeveloped areas, where by and large our presence as a world power is a relatively new experience to both parties.

Here, the indigenous human environment is the product of various cultures and religions, and education systems based on them, that are different from ours, unfamiliar to us,[2] and modified by the impact of recent history to such an extent that they are often no longer fully understood by their own adherents. Governments are strongly influenced if not actually operated by military and economic groups who comprise elite members of the local societies. Much of the economic business of a country might be under the control of a few educated and perhaps wealthy individuals who are political leaders and so may exercise control even under socialist regimes.

While we wish to work for the benefit of the entire population, our desire to encourage orderly economic and social evolution has required us to approach and influence the population through these elite groups. But there may be a wide gulf between the cultural outlook of the elites, who will have assimilated much of Western civilization, and that of the mass of people. The majority of the latter may have far more traditional leanings, alien to ours and inimical to our dynamic concepts of change. Even the elite is not necessarily tuned to our way of thinking. The result is a three-way conflict that is extremely difficult to resolve.

We might wonder, for example, how one instructs a high military leader in new techniques when, as a man who has reached the pinnacle of his society, the very admission of ignorance is a serious loss of prestige. How can military assistance be managed efficiently where traditions of thousands of years' standing require a private share of the "proceeds" for each man down the line as he handles supplies and funds? How can we relate the many abstractions of military tactical and strategic doctrine to the real world in a society where a beautifully logical theory is considered the quintessence of human thought, not to be destroyed by conflicting experimental data? And even if obstacles like these can be overcome in dealings with the elite, it is still difficult to translate them into action through a population that is living hundreds of years further in the past, with whom the elite themselves can barely communicate, whose very language they often do not speak. It is reasonable to expect dedicated, patriotic service from a soldier who, for most of his life, may never have realized that a national government existed?

Of course, such problems are not insurmountable. Our own successes in economic and military aid, the successes of the Communists in the same fields, and especially their success in creating strong military machines and fostering aggression of all kinds around the world, attest to this. But there have also been significant failures; we should not believe that the will automatically creates the means or assures the implementation.

# 7

## How They Fight:
## The Battlefield

ON THE battlefields of World War II, and later in Korea, were developed the tactics and strategies of modern warfare. Foremost among these are armored warfare, the application of air power against military strength on the ground, amphibious and airborne operations by mechanized armies, and sea power transformed into a mobile base for air strikes against enemies otherwise beyond reach.

These developments remain at the foundation of military operations other than the intercontinental exchange of nuclear weapons. But several additions to the technology of warfare since World War II have had a profound influence on the tactics as well as the structure of the armed forces. The most important is the nuclear weapon. Others are guided-missile antiaircraft defenses, vastly more efficient antitank weapons, and changes in the tools of airborne operations. The use of guerrilla tactics as a primary offensive weapon rather than for harassment of regular armies has also led to wholly new concepts of military tactics.

In this chapter we shall describe the effects of some of these developments on the way the armed forces fight.

### The Nuclear Battlefield

Since there has never been an atomic battlefield, what we can say about it must of course be in the nature of speculation. However, there is probably no single question that has occupied the thoughts of ground warfare theorists more than this one since World War II.[1] In what follows, the various theories will be summarized; a number of problems they present will become evident.

The essential fact influencing the configuration of an atomic battlefield is the extreme vulnerability of large concentrations of men or materials to very small numbers of weapons. Yet an essential principle of the application of military force has been that of concentration. Aside from the logistic concentrations necessary to supply troops in the field, the troops themselves must concentrate in strong groups to attack the enemy effectively with nonnuclear weapons.

Since concentrations of troops and supplies, and such focal points of activity as ports and airfields, are at the same time essential to conventional-weapons military activity and most vulnerable to attack by atomic weapons, it has been necessary to rework the principles of concentration to rationalize battlefield operations in the face of the atomic weapon threat. This has meant, in the new doctrines, that battle formations must in general be widely dispersed. The density of men occupying an area must be low enough that an atomic burst will not destroy or cripple a substantial force. Tactical aircraft must be designed to operate from very small fields without large concrete runways; these bases must be shifted often. Supplies must be dispersed among a much larger number of small depots that can be hidden or moved if discovered. A substantial fraction may be contained within the vehicles and aircraft of the supply lines, which are themselves scattered over everchanging paths through the landscape. Artillery weapons will not be massed together to hold positions and fire continuously on enemy concentrations, since their locations are easily traced. They will be dispersed and hidden, in formations designed to concentrate fire on particular targets. They may have to change position frequently. This will be especially true of atomic artillery and missiles, which will be primary targets for enemy fire.

Conventional high-explosive weapons are still expected to play a very important role on the battlefield, even if nuclear weapons are used. Armor will continue to be used for shock action, for mobile exploitation of breakthroughs in dispersed formations, and to provide a measure of protection against radiation.

Some concentration to achieve the full benefits of conventional-weapons firepower, and to penetrate enemy positions in coordination with nuclear fire, will still be necessary. These combat concentrations are supposed to be brought together only when they can close rapidly with the enemy, so that he cannot use nuclear weapons without hurting his own troops. This has been called the "hugging tactic." It has led to the replacement of the "line of contact" between opposing sides by the idea of a "forward edge of the battle area" (known as the FEBA).

In the FEBA, troops on both sides are organized in small, relatively independent and self-sufficient units, which are not ordinarily attractive as targets for atomic weapons. They do not join together lest they become such targets as soon as they do; rather, they remain separated and are interconnected by patrol activity, aircraft, and radio communications. The enemy's troops are similarly disposed, and the area covered by such small groups might extend for many miles into the territory nominally occupied by each side. Many encounters among these interspersed groups of men can be expected, leading to a continuous series of small battles, with supporting fire by heavy artillery or missiles on call from the rear areas as opportunity provides. Behind the FEBA dispersed units will be deployed in great depth, so that in case of a breakthrough the defender can move to contain the enemy, trading space for time.

To break through the FEBA a sufficient concentration of men and weapons must be brought together. This may be done by infiltration into the FEBA, with the resulting concentration "hugging" and applying pressure against the enemy's units. If a nuclear weapon is thought appropriate to remove enemy resistance in the forward areas or to eliminate strongly defended points commanding lines of movement in the rear, the friendly forces may be coalesced very rapidly to move through the hole the weapon creates in the enemy defenses. This must be followed by dispersal on the other side. Conversely, the enemy may try to withdraw his forces rapidly after detecting the concentration so that he can use a nuclear weapon against it.

There is obviously a great premium on speed of movement. Concurrently, it is vital to gain intelligence of the enemy's force dispositions and movements with minimum time delay. The primary targets for nuclear weapons will now have become the rapidly appearing and disappearing concentrations of men and weapons, as well as the dangerous, elusive sources of atomic firepower. Each side must, therefore, maintain continual surveillance of the opponent's activities along with the ability to make timely strikes when suitable targets for atomic weapons are found.

There are a number of severe problems of time and space involved in this concept of the atomic battlefield. Concentrations of troops or weapons, or individual targets such as missile batteries, will have to be discovered, identified, and related to the tactical situation, alternative actions considered, attacks or defensive maneuvers planned and carried out over large areas of landscape — perhaps thousands of square miles, involving hundreds or thousands of troops with their equipment and vehicles — in periods of time that may be as short as a few minutes for individual units. This requires an acceleration of activities that would have required days or weeks under preatomic conventional-weapons combat conditions. On the other hand, because of the risk attending discovery, many more actions of counterattack or defense, including those that could previously have been undertaken on short notice, will have to be preceded and followed by secret troop movements that might under any circumstances be considered major undertakings.

All of this creates problems of communication and control over the dispersed forces which are very difficult to solve. We shall return to these problems in Chapter 15.

In addition, the need for extremely rapid movement over great distances required by dispersed operations increases the logistics problem enormously. Even in World War II, where fuel was about half the total resupply requirement of an armored division, three times as much fuel could be used when the division changed from static to mobile operations. This could more than double again under the atomic battlefield conditions described. At the same time, vehicles and other mobile equipment, being in motion over longer distances in a shorter time, can be expected to require considerably more maintenance than in the past. More supplies will therefore be needed while the time available to obtain them is smaller. To these supplies will have to be added the greater amount of ammunition implied by the FEBA, with its continuous high level of conventional-weapons combat.

With the increasing supply and maintenance problem arises a more difficult problem of distribution. Where a World War II Army of six divisions might require about 5,000 tons of supply per day,[2] with a 10-day reserve in a single rear-area depot occupying several square miles of territory, the total average load requirements could now be tripled, and the reserves would have to be stored in many smaller depots miles apart. The number of vehicles needed for distribution to forward troops could double, or even quadruple if supply bases are kept mobile or far to the rear. The maintenance and fuel problems would obviously be compounded still further. Nor would the widespread use of aircraft instead of surface transport solve the basic problems. Aircraft require even larger amounts of fuel and maintenance, and they face further difficulties of greater detectability and vulnerability on an atomic battlefield. Bases of air supply operations would have to be moved frequently, with their support equipment (such as major repair tools, loading devices, and so on) and crews, itself a major logistic task.

Some of these problems are susceptible of solution, and indeed much of the research and development supporting the evolution of today's ground armies and tactical air forces has had these problems in view. A greater difficulty is inherent in the philosophy of the conception. It is difficult to imagine that the implied frenzy of movement — "perpetual motion," as it were — can take place for its own sake. It must be associated with vigorous attacks that have a goal: destruction of enemy forces and occupation of his territory. The further implication is, therefore, that a nuclear ground battle will be short and intense. Probably, too, the type of force that could accommodate itself to the difficulties of logistic support would be a small one; large forces would find it difficult to remain in motion and to maintain the rapid shifts of disposition over the entire combat area that are needed to avoid static concentrations.

Despite their dispersal and continual changes of position, troops will certainly be struck by nuclear weapons occasionally. A nuclear weapon dropped on concentrated forces in the open is certain to cause a sudden surge of casualties, much greater than that expected from even heavy combat with conventional weapons. The most desperately injured will have to be treated in the field, and all will have to be transferred rapidly to a large number of hospitals in rear areas. Aside from facing the difficulty of marshalling the needed doctors and ambulances in a short time, the forces in the bombed area would probably come under enemy follow-up attacks during this critical period. The shock effect of such a sequence is unknown, but it is easy to conceive of a complete disintegration of organized military activity in a large area as a result.

If mobility is lost, repeated nuclear strikes could be avoided only by providing protection against nuclear blast and fallout for the stalled forces. This would require a substantial amount of "digging in," which makes the retention of mobility still more difficult. Miksche points out, in fact,[3] the likelihood that a series of nuclear weapon exchanges would so disrupt the mobile operations of both sides that both would be forced to seek extreme protection, by digging themselves underground. This leads to a denouement in static confrontation reminiscent of the trench warfare of World War I. The resulting impasse would, in his view, be a stable situation preventing resumption of maneuver, since any initiative in this direction could be easily detected and would immediately be met by a nuclear blast from protected and hidden weapons.

In another variation of the nuclear battlefield concept, the virtual impossibility of massing large armies is accepted. Ground forces are considered to be organized in rather small, self-sustaining units which can move rapidly, carrying several days' supplies with them. These forces will assume dispersed, columnar formations which are difficult to damage with nuclear weapons. Since they will be resupplied along shifting air or ground routes from reasonably distant terminals outside their areas of operation (sanctuaries, presumably), they will not be concerned with major bases or with holding ground. Their task will be to find the enemy and to destroy him as rapidly as possible.

This type of battle has been likened to that which took place in the North African Desert in 1942 in Operation "Crusader."[4] There, whole divisions maneuvered en masse over many miles of desert in but hours, with intense clashes when they met. Divisions and their subsidiary combat units are, in this theory, considered to be almost analogous to ships at sea, and their tactics are considered to be similar to those of naval warfare. Maneuvering military units concealed in the countryside will search for each other, and when they meet the result will be a short, decisive fire-fight. Tactical aircraft associated with these units will also play a role similar to the one they play in naval battles. They will search for the enemy's maneuvering forces and their bases of supply, and when they find them attempt to destroy them at long range.

This concept suffers from many of the same problems and contradictions discussed previously, but it extends the idea of mobility to smaller forces in a large countryside. The extensive maneuvering is thus easier to support logistically, and the forces are more difficult for the enemy to find. If this small force, with its supporting tactical air, meets a massed army the latter is perhaps more vulnerable to nuclear destruction.

If this idea is followed to one logical conclusion (of the many possible) it can be imagined that the combat units would become progressively smaller to evade discovery, and that they would in so doing have to give up more and more of their heavy equipment and come to rely only on such weapons as they could easily carry. (Some atomic weapons, such as the nuclear rocket, DAVY CROCKETT, have already become small enough to be carried in small vehicles and delivered at fairly close range.) It might then be possible for very small groups of men to operate clandestinely, to be sustained by supplies delivered clandestinely from outside the area, and to use their atomic weapons whenever they encounter a similar enemy group or a major enemy installation. In this conception, atomic warfare would assume many of the aspects of guerrilla warfare and would not involve the operation of large armies at all.[5] The "nuclear guerrillas" would face the difficulty that, if a massed army *could* invade a friendly area despite nuclear opposition, rapidly occupying and "hugging" the population centers, the guerrillalike defenders would be in the position of using nuclear weapons among friends.

All of the foregoing has dealt with the area of the nuclear battlefield itself. The problem of entering the battlefield, or theatre of operations, and supporting the limited-war forces on it through the relatively few available port and airfield facilities, is a related but separate factor. These would be as vulnerable to atomic attack as any other concentrations. Although such facilities are likely candidates for a sanctuary role in a limited war, it would probably be overly hopeful to depend on such a role for them if nuclear weapons are used. They make tempting targets and the stakes elsewhere in the theatre would be high.

Alternative tactics might include reliance upon completely airborne operations, with appropriately designed aircraft using small fields in the forward areas; exclusive reliance on dispersed seaborne maneuvers "over-the-beach"; or some combination of these. The first alternative makes for relatively small forces simply because of the restricted tonnages that aircraft alone can furnish with any reasonable expenditure of resources. The second would require means for exceedingly rapid transfer of cargoes from ship to shore to minimize the risk of atomic attack. Supplies and troops would have to be loaded immediately into the vehicles and aircraft of the mobile supply system for rapid dispersal forward.

Resupply requirements for a Field Army might call for weekly delivery by a fleet of about ten ships able to carry 10,000 tons each. If adequately dispersed during simultaneous delivery — with, say, 5 miles between ships — they would cover a strip of beach 50 miles wide. Such lengths of shoreline with suitable beaches having access to the hinterland might, depending on the area, be difficult to find, and the dispersed overland supply routes difficult to control. Spacing deliveries in time (that is, one or two shiploads each day) could lead to critical problems of reserve storage in the event of occasional loss of a ship.

Larger fleets would be required for mass landings. Some 120,000 men landed in Normandy on D-Day from a fleet including 5,000 ships of all kinds. If such a fleet were dispersed to avoid a nuclear strike, it might be extended over hundreds of miles of coastline, or over many days during successive, small-scale landings. It would be a relatively simple matter for small enemy forces to destroy such landings piecemeal, even without nuclear weapons. If the landings were successful the problem of coalescing the separate landing groups into a unified army for deep penetrations into enemy territory might well be insuperable.

All of the theories of the atomic battlefield — "perpetual motion," static confrontation, "ships at sea," and "nuclear guerrillas" — combined with the problems of entering the battle area, lead to the conclusion that a nuclear battlefield works against massive forces.* Moreover, the uncertainties and logical contradictions in all these theories raise the question whether the idea of nuclear weapons on a battlefield is tenable at all, except as a desperate, all-or-nothing measure.

There would probably, in the actual case, be many compromises with the theoretical concepts, even if the use of nuclear weapons were accepted as a possibility. For example, it is likely that ports will be used, that there will be concentrations of supplies and troops, and that there will be a great temptation to fix the locations of tactical airfields. Since neither side could long survive as a cohesive military force if nuclear weapons were to be used indiscriminately, inhibitions against their use may well be as strong as the countervailing pressures in favor. Moreover, if there is any doubt about the use of nuclear weapons, then the advantages of force concentration accruing to the more audacious side will demand that the other side also take the risks, or lose.

## Other Factors Affecting Tactics

Many of the basic principles inherent in the nuclear battlefield can be expected to act even on a nonatomic battlefield as long as the use of nuclear weapons is possible. Deployment in depth, high mobility, rapid communications, sudden application of intensive firepower, and subsequent dispersal of force concentrations are principles underlying every modern commander's doctrines. And since in limited war (as, in fact, in any war) it is most desirable to carry out military operations rapidly and decisively, the development of effective, light, very mobile forces, which is spurred by the vision of the nuclear battlefield, is also desirable even if it is virtually certain that nuclear weapons will not be used.

But many other advances in technology, besides nuclear weapons, have acted to change military tactics. Their effects will be felt as strongly as those of nuclear weapons, even in a conventional-weapons conflict. A few of them are worth emphasizing.

*Antiaircraft Defenses.* Probably the most important nonnuclear weapon system improvement is the modern antiaircraft defense. Supersonic fighter aircraft, their weapons, and the ability of combat controllers

---

* It is uncertain whether the Soviets conceive of an atomic battlefield as described here. Indications from their writings[6] are that they do believe armies will have to be dispersed in the field, and that they will have to rely on lightning strikes to disrupt and destroy their enemy, taking advantage of the hugging tactic as well as the measure of protection provided by armor against nuclear weapons and residual radioactivity. Forces destroyed by nuclear weapons will be rapidly replaced by reserves. The conflict between dispersion to avoid catastrophic losses from a few weapons, and concentration to bring overwhelming military force to bear at a critical point must, however, be as difficult for them to resolve as it is for us.

on the ground to guide aircraft by means of radar to interception of an enemy plane have all improved the likelihood that enemy aircraft could be destroyed in air combat. There are, however, enough uncertainties in the sorting out of multiple targets for the interceptors, assignment of defending aircraft to them, and the monitoring of the details for a complex air battle, that in an attack by many aircraft a number of the attackers, perhaps a substantial number, might still get through.

This likelihood becomes much smaller in the presence of modern antiaircraft defenses on the ground. Radar direction of antiaircraft gunfire and the use of radar with guided antiaircraft missiles have led to a marked change, which in some circumstances amounts to a reversal, in the expected relative effectiveness of defense and attack. In contrast to World War II when thousands of rounds had to be fired with visual aiming of guns to score hits on even a few aircraft, a strong defense complex using missiles can now be expected to destroy so many attackers that sole reliance on the high-speed, high-altitude performance of the aircraft to penetrate these defenses is no longer feasible.

The tactics of air warfare have therefore been revolutionized. Evasion of the defenses and reduction of the time available for tracking and weapon firing require high-speed flight at very low altitudes. The terrain must be used to hide the aircraft. Decoys may have to be used to confuse the enemy and draw his fire. Attacks against the defenses themselves, by a variety of weapons, may have to take precedence over attacks against the target they guard.

If such defenses exist, therefore, the opening phases of any military engagement may have to be devoted to a duel between tactical aircraft and the opposing defensive systems. Air sweeps over enemy territory to seek out his fighters and destroy them in air combat might be part of the engagement, but only part. For if the ground-based defenses are not destroyed, air attacks and reconnaissance in support of the ground battle may be impossible. Without having any aircraft, an army can deny its opponent the use of the airspace over its critical positions and installations. This is a new development in warfare. And it may be encountered outside the heavily defended areas of the Communist Bloc nations. It is known, for example, that the Soviets have given antiaircraft missiles to Cuba, and the United States has sold them to Israel.

*Antitank Weapons.* In the last several years the effectiveness of antitank weapons have progressed far beyond what it was in World War II and Korea.[7] Guided missiles have been designed to hit tanks accurately at many times the range of the familiar "bazooka" rocket of yesterday's infantryman. Their hollow-charge explosive warheads can penetrate even the heaviest armor. They are light in weight, and can be carried by and launched from a jeep or a helicopter. They are therefore highly mobile as well.

This development may significantly reduce the value of the tank as a relatively impregnable, mobile fortress. The large-scale attacks en masse in open country by armored forces, penetrating or sweeping around defensive lines to reach the enemy's supply and reserve areas, may still be a most devastating form of attack if the defense does not have large numbers of modern antitank weapons. But if it does, then a turning point in conventional-weapons war may well have been reached. The armored column may have ceased to be a juggernaut able to overrun everything in its path, and the tank-to-tank battles of Rommel's day may have gone the way of duels between battleships.

*High-Capacity Cargo Aircraft.* When the most advanced military cargo aircraft was the Dakota, able to carry about twenty troops and little heavy equipment, airborne operations by paratroops could be considered only as an adjunct to groundborne attacks. The paratroops were dropped a short distance behind enemy lines to help prepare the way for a frontal attack on the ground. They could hold ground against light opposition, provided a linkup with the main forces occurred in a few hours or a day. This was the successful pattern of Sicily and Normandy in World War II. But if the linkup did not occur the paratroops could become heavily embattled when the enemy moved to surround them, and the ground attack became a rescue operation. This happened at Arnhem during the invasion of Germany.

The problem was, of course, that the airborne troops could not carry with them their heavy combat equipment, such as artillery. This weakness has been overcome to a great extent with the development of cargo aircraft able to carry from 10 to 50 tons of men and equipment over long distances. At the same time, the weight of combat equipment has been reduced, so that lightly armored combat vehicles, artillery, rockets with nuclear warheads, antiaircraft missiles, antitank missiles, and small trucks can be carried in the larger cargo aircraft.

It is now possible to transport an effective fighting force by air over the oceans to places where war is imminent or has begun. These forces cannot be as large or heavily equipped, of course, as those carried by sea. But we can contemplate advanced guards, powerfully armed, which can be dropped by parachute if not landed at airfields, able to maneuver on the ground and sustain themselves for many days with air-dropped supplies. The response to overt aggression far from our fixed bases of permanent military strength can be much more rapid than it was in Korea. And these units can play an important role in sustained military conflict; they give a new dimension to the maneuvers of the ground army.

## The Guerrilla Battlefield

It is in the nature of a guerrilla force that it is invariably small and weak when it starts its military operations. It is not well equipped and cannot maneuver as an army in the field. It must use hit-and-run tactics, never becoming involved in a prolonged battle.

Remaining hidden in the population or in rough terrain that restricts the movement of regular forces, the guerrillas engage in combat only if they feel certain of success. In any local engagement they seek numerical superiority and take advantage of surprise attacks. Ambush and night attack against small regular units are their stock-in-trade. If the surprise attack is successful, they can collect the weapons and equipment they are after; if resistance is strong, they will break off the engagement and vanish in the favorable terrain, since it is not in their interest to hold the ground of the battlefield. They do not usually take prisoners.

The deployment of the defending regular forces usually favors the guerrillas' tactics. There are many attractive targets for the guerrillas to attack, scattered in a wide variety of locations. The regulars are distributed to defend these points, in consort with less well trained, quasi-military forces such as the police or civil guard units. Having been spread thinly, the defending units are more vulnerable to guerrilla attacks, since the latter can more easily amass sufficient force to attain local superiority.

Although any selected defensive position can be made strong enough to withstand attack, there will always be weak points that can be successfully overrun, contributing in the long run to rising guerrilla strength. For this reason, static defense is not enough; the guerrillas must be sought out and destroyed or captured. But since they occupy terrain that is ideal for hiding and since they can, if they are pressed hard enough, disband and merge with the general population, a military sweep in force through an area of guerrilla activity is likely to be ineffective in locating and defeating guerrilla bands.

One method of overcoming these disadvantages is the adoption of the guerrilla tactics and ways of life. The attacking force operates in the area occupied by the guerrillas, in groups of sufficient size to win in most encounters, but not so large that they are easily located and avoided. Surprise and ambush are then important tactics for the regulars as well as for the guerrillas.

The regulars will have certain advantages in this kind of operation. Relative to the guerrillas, they will be able to draw on unlimited resources of weapons, equipment, and logistic support. They will be able to reach remote regions by air and be resupplied by air if necessary, even though their patrolling and combat operations are on foot. They have the advantage of better communications, so that they can coordinate their activities over a large area. The British in Malaya used these tactics to drive the guerrillas out of the jungle into the waiting police forces in more civilized areas.

At the same time, weakly defended posts and villages must be protected somehow. Mobile reserves must be on call within a defended area. Since the guerrilla tactic is primarily one of hit and run, if the reserves move overland and are slow to arrive, the guerrillas can discontinue the battle and disappear into the countryside to strike again elsewhere. They can also set ambushes for the reserves, attacking a post deliberately to lure them into the trap. For these reasons, the rescue forces can be more effective if they move by air, using helicopters (or, in the future, vertical-takeoff airplanes) to reach the battle.

The weapons used by the guerrillas are always relatively simple. Rifles, submachine and machine guns, mortars, bazookas, and some simple radio receivers are available to them. To preserve their mobility, they do not want anything more complicated, even if they could learn to use it. They are most likely to move on foot, on horseback, or in small boats (depending on the local geography), and have no supply lines. Each band takes its supplies from local villages and small food and arms caches nearby.

Since the regulars have only to shoot people and not machines, their weapons are equally simple, if more modern. They may also bring simple tactical aircraft into action for reconnaissance and bombing. They may use helicopters, transport aircraft, and armored vehicles. They have well-established supply lines, which are at the same time free to move everywhere but vulnerable to attack anywhere.

Finally, even though massive sweeps through the countryside may not catch many guerrillas, they may have the advantage, if they are frequent enough, of keeping the guerrillas on the go. The latter will have trouble consolidating their gains, or simply resting for the next fight. If the sweeps are not enough in themselves to defeat the guerrillas, they can be a useful adjunct to the other methods.

The need for intelligence weighs even more heavily here than in conventional warfare, because only through intelligence is each side able to locate and strike the other. If the guerrillas have properly built their base of support in the population, they will, at least early in the war, have better intelligence than the defending regulars. The people will give them information, but withhold it from the government. Analysis of

101

patterns of recurring activity from reported incidents, and careful, extensive, police interrogation and search are almost the only methods open to the government in these circumstances. But if the counter-guerrilla forces are successful their opportunities for gaining voluntary intelligence from the populace will obviously increase.

This, then, is the picture of the guerrilla battlefield. It is war by stealth and ambush, with no front and no rear. Concentration of forces discourages attack at the point of concentration, but encourages it elsewhere. Dispersal of forces invites nibbling attacks everywhere, until the defenders are weakened and bled to destruction. The government must undertake almost every kind of military activity from guerrillalike patrols to frantic rescues reminiscent of the old cavalry-and-Indian days of the American West, against an elusive and crafty foe. The population is a pawn, pressed by both sides for information, and by one for food and shelter.

Although the regulars may use the machines of war, it is not a war of machine against machine as the conventional war can easily become. It is basically a war of man against man, with the simplest of weapons.

# 8

## The Logic of Multifarious Requirements

IT IS now possible to bring some logic into the vast and many-faceted array of kinds of limited war, geographical features of potential conflict areas, and military-technological factors on the battlefield.

All of the correlative factors of physical and ethnic geography permit environments and armed forces over the world to be arranged in an orderly array, or matrix. Within this matrix, the elements can be arranged so that each represents a particular *kind* of limited war for which military forces must be prepared. Such a matrix is an abstract description of a complex reality. As an analytical tool, it can be useful to help clarify the problems of force structure planning. We shall want a representation for this purpose to be simple, accepting a high degree of oversimplification in description of real situations in exchange for clarity of conception.

Let us postulate that only two factors characterize a limited war: the enemy and the location. By describing certain characteristics of the enemy's technological competence and armed force structure, we shall subsume all of his military organization, tactical doctrine, political, economic, and cultural orientation. By characterizing locations or physical environments in terms of their impact on mobility of military forces, we shall subsume all of the other characteristics of force structure, weapons, equipment, and tactics necessary to operate in the environment.

Consider then, three types of enemy, designated $E_1$, $E_2$, $E_3$, and three types of environment, designated $L_1$, $L_2$, and $L_3$, as follows:

$E_1$ An enemy who has much the same military-technological sophistication as we ourselves, although his military machine may differ in detail of weapons and organization from our own. He would have an extensive capability for mechanized warfare where appropriate; nuclear weapons; battlefield ballistic missiles; a full range of artillery weapons; large tactical air forces; well-developed antiaircraft defenses; and the ability to use electronic technology in all aspects of warfare. At present this can describe, among our potential enemies, only the Soviet armed forces and perhaps some of the allies with whom they are closely associated in the Warsaw Pact. Ultimately the Communist Chinese might be included here. However, we are not interested particularly in precisely whose forces are included; only in the kind of enemy we face.

$E_2$ An enemy able to organize and operate armed forces using fairly modern weapons and equipment. The latter might include artillery; tanks if appropriate to the geographical region; tactical air forces that might vary from formidable (for example, in the case of the Communist Chinese) to virtually nonexistent (in the case of any of the newly emerging nations of the world); some antiaircraft weapons (most likely in the form of antiaircraft artillery and smaller weapons, but possibly including Soviet-furnished surface-to-air missiles); and the ability to use radar and radio communications to some perhaps substantial degree, though not to engage in elaborate electronic warfare. This class includes by far the greatest number of military organizations in the world and the greatest variation in equipment and military ability among these organizations. The essential characteristic unifying them all is a degree of technological sophistication that, even though in some cases it might be considered high in comparison with that of the less advanced members of the group, is nevertheless not equal to that of a highly industrialized society.

$E_3$ Includes the primitive forces most likely to engage in guerrilla warfare. They are characterized by an almost total lack of technological sophistication, have no aircraft, no radar, and although their communications systems may include some radios, they are in general rudimentary. Again, there may be some considerable variation from one such force to another. Some countries may have organized armies that are in effect as primitive in their equipment and operations as guerrillas, while some guerrillas may have considerable military skill and the ability to manufacture weapons; still other groups may be virtual bandits unable to equip all of their men with even the simplest firearms.

$L_1$ An environment with extensive industrial development, including, especially, highly developed transportation and communication facilities. In general, cross-country movement of mechanized forces with reasonable flexibility in choice of maneuvering paths is possible. This corresponds in the main with the flat-moderate, and certain small portions of the mountainous-moderate generic regions.

$L_2$ An environment with some industrial development, but with only moderately to poorly developed transport and communication facilities. In this environment, cross-country vehicular movement is possible to some reasonable degree. Included here are the flat-dry and a small fraction of the mountainous-dry and moutainous-moderate generic regions.

$L_3$ An environment which, while it may have some industry, has little or no development of transport and communication facilities, and in which surface cross-country movement of mechanized forces is impossible or possible in local areas only. This includes the flat-wet and most of the mountainous generic regions.

War at sea or in the air must be associated with an enemy and the environment in which he originates. They are therefore included implicitly in the foregoing definitions.

Each type of enemy listed can, with some probability, face us in each kind of environment. Each of the possible combinations of $E_i$ and $L_j$ (where $i$ and $j$ can be 1, 2, or 3) represents a possible kind of limited war, against some enemy in his characteristic environment. The arrangement of all the combinations in a matrix, as illustrated in Figure 8.1, has some interesting characteristics.

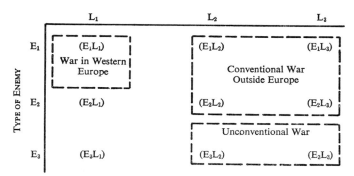

TYPE OF PHYSICAL ENVIRONMENT
(*Locale*)

FIGURE 8.1 LIMITED-WAR MATRIX

*The "matrix" is an orderly array of combinations of enemy (vertical axis) and environment (horizontal axis). Each "element" in parentheses represents a combination of enemy and environment leading to warfare of a distinct character, as illustrated by outlines including various elements.*

105

We can observe, first, that only one element of the matrix, $(E_1L_1)$, represents limited war against the Russians or the Warsaw Pact nations in Western Europe. Second, although the internal variations of force structure in the class $E_2$ are great, these force types vary in an orderly way with location. An army organized for mechanized warfare in the desert is likely to be found in the combination $(E_2L_2)$. In the combination $(E_2L_3)$ troops who move on foot in jungle-type terrains are more likely to be encountered. Thus the matrix element $(E_2L_2)$ might represent limited wars in the Near or Middle East, while $(E_2L_3)$ might represent limited war involving organized Communist forces in Southeast Asia. Third, since the environments $L_2$ and $L_3$ are far more suitable for guerrilla operations than is $L_1$, the wars represented by elements $(E_3L_2)$ and $(E_3L_3)$ are far more likely to occur than $(E_3L_1)$ (which may be met quickly by action of the very effective police forces available in $L_1$, or as the Hungarian rebellion was met by the Red Army). These are the "wars of national liberation."

Finally, we may note that the complete change in the conditions of warfare that can occur with external intervention in a conventional limited war, or with the evolution of unconventional war, is easily expressed by a change of matrix element. A local war in the Middle Eastern desert, $(E_2L_2)$, would change to $(E_1L_2)$ with Russian intervention. The war in South Vietnam, currently described by $(E_3L_3)$, would change to $(E_2L_3)$ if the Communist Viet Cong experience continuing success or North Vietnam were to intervene openly in force. The Korean War remained a borderline case between $(E_2L_2)$ and $(E_2L_3)$ after the Chinese intervention; such intervention in a 1970 Korean War would, if the Chinese Communists achieve nuclear weapons and substantial industrial development by then, change to $(E_1L_2)$ in Korea and perhaps even to $(E_1L_1)$ if extended to Manchuria.

The character of sea warfare changes over the matrix as well. The full range of antisubmarine and antiair operations, as well as strikes against objectives on land, might be expected in war against an "$E_1$" enemy. Strikes against land targets, and amphibious operations, would probably predominate in the naval aspects of an "$E_2$" war. Small-scale amphibious operations and the exercise of vigilance — guard and escort duty — might be the main function of sea power in war against the enemy "$E_3$."

The abstract limited-war matrix of Figure 8.1 thus encompasses the entire scope of limited war for which we must plan. The kind of war represented by each matrix element presents us with particular technical and policy problems in planning a limited-war force structure.

Although it would be naive to think that a separate and unique force should or would be designed to meet the needs of each type of war, the more subtle obverse, that a single force type could meet the needs of all, is also untrue. Each of the elements of the limited-war matrix must be accounted for in creating the limited-war force structure. Specialized forces must be provided where failure to do so would too severely compromise or handicap general-purpose military capability.

## PART III

# THE PROBLEMS
# OF PLANNING

# 9

## The Planning Process

SINCE the military forces exist to support the national foreign policy, the planning of the military force structure should begin at the highest levels of government, where foreign, defense, economic, and all other policies are decided and interact. This does occur in many ways. But it is the weapons and equipment of the military forces that enable them to carry out the particular tasks demanded by specified policies. The design and development of weapons systems and military equipment have their roots in research and engineering processes that are only partly controllable at the policy-making level.

Technical areas where research and weapon development should be emphasized, in the hope that certain desired military capabilities will result, can be selected by the direction of those who make national policy and its derivative defense policies. The weapons and equipment that are ultimately provided, however, must emerge from a host of decisions, important or minor, made by the directors of individual projects in the military Services and in the defense industry. Science and engineering must also have a powerful influence. In the last analysis they are the determinants of military capability because they determine the shape of the force structure.

The national policy must therefore inevitably be tempered by what is possible in technological progress and by the internal workings of the many public and private organizations that influence and control that progress. The defense planning structure is the embodiment of this interplay between what is desired and what is made available. It is the intermediary, trying to translate policy into the tools for policy implementation.

In this chapter we shall review the planning process as it is intended to work. The problems encountered in the attempt to make it work well can then be described.

In the National Security Council the President meets with the heads of the Government Departments to decide the general outlines of national objectives at home and abroad and the military force structure desired to meet them. At the time of policy formulation, the Central Intelligence Agency and the Defense Intelligence Agency will have described, through the Director of Central Intelligence, the current and estimated future state of the military capability of nations the world over. They will have made estimates of the likely strategy of potential enemies, and assessed the future military balance among friend and possible foe. The State Department will have described local situations in various specific areas and suggested political strategy and tactics to meet local pressures in ways suited to local conditions.

With this information, and the advice of the Council, the President lays out the strategic needs. The military support of those needs is the responsibility of the Secretary of Defense and the military Service Chiefs. Based on their knowledge of weapons and forces in the inventory and in process of development, they recommend the kinds of forces, their size, and the worldwide deployments that will be needed. The availability of resources and fiscal policy to maximize their usefulness are then the concern of the Treasury Department and the Bureau of the Budget. From all these separate considerations, with pressure and influence by all the participants, the military needs will be projected and the broad outlines of a future force structure agreed upon.[1]

These broad policy statements initiate a more detailed planning cycle for the military forces, their weapons, equipment, and organization. The process begins with a series of descriptive statements of military "requirements."

In technical military parlance, a "requirement" is the expression of the mission and form of a military system. It is based on a view of what needs to be done, which is based in turn on the nature of the opposition the potential enemy is expected to present. Each military Service, using the policy guidance transmitted through the Secretary of Defense and the Joint Chiefs of Staff, as well as the strategic and technical forecasts of the intelligence agencies, prepares and keeps current a set of documents describing what its weapons, equipment, and organization should look like in 5 to 10 years. These statements are usually rather general in nature. But when a new system development is imminent the "requirement statement" is made quite specific, often down to the last detail of its form and performance.

The writing of the requirements involves almost all parts of the Services, including the top policy-making level and all the groups concerned with doing the research and development on new systems, testing them, and using them. Collectively, they must examine the military need and the various ways of meeting it. Various points of view must be reconciled; the final statement must represent either a compromise among conflicting demands or a decision of the Service Chief of Staff, Secretary, and Assistant Secretaries that a particular approach should dominate.

A requirement, if adequately considered, does not represent an abstract statement of need. For this would have little meaning if the expressed need were not related to the possibility of implementation. It starts with some situations, locales, and potential enemy capability in view. It must then be tested by exploration of the technical feasibility of building the system called for. Only if the requirement still appears reasonable in the light of possible extensions of technology, can it be considered valid. If the original statement is found to be unreasonable, it must be modified; perhaps a lesser capability than was originally desired must be accepted. Very often, the test of reasonableness, of technical feasibility, is omitted. The resulting "requirement" either becomes a major headache or is ignored.

Each of the Services is divided roughly into an action or "operations" part (including logistics and other force management), and a planning, research and development part. Within the latter portion of the Services exist separate commands whose concern is the specification and promulgation of requirements for future military systems on the one hand, and the creation of those systems on the other. The requirements portion of this activity is in general tied very closely to the action part of the Service, so that there is a close coordination of the effort that implements plans for warfare contingencies and that which specifies needed future capability to meet them better. It is through the requirements side of the house that the Service Chiefs of Staff are able to control the description and creation of the forces they will need in the future. A highly simplified diagram of this organization and its relationship to the weapons acquisition cycle is shown in Figure 9.1.[2]

The creation of weapons systems and new organizations is, of course, a lengthy and arduous procedure.[3] Within the technical commands responsible for this task are many subsidiary units including research laboratories, systems management organizations having teams that direct specific major projects, as well as individual contract managers who call

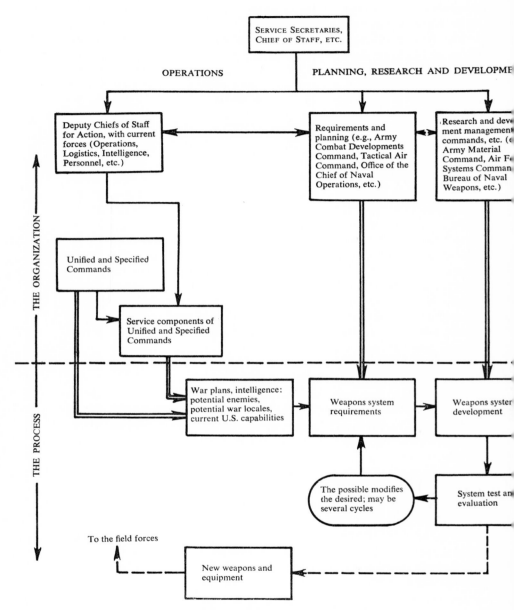

FIGURE 9.1 NEW SYSTEMS ACQUISITION

on the laboratories for technical assistance in management of the work of the defense industry. There are also a number of specialized test commands whose responsibility it is to test equipment in the field and rule on its adequacy for incorporation in the Service structure.

As a system or piece of equipment passes through the research, development, and engineering phases, it eventually comes under the cognizance of the various testing organizations, who then coordinate closely with the requirements command. The latter, having described the new item, is now concerned to see that the system and the organizations using it do in fact perform as originally specified.

Because it is never certain *a priori* that the technological resolution of a military problem will, over the course of many years, come to meet the original specification, it frequently happens that performance is different from that which was originally intended. In this case, the requirements planning and action parts of the Services must judge whether the performance of the system is nevertheless acceptable or whether the system must be changed. If it is estimated that, despite changes, the system will not meet original requirements, it must then be determined whether a new set of requirements, modified to take account of the possible rather than the ideally desirable, should be promulgated and the system modified to meet these. Alternatively, it may be decided at this point that the requirement cannot be met, that the performance which *can* be achieved will not be adequate to do the job significantly better than it could have been done originally, and that the system development should therefore be discontinued.

The Services do not engage in all of their planning activity unwatched and undirected. The Secretary of Defense and his Assistant Secretaries, such as the Comptroller and the Director of Defense Research and Engineering, are required by law to oversee the Services in the planning and renewal of military forces. All of the Service work is therefore subject to annual review in several different parts of the Defense Secretary's "office." The Director of Defense Research and Engineering reviews programs from a technical point of view; the Comptroller must see that the resource allocation among various programs is the best that can be achieved to accomplish the ends of military and foreign policy. The Assistant Secretary for International Security Affairs is concerned with how the military structure will meet foreign policy commitments, and especially with how the military program relates to and feeds the various military assistance programs. There are also Assistant Secretaries responsible for procurement and support of accepted military equipment, and for the allocation of resources within the defense industry for this purpose.

Each year at budget review time, and also at periods in between, the top management of the defense establishment decides whether the specification of requirements for military systems, the Service allocations of effort and funds in various research, development, and procurement areas, and the technical quality as well as costs of all the defense program components are adequate and meeting schedules. In this review process, the various civilian defense management offices work closely with the Services to review requirements and programs. They have the final responsibility to approve or disapprove programs, and also responsibility to attempt to shift Service programs in new directions or initiate new efforts if in their view the individual Service efforts are unbalanced or inadequate.

It will be recognized immediately that any program or proposal must, during its life, go through an extraordinarily large number of steps of management review. The possibility of redirection by adding to or modifying programs to meet new plans or accept new products of technology; acceleration; delay; or elimination exists at virtually every step. And the process repeats itself, year in and year out.

A proposal for a new system can start at almost any place in this cycle. It can be made by the topmost military commands in the field or in the Pentagon; by subsidiary military commands in the field; by the civilian directors of the defense establishment; by the various government laboratories or management organizations; or by various segments of the defense industry. Wherever such a proposal originates, it must be examined by the operations and requirements commands. If the idea is wholly new and a statement of requirement for it does not exist, the "rules of the game" demand that it be reviewed with respect to its potential role in the military organization. If it appears interesting and useful, a "requirement" must be written. The idea must be sent to the appropriate commands for technical review before it can be approved; they must, if they find the idea technically feasible, prepare a technical development plan. Approval of the technical plan must be given by the requirements and operational commands, and the Service Chief of Staff. If the program will absorb more than some relatively modest amount of money (such as, perhaps, a million dollars in a year, or ten million altogether), it must also be reviewed and approved by the civilian defense managers in the Office of the Secretary of Defense. It is then carried from development through testing by the technical commands, with annual review throughout its growth. Upon completion of tests and evaluation, the entire organization must decide, serially and collectively, whether the system or equipment should be procured in quantity and integrated into the armed forces. The procurement and integration itself is monitored at various levels in the Office of the Secretary of Defense and in the Services.

Within this broad pattern, there is a continuing interplay among the various components of the technical commands, and between the technical and operational commands. This is associated with the numerous day-to-day decisions needed to resolve the problems that invariably arise in a new technological and organizational development. What should be done, for example, if a contractor does not meet a deadline, if available money is spent before a development phase is completed, or if a critical test fails?

At any one of the steps of major or minor review, at any "milestone" in a program, it is possible to redirect it somewhat. Major redirection requires another journey through the entire planning and management organization, with all the time that it takes.

The planning and review structure just sketched out does not yet include all of the steps through which military programs must pass in the process of implementation. After approval of a new system or continuation of efforts previously begun, at all the various levels in the Defense Department, the programs enter the military budget. This is then reviewed by the Bureau of the Budget, the President, and the Congress.

The Bureau of the Budget is concerned with the synthesis of defense and other national resource expenditures. If these expenditures appear unbalanced, in view of the resources available and Treasury Department fiscal policy, the Bureau of the Budget may stipulate reductions in defense outlays. Presumably their nature is the responsibility of the Secretary of Defense and his organization; it is not inconceivable, however, that the Bureau of the Budget may offer suggestions of a technical nature as well. The impact of budget review at this level is again felt in all the Service programs, since, according to the priorities which the Service and other defense chiefs establish, many programs will have to be either eliminated or curtailed. After these changes are incorporated, the President, aided by his staff, has the final power of approval over the recommended defense effort.

But it is the task of the Congress under our Constitution to raise armed forces. The Congress naturally gives very close attention to the distribution of resources and effort in the implementation of defense policy, to which it contributes and which it must approve. As anyone knows who follows the Congressional defense budget hearings and actions, the Congress concerns itself first with major weapons systems and the defense policy under which they are implemented. The argument between the Air Force and Navy about the relative merits of B-36 bombers and aircraft carriers; the question of the "missile gap"; the controversies over the RS-70 strategic reconnaissance/strike aircraft, the SKYBOLT air-launched ballistic missile, and the TFX tactical fighter are all examples of Congress' concern with major defense policy and systems.

The Congressional review does not stop at that point, however. The records of the Congressional hearings show that its Armed Services and Appropriations Committees may well be concerned with individual weapons or areas of research. They have, for example, questioned the Army's effort in developing and modifying tanks,[4] and they have taken positions on small social science research projects related to the defense problem.[5] Here then, is another area of uncertainty wherein programs, large and small, can be affected in many different ways.

Within this whole procedure the defense establishment and higher Executive and Congressional authority are dealing with military systems that include weapons, supporting equipment, the organizations that use them, associated training and maintenance, and the relationships of the various subsidiary organizations (with their equipment) to the over-all armed forces structure. It is inevitable that as program direction percolates through the system to various lower echelons of management, it will, in some degree, be fragmented. In the actual business of creating a military system, efforts at the working level are more often devoted to the creation of components than of entire systems. More people work at providing specific airplanes, missile guidance systems, guns, or radio sets than entire air defense or communications systems.

The responsibility for merging the components into the complete systems resides at the upper levels of management. This is an extremely difficult task for which the managing organization needs a great deal of technical and scientific assistance. A whole new scientific discipline, whose components have such names as "military operations research," "systems analysis," or "econometrics," has grown in the last 10 or 15 years to provide this assistance.

To describe this discipline in all its intricate detail would require a separate book; in fact many have been written.[6] But it is worth reviewing very briefly. It provides analysis, following scientific and mathematical procedures, of the interrelationships among military systems and their components, and of the interchange of military capability with resources when various kinds of military systems and organizations can carry out specific military tasks. The scientific method is applied to the management problems of selection among many alternatives and allocation of resources.

The use of this discipline requires that the analysts work closely with the military establishment. Requirements for military systems must be

118

defined in quantitative terms. For example, the distance to be covered and the load to be carried by transport aircraft, the lethal radius of weapons, the minimum size of target that must be photographed in detail by aerial cameras, or the words per minute that must flow through communication systems must be determined by scientific analysis. The technological possibilities for meeting these requirements must then be forecast. The technical feasibility of meeting them in particular ways must be assessed. Finally judgments must be made, according to quantitative descriptions of potential performance, regarding the ultimate utility of postulated systems. Analyses of this kind lead to the comparison between proposed requirements and estimates of attainable performance, which assures that requirements statements are reasonable.

Several alternative ways of carrying out military tasks generally result from this procedure. (They may also result from various Service and industry proposals for systems to meet requirements previously stated.) These must be compared on the basis of their respective performance and costs (that is, cost/effectiveness), so that the system which will give the best performance, or be the most effective, for the least cost can be selected.

The critical problem in making this selection is to define precisely the criteria of effectiveness. In general, a "measure of effectiveness" is taken to be some number or group of numbers that describe the end result of a system's operation. This might be bombs on target, targets destroyed, aircraft intercepted or destroyed in an air battle, amount of cargo delivered in a given time at a given distance, submarines detected — the possible measures outnumber the systems by far.

The cost of systems is compared on the basis of incremental effectiveness for incremental dollars. If two systems perform in the same way and they are equally effective, their costs might be compared directly. But if one is more effective than the other, according to the same measure, then the difference in cost that yields the margin of added performance is of interest. If that margin is small but the cost large, the gain may not be worth the added resources. If a large performance gain can be achieved for little cost, that is ideal.

But the comparisons are rarely so straightforward. For one thing, it is difficult to forecast with certainty the cost of a future system based on an untried advance in technology. There is also great uncertainty in the selection and quantitative expression of "measures of effectiveness." It is difficult to say, for example, how well a proposed defensive system will counter an enemy offensive weapon when we cannot state precisely what either will look like at some time far in the future.

It is difficult, too, to specify the military tasks that should be stressed in a system design. A fighter-bomber, for example, must fly through enemy defenses as well as destroy targets. It may be found that one which can do a better job of destruction might not be able to reach its target as easily as another, whereas the better-penetrating system may not drop as many bombs as accurately. The criterion for "destruction" may vary over a whole range of possibilities, from enough damage to keep the enemy from using the "target" for a time to total obliteration. Estimates of both destructive and defense-penetrating ability are uncertain. What, then, is the net ability of the system to wage war against the enemy? Even if this could be expressed, it might then be found that the system with better performance may cost an intolerably higher amount, or have undesirable subsidiary characteristics. Or, two systems which can do the same task may each carry out other, different tasks, so that their relative military value cannot be expressed quantitively for direct comparison.

Uncertainties of this kind defy quantitative expression, and prevent the establishment of firm bases of comparison among alternative systems. This "criterion problem" has been discussed many times in great detail and need not be described further here.[7] The essential point to be made is that this type of analysis has many limitations and includes many uncertainties which cannot be overcome by mathematical formulation of the problems. The element of judgment is very great. All that operations research or systems analysis can do is indicate to the decision maker the components of his problem, a number of the alternatives from which he must choose, and some *possible* consequences of various decisions in the selection process.

Despite the limitations of this form of technical assistance to management, it has proven to be indispensable in sorting out the enormously complex array of possible solutions that technology presents in answer to our worldwide military needs.[8]

In another area, that of managing large programs, such as the POLARIS, with hundreds of component efforts (rocket engine, launch system, guidance system, and so on) that must all join together at some far future date, the operations research community has presented to the defense managers an information-processing technique called PERT[9] (for Program Evaluation and Review Technique). PERT, and its many variants with other names, uses electronic computers and statistical forecasting methods to solve scheduling problems and to forecast critical delays in component programs.

Secretary of Defense McNamara has come to rely heavily on cost/effectiveness analyses when making difficult decisions. Mr. Charles Hitch, the Assistant Secretary (Comptroller), has introduced the methods of systems analysis and the formalized Defense Program[10] for planning and review of the defense effort, as an aid in making decisions on long-term allocation of resources among various individual programs.

All of the military Services and the Joint Chiefs of Staff (through the Secretary of Defense) have let contracts to nonprofit organizations — such as the well-publicized RAND Corporation, which does most of its work for the Air Force — to assist them in these very difficult decision problems. Diverse contracts to similar independent organizations, profit-making or not, are also let as the need arises. Because of the latitude possible in judgment and selection of system performance criteria, which can be disguised by apparent mathematical rigor, the work of this scientific-analytical community represents still another multiple source of ideas and judgments that can either expedite or introduce conflict and delay into the whole, ponderous defense-planning procedure.

# 10

## Resource Allocation:
## Levels of Decision and Constraint

### Levels and Kinds of Decision

MANY kinds of decision have to be made in determining the nature of the limited-war force structure. There is, first, the sequence of decisions regarding the distribution of the national budget, and of the military budget among major components of the defense and foreign policy sectors. After resources are allocated for the defense budget, these must be divided among the strategic forces, the limited-war forces, and other areas in support of the defense effort (such as the Defense Communications Agency).

A number of decisions about the limited-war force structure itself then have to be made, as illustrated in Figure 10.1. The system selection process is seen to be part of an endless chain of events in the maintenance and renewal of that structure. There is, here, a continuous interplay between two components of the decision process:

- The conscious decision to mold forces in a desired direction, consistent with current policies.

- The need to accept military capability as it becomes available from prior commitments to perhaps outdated policies, through the completion of long-term weapons developments.

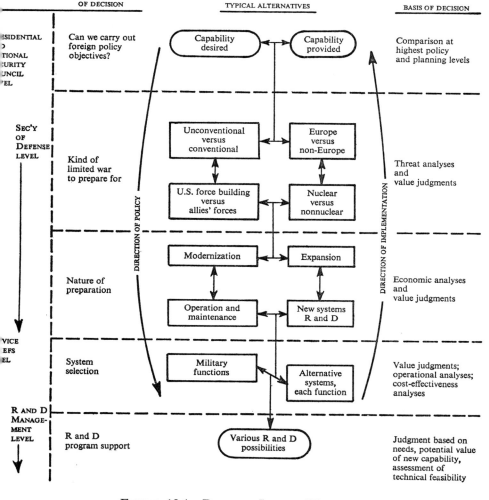

FIGURE 10.1  DECISION LEVELS WITHIN
THE LIMITED-WAR PLANNING AREA

The stronger the second component of this process, the more likely it is that desired policies will have to be compromised and adapted to the capability available.

Since at any time the defense program is in a continuous state of evolution, with new projects beginning and existing ones in process or approaching fruition, the top-level planner who hopes to institute new policies can change its direction only gradually. He can start some new

123

projects, cancel or redirect some that are ongoing. But he cannot do this all at once.

To appreciate the constraints resulting from this interaction between the desired and the possible, we should first examine the nature of some of the decisions, other than system selection, illustrated in Figure 10.1.

*What Kinds of Limited War?* At the policy-making level, this decision appears, at first, straightforward enough. It is made in response to questions such as the following:

- What is the relative emphasis to be given to conventional limited war and unconventional warfare?

- For conventional limited war, to what degree should we concentrate on future systems for wars described by $(E_1L_1)$ in the limited-war matrix (that is, military actions by the Russians or their major satellites in Europe); on those described by the matrix elements $(E_1L_2)$ or $(E_1L_3)$ (that is, overt aggression by the Russians or the Chinese Communists, outside of Europe); or on those represented by the matrix elements $(E_2L_2)$ and $(E_2L_3)$ (that is, wars, like Korea, started by the proxies of the major Communist powers, or even non-Communist powers such as those in the Middle East)?

- Relative to some of these alternatives, should we emphasize nuclear or conventional-weapons warfare, and to what degree?

- For limited wars outside Europe, how much reliance do we place on the military assistance program and the conventional military strength it gives our allies; to what extent do we build capabilities for unconventional warfare into our own forces, and to what extent do we equip, train, and rely on indigenous forces?

These questions are not mutually exclusive, nor are they sequential; they all interact, and any answer to one will affect the answers to the others. While they might be separated for purposes of individual consideration and decision, none of them can be considered alone.

*Keeping Current Forces Going.* Maintenance and operation of existing forces is a relatively fixed expense that cannot be evaded. It includes the support of ready forces in forward areas and reserves in the United States. It includes the cost of force rotation to overseas locations in accordance with the demands of policy and world events; the cost of basic and specialized training that goes with constant rotation of personnel in and out of the Services; and the costs of live war games or maneuvers and training for readiness of both the reserve and deployed forces. Finally, we must add to these routine operating costs those that come from the *ad hoc* use of forces for political and deterrent purposes: the movement of battle groups into and out of Berlin to re-emphasize access rights, the 1962 deployment of Marines to Thailand during the Laotian War, establishment of the quarantine of Cuba, and the like.

But while the forces in being must be paid for, the size of forces that we feel can or must be supported is a matter of judgment and decision, affected by other parts of defense and extra-defense planning.

*Force modernization and expansion* are related in a fairly obvious way. It may be decided, as it was at the time of the Berlin Crisis in 1961, that the limited-war forces must be rapidly increased in size to meet our immediate and urgent international commitments. In expanding these forces, we can continue to rely on existing military capabilities by increasing production of current types of equipment or using "off-the-shelf" equipment that has been stockpiled against such contingencies (in many cases since World War II). Or we can add new capability from among the products of new weapon developments that are coming into being, perhaps even committing them to production earlier than originally planned.

Even if force size is not changed, equipment, organization, and tactics must be improved to meet corresponding improvements on the part of potential enemies. It may well be found, on analysis of our commitments, that existing forces could fulfill them if their total military structure were to be transformed into the most modern possible. Then it might be decided to accelerate modernization, which usually takes place through replacement of obsolete and worn-out equipment at the end of its service life, with new types of systems and weapons.

The modernization decision for existing or expanded forces depends, for many items, on the answers to the questions about the kinds of limited war that should be emphasized. Although a general level of expenditure for modernization may be decided upon by the Defense Secretary, the nature of the modernization may call for hundreds of individual decisions within the Services, about specific equipment and weapons.

Decisions on modernization are often complicated by the alternative of "retrofixing" old equipment instead of obtaining new. The life of an existing system — a destroyer, for example — might be extended, at some cost less than that of a new system, by changes to improve its performance (such as replacing the ship's engines with new ones of a more modern design). The penalty may be that higher costs will be incurred later, when even the refitted equipment becomes obsolete.

Future obsolescence may incur even greater costs than anticipated if the future replacement turns out to be a more complex, and therefore more expensive, system. On the other hand, it may offer a capability not available earlier at any price. Acquisition of this capability may be delayed undesirably if a commitment to more moderate improvement is made earlier. Thus a current, definable capability with ascertainable cost must be assessed against anticipated performance associated with speculative cost estimations.

*Research and Development.* In the development of weapons systems and other equipment associated with military activity there is a normal flow of events, starting with the basic research that leads to new understanding of scientific phenomena. The new scientific knowledge is broadened and applied to practical things in applied research, from which ideas for military hardware emerge. Proof of the feasibility of a new scientific application may then lead to tentative development of a piece of military equipment, or in some cases a complete system, even though the possibility of final success may entail many scientific and engineering gambles. An "engineering development" phase, with ultimate procurement of the system in view, will be entered when it is reasonably certain that estimated performance can be achieved after the work of design, construction, and proof testing.

Basic and applied research studies deal in general with a single phenomenon and require but few people and relatively simple experimental facilities. (This is, of course, not true of major space research projects or such programs as particle accelerators for studying the physics of the atom.) Progression through the various phases of development presents an ever-increasing need for extensive design and shop facilities, and often calls for the manufacture of major hardware components that become part of the system under development. Cost at each stage therefore increases very rapidly through the entire process. Research projects can require as little as a few thousand dollars. In the early phases of development a number of different approaches to a problem may be tried; none of these parallel developments may, itself, cost very much. As the proper direction for further development emerges, the alternatives are narrowed until, in the engineering development, all effort is bent in one direction, manpower and facilities are added, and costs are high.

When a decision is made to undertake a major system development, it is obvious to everyone that it must be carefully considered because it will demand large resources. Decisions to undertake research projects are easier and less carefully controlled. The total cost of all basic research projects might be lower than that of even a single development such as a new missile system. Many research projects can be started without review at the upper levels of management. They can, however, ultimately trigger the major developments.

## Countervailing Constraints

Decision for changes in force size, modernization, or new-weapons-system development programs are tempered by the resources demanded and available for each. Each phase has characteristic costs that must be accepted, and all interact together in the final decision. Given certain forces in being, the fixed costs of supporting these forces must first be set aside. Part of the resource base must always be devoted to providing modern weapons and equipment currently available from the research and development process. There must exist, continuously, a certain number of research and development projects that will assure timely provision of new capabilities as existing equipment becomes obsolete or worn out.

Since the maintenance and operation cost of a force of given size is unavoidable, modernization from a fixed resource base must be traded against research and development in the allocation process; one will have to give if the other is stressed. Conversely, while allocation in both of these areas might ordinarily be based on funds available after the size of forces is determined, it is conceivable that dissatisfaction with the operational capability of the forces would lead to stress on modernization and research and development at the expense of the forces in being.

Table 10.1 shows the amount of money required for the various phases of the force building and maintenance process for two budget years.[1] The operation and maintenance costs for the entire defense establishment are seen to be larger in relation to the other components than in the case of the limited-war forces alone. Some undeterminable part of this difference is due to the department-wide support for activities and agencies, and the demands of the strategic forces with their large proportion of highly complex systems. Further, the over-all research and development costs are about 40 per cent of those for modernization (procurement), while for the limited-war forces alone this ratio is closer to 25 per cent. Modernization is evidently proceeding at a faster relative rate in the limited war forces than in the strategic forces. The over-all budget includes, also, a number of costly space programs that were, in the years shown, in the development stage. They will, when available, be individually more expensive to operate than the limited-war systems.

127

It becomes apparent that the relative expenditures for different parts of the armed forces and for the different phases of their evolution are hard to change drastically from one year to the next.

Precise control of the current state and future evolution of this monstrous organism, in response to policy demands, requires sound judgment and decision based on logical analysis at and within each decision level shown in Figure 10.1. This precision of control can easily be defeated if the cycle of force planning and implementation permits commitment, willy-nilly, to extensive research and development without a clear view of the requirements for the resulting systems. There is an implicit chicken-and-egg question here: Do we set a requirement and then look for a system, or do we find ourselves with a system and look for an application? Both approaches are taken.

TABLE 10.1

BUDGET BREAKDOWN AMONG MAJOR PHASES OF
MILITARY ACTIVITY — BILLIONS OF DOLLARS

| *Total, Defense Department* | | |
|---|---|---|
| Fiscal Year | 1963 | 1964 |
| Operation and Maintenance* | 24.8 | 26.2 |
| Procurement† | 17.0 | 17.7 |
| Research, Development, Test, Evaluation | 7.2 | 7.4 |
| | 49.0 | 51.3 |
| *Limited-War Forces‡* | | |
| Fiscal Year | 1963 | 1964 |
| Operation and Maintenance* | 9.4 | 10.0 |
| Procurement† | 9.6 | 9.7 |
| Research, Development, Test Evaluation | 2.3 | 2.8 |
| | 21.3 | 22.5 |

* Includes cost of "Manpower" plus "operation and maintenance," that is, total operating cost.
† Includes force expansion as well as modernization; in budget years shown, most cost was for modernization.
‡ Estimated from "program package" breakdown; includes General-purpose forces, Air and Sealift, and certain reserves, but no proportionate share of Service-wide general support.

The development of a new aircraft, engine, tank, or artillery piece generally begins with a prior view that a requirement for the item exists. The logic of the process can be followed. Often, however, a radical new capability appears from research undertaken independently of any criteria except an almost fortuitous judgment that the research is interesting and might have ultimate utility. The products of this research are then acquired for use in military missions that remain to be defined clearly. An example from the past is the acceptance of airplanes or, more recently, helicopters, by the armed forces. In the electronics area the inputs of research in solid-state physics have led to the development of new radio equipment that offers many benefits, and for which military requirements can be found without a great deal of trouble. There is currently an intuitive feeling in many quarters that the evolving man-in-space capability should be put to military use.[2]

These are not examples of poor or undesirable changes in military technology, but they do demonstrate that there is freqently a substantial commitment to development of military systems prior to a clear understanding of the requirements for them. And to a very great extent, this must be accepted as unavoidable — we cannot ignore the new technology.

The presence of these developments, however, narrows the flexibility of selection in areas where conscious judgment indicates that serious deficiencies of equipment exist. Too often, decisions leading to substantial expenditures in one direction at the expense of another — to develop communications satellites in preference to new types of ships, for example — are made by default. A program is started because a desirable capability can be foreseen; when resources are needed for another program that becomes urgent, it may then be found that they are committed and not available for that program. If more resources *must* be made available, this can be done by eliminating lower-priority programs well along the development track, or increasing the budget. Both are more painful than would have been a more prescient selection in the first place. (The cancellation of the SKYBOLT air-launched ballistic missile, which had international repercussions, is a case in point.)

Once commitments to a major program of new system procurement are made, it is still more difficult to exercise the prerogatives of selection. The costs of the system include all those, in the past and future, of research and development, test and evaluation, procurement, operation and maintenance, as well as a number of indirect costs that may be incurred for training, reorganization of forces around the new system, and procurement of related systems that the new capability demands.

The impact of the latter can easily be underestimated if the evolutionary process in the military forces is not viewed as a whole. For example, we may obtain a surface-to-surface missile only to find that a complete renewal of targeting systems is necessary.

While the opportunity does exist to change or eliminate a system well after the commitment to it, such change, again, means a loss (except for "experience" and minor "fallouts") of substantial investments, with perhaps severe economic and political consequences. Clearly, once a line of advance is undertaken, it is much harder to make choices among alternatives than it was prior to commitment; and the commitment is to the total cost of the system, direct and indirect, foreseen and not.

After an item of equipment or system is procured and integrated into the armed force structure, it is necessary to capitalize on its useful life, to get value received for our investment. Organizations and secondary systems will have been modified and reshuffled to accommodate it. The logistic system will have been changed to support it. A change eliminating the new equipment or system at this point would mean restarting the entire cycle without having taken full advantage of the prior investment. (This is obviously more true for major systems than for minor pieces of equipment. But in all cases the pressures tend to act in this direction.) Changes in the force structure at this point are therefore even more difficult and far less likely, short of a major change in national policy, than they were during the previous steps.

Even if the decision is taken to change policy and therefore to modify the force structure, the policy directives do not deal with details at the level of individual systems or even individual military functions. Implementation at these levels is properly the task of the military Services. Assuming that agreement is perfect at all decision levels on the details of force structure to meet policy objectives — an assumption open to serious question — policy and its implementation are still not likely to be in phase with each other. Policies must change direction in response to external events, while implementation may take a relatively independent path that depends more on the internal workings of the planning and force-building organizations. Implementation of policy changes is constrained to follow the sequence from change in force size through fundamental modification of force capability capitalizing on the results of research and development. This cycle may require a period of 5 to 10 years, while the demands on the military system may shift a number of times during the course of an administration or with a change of administration. Consider, for example, the change from a limited-war to a massive-retaliation strategy after Korea, the gradual drift back to a tacit limited-response strategy until and beyond the Lebanese landing, the direction for greatly increased conventional-weapons capability and the new emphasis on unconventional warfare during the years of the Kennedy administration.

It is entirely possible that when the force structure finally assumes the characteristics planned at the beginning of the implementation cycle, the strategy for its use will have changed in such a way that it is no longer well suited to the new policy. One of the critical problems, then, is to provide sufficient flexibility in the orientation and details of the military program so that it can respond to changes of need and strategy. This can only be done if we can control the march of military technology.

# 11

## *The Impact of Technology*

WHILE technology can give us the ability to carry out innumerable military tasks in many different ways, the attempt to achieve all the desirable solutions to the problems of all possible military situations would most certainly lead to efforts exceeding the resources available. It is obviously necessary, from both time and cost considerations, to anticipate needs with some degree of precision, whatever the uncertainties, or else to find solutions providing a great deal of flexibility in individual systems.

To some extent, anticipation is possible. If the potential enemy is known to have submarines, we know we will need equipment to detect them so that they can be destroyed in war. And the solution is not easy; finding submarines requires all the scientific ingenuity at our command. Flexibility, too, begets technically advanced systems. The tactical fighter-bomber described earlier can carry out many tasks of attack and defense in many types of war. And it, too, with all its subsystems, presses the frontiers of science and technology. In the last analysis a considerable amount of technological sophistication is unavoidable in the solutions to the problems of modern-day limited war. This is, indeed, one of our strengths.

But control of that strength and its growth brings problems of its own. That of allocating resources within the enormous defense budget is one of the most obvious. What are some of the more subtle pitfalls into which the defense planner can be led by the search for military capability through technology?

## *Priority According to Expense*

The first and most obvious problem in the pursuit of sophisticated technological solutions to military problems is that they are extremely expensive. The development and support of major weapon, transport, or communications systems can run to hundreds of millions if not billions of dollars. Entire military organizations must often be created to operate them. But all items of military hardware are not equally expensive. In fact, three quarters or more of military research and development projects and separate items of hardware entail expense of a lesser magnitude than the few major items — ships, airplanes, missiles, worldwide communications systems — around which the armed forces are built. (See Figure 11.1.)

The large range of cost among the separate elements of the entire force structure creates a disparity in the attention given these elements in military planning. The relatively few multimillion dollar systems that absorb the greatest expenditure of resources are the ones which must be watched most carefully in the planning and management of the defense effort. The need to assure that a major system will be brought into being successfully inevitably concentrates effort on that system. Since management resources are not unlimited, the much greater number of smaller systems is not observed as closely or as carefully.

This does not mean that minor weapons and equipment are ignored. One of the forces making for size and complexity in the management structure is the fact that there is, somewhere, a manager for each and every program that will result in a piece of military equipment. But as higher levels of management are approached, the criterion that establishes the need for specific attention is usually the level of expenditure. The smaller projects tend to be aggregated and reviewed in classes or groups of equipment.

The larger projects, however, exceed the cost level permitting aggregation. A cost overrun of a few per cent in one of these can swallow up the resources needed for dozens of the smaller ones. A year's delay in completion of a major development can affect plans for organization and re-equipment of important parts of the force structure. Lack of funds in the midst of such a development can affect the level of employment in a major industrial plant and among many subcontractors.

The development of a surface-to-surface missile system like PERSHING,[1] an antiaircraft missile system such as MAULER,[2] or a tactical fighter for operation from an aircraft carrier are therefore followed very closely from inception to integration in the armed forces. If they fail to meet target dates or demand funds beyond the original estimates,

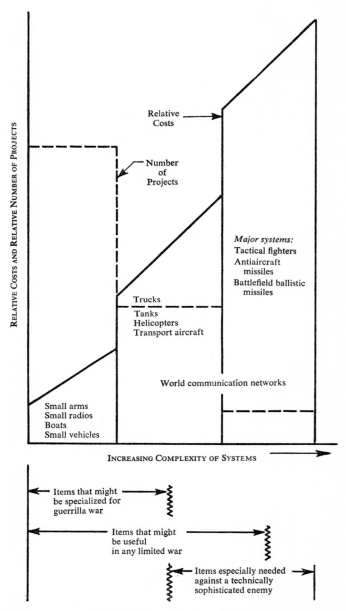

FIGURE 11.1  RELATIVE COST RANGES OF TYPICAL LIMITED-WAR
EQUIPMENT AND SYSTEMS, WITH ASSOCIATED RELATIVE NUMBER
OF INDIVIDUAL DEVELOPMENT PROJECTS

134

the consequences are great enough that even the Congress wants to know why. If efforts to create such systems are at all duplicative, the pressures for conserving resources by selection of the best one and elimination of the others are great. On the other hand, a large number of small items experiencing similar vicissitudes of research and development effort, or delays in procurement, may go for years without critical examination at the centers of program management.

Almost always, the projects receiving individual attention are those designed to meet and exceed the capability of an enemy who is able to place very sophisticated military equipment in the field. While it might be argued that the development of a new, lightweight rifle would substantially increase the effectiveness of a soldier against guerrillas, there could be valid counterarguments that (*a*) the effort is not warranted because guerrillas can after all be attacked with existing weapons, and (*b*) in the long run the real solutions to the guerrilla warfare problem are political and do not lie in the area of weapons at all. It could never be argued, however, that if a potential enemy has supersonic aircraft and antiaircraft missiles there should not be weapons in our inventory capable of defeating them. Weapons of this type demand the greatest expenditure of resources in the defense effort, and are also the ones to which major management effort is devoted.

The variation of management attention over the project structure, demanded by the variation of costs, automatically lends first priority, in the evaluation of military capability and direction of its evolution, to the few major projects. There are two consequences of this orientation in the program.

First, while a few major new weapons systems will be brought into the armed forces, the evolution of the force structure that is realized will represent only a part of what is desired and needed. A much larger number of *relatively* minor pieces of equipment, which in the aggregate represent much of the desired over-all military capability, may appear only tardily if at all. The military Services become unbalanced, with some obvious new strength but a substantial fraction of obsolete or obsolescent equipment.[3] There is concomitantly a certain amount of waste on items which are perpetually under development but which may never reach fruition, or may reach it too late to be of real value.

Second, and even more significant in its repercussions, is the fact that priority is implicitly given to preparation for warfare represented by the $E_1$ component of the limited war matrix of Chapter 8. But this does not mean that we are at the same time creating a military structure that will be as useful as desired in other elements of this matrix, for other limited wars. Rather, since a substantial fraction of our resources is devoted to the problems of defeating the sophisticated enemy, there is little left over for creation of ideally designed equipment and forces to meet the other threats. For this we are forced to use what we have, and what we have may well represent a substantial compromise with what we need.

The pursuit of technological sophistication thus lends the entire defense program, outside the strategic weapons area, a strong bias. The question "What kind of limited war should we design for?" is implicitly answered: "Limited war in Europe, first."

Of course, considered judgment may still dictate that most effort be devoted to meeting the Soviet-European threat. The real danger is that system selection and management according to system expense can easily cause neglect of other capabilities needed for more likely contingencies.

## The Pressure for Progress

Suppose it is assumed, in the most optimistic view, that there is no problem of military movement, delivery of destructive power, or communication among military forces which technology will not *ultimately* be able to solve. It will remain true nevertheless that all these solutions will not be simultaneously or immediately available. The entire process of creating a military capability using the fruits of technology is evolutionary. With rare exceptions each step is built on the success of the previous one.

An important part of the problem of capitalizing on the evolutionary products of science and engineering is the need to sort out the many directions of their possible evolution, to recognize when there is no value in trying to press forward in a particular direction, and to identify the directions that promise to continue the process usefully. We must recognize, that is, when improvements in wagon wheels and harnesses will no longer contribute to the speed and load capacity of cargo hauling on the ground — when it is necessary and desirable to press for such improvements through motor vehicle development.

The issue will not always be so clear-cut. For there may well be better ways of doing the old job; better wheel bearings can make it much easier for a horse to pull a wagon, and increase his net speed by reducing the time between rests. Further, the motor vehicle will not displace all horses overnight, and in its early versions it is neither fast nor reliable. Can one see far enough ahead to know that it must eventually become dominant? When is the time right to stop improving wagons and concentrate all our resources on trucks?

The trouble is that, although failure to take advantage of a new line of advance is costly, the new direction is costly as well. Several examples from more modern times can be cited.

Speed of movement on the ground advanced rapidly from the invention of the automobile, until the average passenger car or truck can move easily at a cruising speed of 60 to 80 miles per hour on a good road surface. At the same time, vehicles designed for off-road or cross-country movement have progressed in a different direction, that of riding over obstacles such as ditches or logs, and moving through sticky or soft earth. Both of these achievements have required a great increase in energy expended for movement — an increase in power reflected as a higher cost of purchase and operation than was paid for the horse which could, within its limitations, do both jobs.

We have now reached the point where the cost of increasing road speed or terrain negotiability by even small amounts may be very expensive.[4] A new approach is offered by the helicopter, which combines speeds of a hundred miles per hour or more with the ability to move cross-country even though large airfields are not available. But helicopters, too, are much more expensive to build and operate than autos or tractors.

Another example is given by the development of travel over water. The average speed of transoceanic travel increased from an average of perhaps 50 to 100 miles per day for sailing ships to between 300 and 500, or even as high as 1,000 miles per day, with the modern steamship. This occurred largely because a ship that does not have to depend on wind for power can more easily select and maintain its direction and average speed of travel. (The clipper ships in the Oriental tea trade of the nineteenth century could sail faster over short stretches than many modern cargo ships.) Steamships are much more expensive than sailing ships, but we gain compensating advantages, such as size and load capacity, so that the *net* cost, or cost per unit load to move cargo, is reduced. The rate of increase of the speed of sea transport has now tapered off, however. If we wish to pay the price, we can make large ships travel twice as fast as the sailing clippers, and small ones faster still. But by and large the speeds at which most ships can move through the water will not go very much above 30 or 40 knots in the future — we have reached a technological plateau.

If we want to move over the water faster, we shall have to do it by getting away from hydrodynamic drag. We can use the airplane, where net cost is higher than that of ships and cargo capacity smaller. These penalties may be reduced in the future by development of the "ground-effect vehicle," which rides near the surface on a cushion of high pressure air, or hydrofoil and hydro-ski ships, which take advantage of small wings or skis just under or on the surface to support a hull out of the water at high speeds. These "ships" may travel at from 70 to 100 knots. The net cost of moving cargo in them will be between those of the true ship and the airplane.

Almost always, in such technological evolution, we reach a point where the attempt to continue in a particular direction yields little gain but is extremely expensive. The problem is to recognize when this happens, and to seek other approaches; to change from piston-engined to jet aircraft, or from long-range bombers to intercontinental missiles.

This does not mean that we necessarily cease to improve existing machinery. Often improvements are possible in directions that may be considered orthogonal to the main line of advance. Thus, while it may be very difficult to increase the speed of trucks, there may be improvements which can still reasonably be sought in off-road terrain negotiability. Subsonic aircraft can be made more useful through reduction of required airfield length, and helicopters through increased service life of their moving parts. It may be possible to increase the killing power of a weapon and reduce its weight without increasing its range very much.

Whether we wish to pursue these directions of evolution depends upon the value of the additional capability they give us. All of them may approach technological limits of the kinds we have been discussing. All of them require expenditure of resources, just as do the radically new developments for extending capability by "quantum jumps." In addition, the radically new does not necessarily replace the old; rather, it complements it. Cargo ships, trucks, and rifles remain necessary even as we invent airplanes, helicopters, and machine guns. Conventional artillery was not given up after the invention of the atomic bomb.

What is retained is also continually improved, even though the change here is not as great as the change to the new system. The 1970 truck may ultimately represent a lesser improvement over that of 1940 than the latter did over the 1910 model, and less, still, than the 1910 truck over the horse. Nevertheless, possible advances in truck design from 1940 to 1970 appear attractive and are useful. Certainly when the 1940 truck wears out, it is easy to argue with much validity that we can now have automatic drive to ease driver fatigue, large and soft tires to pull through mud, and more efficient engines to conserve fuel. It can be made evident that the truck's replacement ought not to be simply a new item of the same model but an improved and modern version.

And so we are faced with continuing additions of better models of machines and weapons of a kind that we have had for a long time, while entirely new types enter the inventory and join the cycle. The net effect is a continuing increase in the cost of building and maintaining a military force.

If the reader will identify himself with the military planner, he will see that he has become enmeshed in a nightmare of interacting effects and pressures. He has first had to find where equipment improvement has reached the limits of useful evolution in a particular direction. He has then had to search for, or has had thrust upon him, new technological approaches to military tasks, permitting further progress. But he has found the old types of weapons and equipment to be still important, so that he cannot give them up. It is in fact possible to improve them still further through changes in direction of *their* development; and even if this is not possible he wants the small changes that make replacement items of worn-out equipment more modern and up-to-date.

All of these things cost money, so that the cost of an equipped military unit keeps rising until the limits of available resources are approached. The planner therefore has to select the items for which he wants to expend the limited resources. Difficult choices have to be made among a bewildering array of alternatives that have proliferated almost surreptitiously. Moreover, these problems of selection are multiplied by the number of military functions that have to be carried out — the same problems face the planners of communications, weapons, or mobility systems, and the problems of all face the planner who must maintain an overview of the total force structure.

In the face of this problem, the rotation cycle for military personnel in assigned positions is in most cases 2 to 4 years, and for political appointees 4 years, more or less. These turnover times are substantially smaller than the lead times for new equipment development or the service life of current equipment. Thus a large fraction of the planning body finds the selection problems already full-blown and urgent. Only an intermediate group of harried civil servants, who have had to weather several cycles of policy change and redirection, provides continuity. And their actions with respect to the selection criteria must depend on the views of the others in higher positions, where continuity does not necessarily exist. The technology and the organization which manages it are ill-matched. This simply makes the planning and selection problems more difficult.

## The Pressure Against Progress

The creation of new types of weapons systems and other major equipment must inevitably be followed by the creation of new types of military organization, new tactics for these organizations, and even new strategies in the application of military force. The advent of the steamship, the airplane, radio, radar, the nuclear weapon, and the guided missile all had this effect. The onset of the new and the radical has radiating effects throughout the armed forces' structure, and some of their elements and doctrines must, as a consequence, wither and disappear.

Occasionally, the most important potential effects of a new system are so clear that the entire military organism overreacts, seizing upon the obvious before its full import is recognized. The acceptance of nuclear weapons as an instrument of all types of war, to the detriment of conventional-weapons capability, is the most well-known recent example.

More often, however, the impact of a new military technique takes much longer to make itself felt, and its full acceptance must await an obvious demonstration of its effectiveness. Before the United States entered World War II, for example, British naval power, and American, was based largely on the massed firepower of fleet cannons, including those of the battleship. Even after England had lost almost her entire Mediterranean fleet to German airpower, after she had lost her newest battleships, the *Repulse* and the *Prince of Wales,* to an almost minor Japanese air attack, and America had lost a substantial fraction of her Pacific fleet to Japanese carrier-based airplanes at Pearl Harbor, so brilliant a strategist as Winston Churchill was impelled to comment that the American fleet would redress the balance of naval power in the Pacific when battleships then under construction were brought into service.[5] It was not until after the battles of Coral Sea and Midway that the implications of seaborne airpower were generally realized. Then the entire structure of the Navy and its tactical doctrines were overturned, and a new era of naval warfare opened.

It is easy for the forces of conservatism to act against technological innovation. The difficulty of fathoming the implications of a radical technological advance interacts with the long lead time associated with developing a new system and incorporating it in the military forces, and with the fact that most new systems are very demanding of resources for which strong prior commitments exist. Since the implications for military strategy and tactics are not obvious, and since it takes a great deal of argument, analysis, and testing to bring the essential points on each side into the open, the first reaction is to delay any major change until the arguments are resolved. The decision time can easily exceed the time of actual technical development, and a decision in favor of change can be half-hearted.

If it is hard to see where *major* technological change can lead and to change our military posture accordingly, it is much more difficult to foresee, over the short run, the aggregated impact of a whole series of smaller technological improvements. The armed forces may therefore continue to exist in a relatively static condition for a long period of time until the accumulated effect of these new additions to military capability is fully understood. The transition to a new force structure is then difficult and expensive, because of the lead time involved in effecting it and because of the conflict for resources between the fixed operating costs of the existing structure on the one hand, and the new funds demanded for its modernization and reorganization on the other.

The problem is even more subtle and complex than that of a simple reaction against the new and untried. One of the great effects on military thinking wrought by World War II and subsequent events, which spawned radar, jet aircraft, nuclear weapons and missiles, was the acceptance of the idea of technological change. Resistance to change on the part of a military society moved by "honest disbelief in the dramatic claims of the new process [and] protection of the existing society with which they [are] identified"[6] has been to a great extent overcome if not shattered, on the surface. The entire technological base of the armed forces has been overturned several times. The vast expansion of research and development, and continual acceptance of an adjustment to its products, has been accepted as a way of life.

Yet this may not all be to the good. All sorts of external forces, extraneous to the technical problems of force structure, have insinuated themselves and distorted the revolution. Among the reasons for the avid acceptance of nuclear weapons were not only their obvious potential effectiveness in various tactical and strategic applications but also the attempt on the part of a new military service — the Air Force — to gain the ascendancy in the defense structure. The older Services had to "go modern" to stay in the race, regardless of the logic of their own tactics and strategy. The search for an easier, cheaper way of carrying out the over-all military mission as it was then conceived, of getting "more bang for a buck," dictated that everybody would concentrate on nuclear weapons systems. Yet while the theory of strategic air and missile warfare using nuclear weapons could be expounded logically, many aspects of the theory of land and naval warfare, as we have seen in Chapter 7, could not. It almost appears that the idea of change for its own sake had, for various reasons, to be accepted despite the difficulties that it brought. And the philosophy carried over into other areas of defense. The increasing rate of technological evolution everywhere, including that in the enemy camp, would seem to demand it.

Such acceptance may, however, simply reflect a modern aspect of the more obvious resistance to change of the earlier military structure.[7] The idea of change has become acceptable, but changes are channelled in "safe" and acceptable directions. Research and development can be made to turn out continually new products representing improved ways of carrying out old missions. Innovation can follow certain accepted patterns of ever-increasing performance of weapons and equipment of existing type, whose use and role in the organization are understood by the current military generation. There are always better radars, better air defense missiles, better fighter-bombers, better radios and guns. Or change can follow the popular and approved pursuit of an obvious and inescapable new departure in technology, such as nuclear weapons, and the body of theory built up around it, however imperfect or controversial it might be.

But when new products of technology with more ambiguous benefits threaten the existing form and structure of the armed forces, when they call for structural changes that cannot be effected by slight modification of an existing organization, these changes are resisted. The dynamics of technological evolution then assume a rigid pattern not unlike the previous patterns of resisting innovation in a more obvious sense. The pattern may now be one of perpetual improvement of current equipment types whose implications are not threatening, accompanied by delay in accepting the really new and different. Equipment modifications that are not really significant, but which can be expensive, may be accepted at the same time that other, more revolutionary tools and weapons of warfare, with the different organizational and doctrinal structure they imply, are overlooked or delayed. The result is that flexibility in adapting to continuously evolving patterns of warfare is lost even while new products of technology are incorporated in the armed forces wholesale.

This rigidity is of course not a strict rule. But to the extent that the pattern is rigid the force structure will suffer in its ability to meet the needs of limited warfare in the modern age.

## Something Better Around the Corner

It is often found that when a new piece of equipment or a new system is ready for integration into the armed force structure, just a moderate additional expenditure of time and money can further improve it and extend its performance. To take a few hypothetical examples, a helicopter started 5 years ago, and designed to use an available engine, might carry 20 per cent more load if it is modified to accept a new, more powerful engine whose development is nearing completion. A new computer using transistors instead of vacuum tubes can reduce the weight and increase the reliability of a tactical bombing system. A new rocket motor might extend the range of a missile, making it a more effective weapon for air defense. A better gyroscope will increase the accuracy of an inertial navigation system.

Opportunities such as these arise legitimately as the normal consequence of a vigorous research and development effort. But they present the uncomfortable choice of foregoing the possible gain for the many years of the life cycle of a piece of military equipment, delaying procurement of the system in favor of continued development, or discarding equipment before it has given us our money's worth.

The decision goes sometimes one way and sometimes another. While this is known to the decision makers, the cumulative effect of a large number of such decisions is not always clear to the remainder of the defense community. The industrial part of that community, especially, must live on the fruits of new and improved products. It is always proposing them; many are accepted; and still newer ones proposed. The weapon developers think in terms of systems that are many years ahead of the actual capability of the armed forces.

As soon as a system is developed and turned over to the armed forces for test, the proposal for the next, better version is presented for consideration, whether the original version enters production or not. Moreover, with the turnover in defense management personnel, any one project director is not likely to be as familiar as he should be with the past history of many systems that preceded the one currently under consideration. As a result the pressures for continual technological development intensify. At the same time, if a major line of development goes through several stages of renewal before procurement, 10 or 20 years can easily go by without substantial change in the equipment actually in the hands of the troops.

It is easy, without a hard look at the actual situation, to assume that achievable capability actually exists, when in fact it does not. New systems can be planned with the idea that they will mesh, in the military organization, with others that may in fact not reach fruition. As one general put it, we come to think in terms of "fighting today's war with tomorrow's weapons against the enemy we knew yesterday."

The perpetual search for something better has serious economic consequences as well. The first few production units of any newly developed equipment are relatively expensive because the development and tooling costs are considered part of the total purchase price, to be apportioned among all the individual items (guns, aircraft, tanks, and so on) procured. As greater numbers of the item are obtained, the initial costs are apportioned over all the units, and the cost of each follows what is known as a "learning curve" having a shape like that shown by the solid line in Figure 11.2.

143

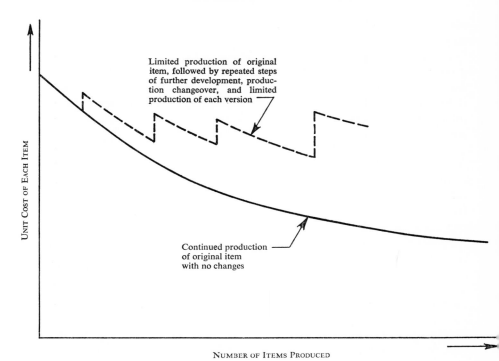

Limited production of original item, followed by repeated steps of further development, production changeover, and limited production of each version

Continued production of original item with no changes

UNIT COST OF EACH ITEM

NUMBER OF ITEMS PRODUCED

FIGURE 11.2   LEARNING CURVES AND THE EFFECT
OF CONTINUED REDEVELOPMENT

If this cycle is inhibited by premature curtailment of procurement, then not only is the unit cost high, but the development costs of the next model are added to *its* unit cost, so that the benefit from the cost reduction of the learning curve is never realized. The ultimate capability of the military forces may not be improved to a degree commensurate with the increased cost, while the latter follows the dashed line in Figure 11.2. The defense planner suffers greater constraint in resource allocation. In the long run, we shall have used unwisely resources that might be needed to advance military strength in a completely different area.

## Technology Misapplied

It is perhaps fitting to close this chapter with the observation that technological solutions to military problems can too often be sought when the needed answers lie elsewhere. Since the creations of technology have such a large impact on the shape of the military forces and on their effectiveness, much of the thinking of the civilian defense establish-

144

ment, the military forces, and the defense industry must be devoted to the problems of designing and using hardware. It is only natural, therefore, that thinking about the use of military capability should also direct itself toward technological solutions to the many problems that limited war presents.

In many important situations, however, these are not the types of solutions needed. It does little good to develop better weapons for a government's forces to use in fighting Communist guerrillas when that government's ineptitude causes its people to sympathize with the guerrillas. The development of new types of weapons may not discourage Communist pressure on Berlin when a significant increase in the size of the existing forces in Europe could. Communications delays between command centers can often be reduced by better discipline in the use of radio as well as by new, higher-capacity communications networks.

These are but a few instances of where and how technology might be misapplied; the list can be extended at length. We shall, in fact, devote a good deal of attention, in the remainder of this book, to many more examples of military problems where either ($a$) the technology already exists but we are not certain of how we should use it, or ($b$) technology is relatively minor in importance to the over-all picture.

If we look to technology alone for answers to the problems of limited war, we place ourselves in the position of coping with only a portion of these problems, while other aspects may become overpowering. We must therefore be ready and willing to recognize when still further advances in technology cannot and should not be asked to meet our military-political needs. This can be difficult indeed for Americans, with the traditional orientation of our society towards perpetual technological progress.

145

## PART IV

# THE STRUCTURE OF
# THE REGULAR FORCES

# Introductory Note

*In the next five chapters we shall try to show, by discussing a few of the problems faced in preparing the regular forces for limited war, that there are several directions in which their structure can evolve. These directions are not mutually exclusive; it may be possible and even necessary to move in several at once to prepare for the many unpredictable eventualities of limited war. But they are all interdependent in some way.*

*The Navy is undergoing a technological revolution forced, in part, by simultaneous revolutions in the ground and air forces. Changes in the form and tactics of the ground forces demand accompanying changes in the forces devoted to tactical air warfare. Heavier reliance on airlift for intercontinental mobility requires new philosophies in the design of major ground force combat equipment and the units that use it. Rapid and controlled response in a strategic sense requires parallel changes in the command structure and that of the long-range mobility and logistic system.*

*Indirectly, one form of military force structure is implemented at the expense of others when both compete for the same, limited resources. We can continue to develop the armed forces in directions that have become clear and acceptable in the last several years, and so forgo the possibility of certain military capabilities that can be decisive at some future critical time. Or we can take the risks attending further military-technological change, with unforeseen consequences. There is no clear answer as to where to go in planning the structure of the regular forces. But some of the alternatives can be intriguing, indeed, as we shall see.*

*One further note. The reader will find that most of the problems treated here are associated with land and air war in a theatre of warfare. The question of long-range airlift and sealift to reach the theatre is also considered. To the extent that these problems are related to the Navy's tasks in limited war, the discussion is pertinent to the structure of the Navy's forces. But the Navy's problems could not be treated here in the same detail as those of the Army and Air Force.*

*This should not be taken to imply that the Navy's role in limited war is not extremely important. In virtually all of the engagements listed in Chapter 1 where the United States was involved, the Navy was the first available force called upon by the President. It was the first in action. The naval forces have the virtue of being ready and mobile in response to strategic warning without the need for the publicity or fanfare that must accompany the movement of divisions or air wings. They can be in place, ready for action, without entering the areas of other nations' sovereignty. They can achieve strategic surprise by appearing at a critical spot with little or no warning.*

*A cursory examination would show that, the Fleet Ballistic Missile Submarines aside, the fundamental structure of these forces — the attack carrier and anti-submarine task forces, the amphibious task forces with the Marines, the combat ships for screening and defense of the fleet, and the auxiliary ships and aircraft for its support — is basically correct for the limited war mission. This structure will, perhaps, not change in its broad outlines. But there are profound changes in progress in the internal structure of the Navy.*

*The shore bombardment role of the battleship and heavy cruiser has been taken over in great measure by tactical combat aviation, as the cruisers, destroyers, and frigates have been armed with missiles for antiaircraft defense. While smaller ships are being specialized for anti-submarine warfare, others are specialized for air warfare and war against the enemy on land; war between surface fleets has decreased in importance. Atomic power offers the possibility of much greater endurance of ships, increases their cost, and adds to the pressures to change the kinds and numbers of ships in the fleet. Nuclear weapons increase the risk of catastrophic loss in a single engagement at the same time that the fleet remains a mobile air base on which shore-based missiles cannot be zeroed in well in advance.*

*All of these technological changes, and others not mentioned, will affect the form of tomorrow's Navy, as they have already influenced the structure of today's. There is not, in the public literature, a thorough and comprehensive analysis of these changes and their implications for the evolution of the Navy in the future. Such an analysis is needed.*

149

# 12

## *Battlefield Ballistic Missiles*

MANY different kinds of missile are used on the battlefield: for air defense from the ground, attack of both air and ground targets from the air, and delivery of firepower from one point on the ground to another beyond the range of artillery. We shall discuss here the latter type, which is known as the surface-to-surface missile, or SSM.

Such missiles are considered to be tactical weapon systems that can be used in a limited war to destroy important targets deep in the enemy rear, much as tactical fighter-bombers do. A glance at Figure 11.1 will show that they are among the most expensive developments with which the defense establishment has to be concerned. Their development costs are comparable with those of a new tactical fighter-bomber system.[1] Entire battalions including hundreds of men and dozens of vehicles may have to be organized to operate a few launchers.

These systems must therefore absorb a significant fraction of the resources available for all the ground forces. This expenditure should be a wise one, strategically and tactically, to be justified; if not, it might be made to better advantage elsewhere, or simply be saved.

The reasons usually given for the existence of SSM are the following:[2]

• They can operate in all weather and so be used at times when tactical aircraft cannot fly.

• They are directly under the control of the ground commander and therefore, by eliminating one step in the command process, would appear to avoid the restrictions on his freedom to use heavy firepower that could be caused by tactical air mission conflicts.

151

- By virtue of their speed, they are not vulnerable to the very effective defenses that can stop tactical aircraft from penetrating enemy territory.

- By virtue of their mobility, they do not need fixed bases, and so are more difficult for the enemy to find and destroy.

What are the disadvantages, and what are the tradeoffs relative to the competing tactical aircraft systems?

Let us start with the economic tradeoff. There are errors in location of the targets against which the missiles are fired: the missile cannot see the target and make corrections in its aim as a pilot on a bombing run would; and there is also an intrinsic error in the ability of the missile to hit a specified location. For these reasons, the accuracy of surface-to-surface missiles can be assumed at best to be of the same order as that of tactical bombing systems using aircraft. While an individual missile is considerably less expensive than an individual aircraft, an airplane can be used many times over, but the missile can be used only once. Furthermore, each missile carries a substantially smaller load of explosives (or payload) than a tactical fighter-bomber.

Because of the high cost of the missile per pound of payload, and its less-than-perfect accuracy, we are almost compelled to use nuclear warheads on all but short-range SSM's or rockets. (We are discussing here only the missiles that will be used in tactical operations, not IRBMs or ICBMs designed to be part of the strategic deterrent or offensive forces.) For if these weapons are armed with conventional high-explosive warheads, then it is well-nigh impossible to place the weight of destructive firepower on a target for a cost approaching that of aircraft bombing or artillery.

The difference can be illustrated by a hypothetical example. While the figures used will be fictitious, it will be easy to show the implications of attempts to shift the balance in favor of one system or the other.

Suppose experience shows that it takes 10,000 pounds of high explosive delivered with a certain accuracy to destroy a target: a bridge, a complex of buildings, or a group of aircraft on the ground. Suppose the target is beyond range of conventional artillery and small rockets or missiles, so that we are faced with a choice of using one of the longer-range SSM or a tactical aircraft. Assume that a single tactical missile with its warhead costs $100,000 and that it can carry 1,000 pounds of high explosive in the warhead; the aircraft might cost $2 million dollars but it can carry 10,000 pounds of conventional bombs, which might cost $1 per pound. Both weapons systems will also have to be charged with long-term operating costs for training of technicians, support, and maintenance in the field. We shall assume here that these costs, prorated over each mission, are roughly equal for the two systems and so can be neglected in the comparison.

The cost of the airplane flight crew must also be charged against that system. This is difficult to assess accurately. Suppose it costs a quarter of a million dollars to train a pilot. If he is lost, his government-supported insurance and other benefits to his family might run to an equal amount. But what value should we put on a human life, and the contribution of a man to the war effort? Certainly, we cannot say. But since the missile battalion will be subject to enemy attacks, just as the airplane will, we might assume that roughly equal numbers of men will be lost, so that the intangibles will balance out. We can, however, to give the missile the benefit of the doubt, add to the airplane cost another $1 million to cover the tangible expense of a two-man crew.

We can see immediately that with these assumptions the delivery of 10,000 pounds of high explosive against the target would require 10 missiles at a total cost of $1 million dollars, exclusive of support costs. To estimate the comparable cost of weapon delivery by aircraft is somewhat more complicated because we cannot assume that the aircraft will last forever, nor that it will be lost on the first combat sortie; its cost will have to be distributed among all the sorties it might carry out in its combat lifetime. If on the average the tactical air force in this hypothetical war suffers an attrition of 1 per cent, or one aircraft lost per hundred sorties, then 1/100 of an airplane's cost, or $30,000, must be ascribed to a given sortie. The total cost of the mission using aircraft will be this $30,000 plus $10,000 for the bombs delivered. Thus we will have destroyed the target at a cost of $40,000 using aircraft compared with $1 million dollars using missiles.

These figures, since they are assumed, did not, of course, portray the true relationship. The mission could be carried out with missiles at the same cost as with aircraft if the missiles cost $4,000 each. Conversely, the attrition to the aircraft system would have to be about 34 per cent for the mission cost using $3,000,000 aircraft to be the same as the mission cost using $100,000 missiles.

The alternatives then become apparent: either we must produce an inexpensive missile to match the aircraft cost in a "low-attrition environment," or the missile becomes profitable in a "high-attrition environment." If the aircraft cost has been underestimated, then the missile can be more expensive for equal costs. But the cost of a single airplane will never become high enough to let the missile cost for equality approach the assumed $100,000. Aircraft losses of 34 per cent are unusually high, so that the missile probably becomes desirable at some lower attrition value. Nevertheless, this general expression of the economic relationship between the alternatives will hold.

The technological problems and the costs of achieving various technical solutions that can change this relationship must be examined for their effects. Since a large part of the missile cost is absorbed by the guidance system necessary to achieve high accuracy, a very cheap missile might be made if accuracy is sacrificed. But then we would have to deliver much more than 10,000 pounds of explosives on the target in the previous example. Alternatively, we could try to develop a cheap missile having the same accuracy; this would require some perhaps substantial research and development expenditure, assuming it were possible to extend the technology that far. This expenditure would have to be charged at least in part against the missile, so that the indirect cost of bringing the price of the missile down could be extremely high. (This example has considered the case where artillery cannot be used. It is quite possible that relatively short-range missiles can be produced in the required cost range, but these missiles will then be competing with artillery, in most cases a more accurate and less costly system than either missiles or aircraft.)

From the other direction, while it is possible that losses on the order of 25 to 35 per cent can be suffered by tactical aircraft in warfare, this is likely to occur only under rare circumstances. Ordinarily the destruction of the enemy air defense system will be the first order of business before other targets are attacked. The high-attrition situation can occur, however; moreover the aircraft cost may increase sharply as all-weather attack capability is built in, so that the point of equal costs would occur at a lower attrition value, making the missile more competitive.

But now we must move from the economic to the military realm. If both systems are to be used in a high-attrition environment, the nature of the war is likely to make the use of nuclear weapons highly probable. The enemy will be the most technically sophisticated, and the cost of conventional-weapon delivery by aircraft will be increased enormously by the presence of highly effective antiaircraft defenses. This makes the use of nuclear weapons, with their vast destructive power, appear more profitable and, in fact, necessary. The systems will then compete on a different basis: a single missile may suffice to destroy a target; nuclear warheads for bombs or missiles are in a different cost range; and the cost comparison will be entirely different — it will be much more likely to favor the missile.

From this it appears that the use of SSM hinges on the question of whether we will fight a nuclear war. This is a separate question of political, tactical, and strategic theory, which we examined earlier.

Whether or not limited nuclear war is feasible or probable, we might agree that nuclear delivery systems of this kind should be available in reserve against the eventuality of nuclear war and the military environment leading to high aircraft attrition.

But now we run into some contradictions. Antiaircraft defenses can be equally effective in nuclear or nonnuclear war. If we are to rely on aircraft to deliver conventional weapons, and if we are to lay stress on the capability for conventional-weapons war (which current defense policy has emphasized), then we must in any case build tactical aircraft with the appropriate performance and electronic and weapon systems to penetrate sophisticated defenses.

This is being done. A considerable effort is being expended to improve the ability of tactical aircraft to operate under almost all weather conditions, with every possibility of success in the not-too-distant future. Supersonic speeds, making the defense problem more difficult, have already been designed into existing tactical fighters. Newer generations of tactical aircraft will be designed to use small, relatively crude airfields, so that their vulnerability to enemy detection and attack on the airfields will be reduced.

The aircraft have the additional advantage that, in tactical missions, the pilot can contribute to finding targets for attack. He has the option of looking for and striking targets of opportunity, or attacking preselected targets whose general location is known and which he can pinpoint before dropping his bombs. This advantage can be stated differently and more positively: the nuclear missiles depend heavily on tactical aircraft for reconnaissance or continual observation of the battlefield to find their targets for them.

This restricts the utility of the missiles to particular kinds of targets. The aircraft that goes out to gather the target information must return with it, and it must be processed, evaluated and transmitted through the appropriate channels to the missile command before the missile can be fired. However much this process can be streamlined and accelerated, it is bound to be lengthier than the process in which the pilot himself finds targets and attacks them directly. In view of the anticipated dispersal and mobility of the ground forces in tactical nuclear war, targets such as enemy missile trains or moving formations of troops are not likely to remain in one location very long. Rates of movement are, in fact, such that even the best information-gathering system which the missiles can use are likely to be marginal, if not inadequate, for enabling the missiles to fire on "fleeting" targets before they disappear.

Therefore, even in nuclear war the missiles are most likely to be used against fixed or relatively stationary targets such as tactical airfields, supply depots, and major fixed transport facilities. A large variety of important targets will remain against which tactical aircraft will have to be used.

To summarize then, we face the following:

• If we rely too heavily on SSM for long-range firepower on the battlefield, we are likely to be forced to nuclear war by economic considerations.

• To retain the option of nonnuclear war against a technically capable enemy, effective tactical aircraft systems will have to be developed for it.

• These tactical aircraft will, in addition, have to play an important role in finding targets for the missiles, in any kind of war.

• The SSM are not the answer to comparable enemy missiles and other very mobile systems because of a combination of target location and response time problems. Therefore, aircraft will have an important attack role to play against certain targets in nuclear as well as in nonnuclear war.

In assessing the relative need for SSM, we do not know the conditions under which limited nuclear war will be possible or probable; certainly it is less likely than conventional-weapons war. The utility of the SSM is in any case difficult to assess in the face of the uncertain viability of a nuclear battlefield. Nor, in these circumstances, is the argument that we are faced in Europe by Soviet armies equipped with such missiles in profusion necessarily a pertinent or valid one.

The Soviet needs are different from ours. Their targeting problem is probably easier, given the knowledge they can gain of the NATO powers' installations in the open West European society. It is generally considered that massive war in Europe will be initiated by the Soviets. Their short and medium range missiles in such circumstances would be ideal first-strike weapons against the open NATO tactical military complex, and so they are in a sense strategic rather than tactical or limited-war weapons.

All of this raises the question, why have battlefield SSM? The reasons given at the beginning of this chapter can now be reinterpreted.

• The SSM represent alternative firepower delivery systems designed for the very case when the airfields and the tactical air forces are knocked out of the battle.

• Even though SSM cannot strike all targets, they can strike many. And even though it may take days, there are other ways than tactical air reconnaissance (through secret agents, for example) to find targets. This can be compatible with the "static confrontation" theory of the nuclear battlefield.

• The SSM are offensive systems which can eliminate enemy airfields and other installations in the same way that the enemy missiles can attack ours. They are hard to find and so difficult to counter in the same way that the enemy's are difficult for us to counter.

These may be valid reasons for retaining, renewing, and augmenting the SSM capability. But it becomes clear that we are not faced here with a choice between truly alternative means for carrying out a particular military task. Rather, one of the systems will exist regardless of the fate of the other. The second system (SSM) is largely redundant, less viable, and in only limited circumstances unique. Its value depends on the defense planners' view of the possibility and permissibility of nuclear land war between armies, and their estimate of the need, in these circumstances, for an alternative or backup system to the tactical air forces that will have to exist in any case.

This estimate will have to keep in view the high cost of the backup system. For the resources it demands might otherwise be used in different ways, to meet the far more likely threats of unconventional warfare, where the surface-to-surface missile systems are not applicable at all, or of conventional nonnuclear limited war, where their utility is marginal.

# 13

## Battlefield Mobility: By Land or by Air?

THE armored personnel carriers, tanks, self-propelled artillery, trucks, transport aircraft, and helicopters that carry troops and their weapons into battle comprise what might be called a "combat mobility subsystem." There is also a "logistic mobility subsystem" in the theatre of warfare that transfers supplies and troop replacements from ports of entry to base areas adjacent to the battlefield by means of railroads, trucks, trailers, and transport aircraft.

The combat and logistic mobility subsystems interact with each other in the obvious way that troops moving against the enemy in combat vehicles must be supplied by logistic vehicles, and the two parts of the entire system must be in balance with each other. A fast-moving army loses much of its potential striking power if it must halt periodically to wait for supplies. A logistic system that can move large tonnages over long distances in a very short time is a needless luxury if the maneuver of the combat units is always slow and deliberate.

### The Mobility of a Modern Army

Armies today are designed, in keeping with their universal heritage, to move and fight on the ground. Major combat equipment — artillery, combat vehicles, communications gear, and the like — is designed to withstand the punishment of bouncing over rough terrain as well as that delivered by enemy weapons. Such equipment is heavy. Most resupply and equipment replacement must be groundborne as well, simply because aircraft are unable to carry many of the heavy pieces of gear. Of course, certain weapons and supplies, and light troop units that do

158

not have extremely heavy equipment, can be carried in aircraft. The ground army can receive some urgently needed supplies by air in times of shortage, and aircraft can move some troops about the battlefield or to it very rapidly. But aircraft must remain in a supporting role.

A military commander, in planning the strategy and tactics of military engagements, must think primarily in terms of forces maneuvering at ground speeds. The distances over which troops can be dispersed and supplied are limited to those characterized by hours or days of travel cross-country at ground vehicle speeds. The supply system must have its formal terminals close to the combat area, and the speed and strength of attacks beyond enemy lines into the enemy rear depends in great measure on the speed with which the supply terminals, imbedded in a mass of auxiliary, reserve, and protective troops, can be shifted.[1]

How fast can an army move on the ground? Typically, the speed of vehicles moving cross-country is about 2 to 4 miles per hour. Higher speeds are possible for short periods of time when the terrain is particularly favorable; the commander who can take advantage of such situations can win a battle by superior skill in maneuver and surprise. But such opportunities are local. The presence of terrain obstacles of various sorts acts to reduce drastically the sustained speed of cross-country movement. Even such very slow speeds cannot be maintained indefinitely because a combat unit must stop to refuel and repair its vehicles and to rest and feed its men.

The average speed of the Third Army during the breakout from Normandy and pursuit of the Germans across France during World War II was 15 miles per day; at its best it covered 30 miles in one day.[2] In Operation Crusader, where Rommel's forces engaged the British 8th Army in Cyrenaica, maneuvering speeds of entire divisions varied from 20 miles in 24 hours to 40 miles in 4 hours, that is, from somewhat less than 1 to about 10 miles per hour.[3]

Can we look for any substantial change in the speed of ground mobility in the future? Vehicles are being developed that will negotiate difficult terrain more easily than those we have known in the past. Many of them will be able to cross rivers without the need for bridges. These vehicles will allow the ground forces to select more paths for maneuver, but none of them will achieve substantially greater speeds than those known heretofore. Nor will they offer substantially greater freedom from the most serious terrain obstacles, such as mountains and dense forests. And these will be combat vehicles, in great measure. Although some future logistics carriers are being designed especially for cross-country travel, most of the logistic vehicles are, and will continue to be, designed primarily for travel on roads.[4]

The implications of this constraint can be illustrated by a highly simplified example of a hypothetical combat-supply situation. We shall, in this example, be particularly interested in seeing what happens to the supply system when the situation changes from one in which roads are available to one in which they are not.

Consider a division that, while in action, must receive a certain amount of supplies each day: food, medicines, fuel, ammunition, repair parts, and replacements for its men, weapons, and equipment. Depending on the kind of battle (defense, attack, or pursuit) and the kind of division (infantry, mechanized, or armored), the supplies needed could amount to between 500 and 1,000 tons per day. Let us assume that there is a single supply line between a major depot and a point, at the rear of the area occupied by the division, to which the supplies flow. The distance between these two points may be several hundred miles. (In the countries along the southern Eurasian periphery the distance between ports of entry on the seacoast and potential combat areas along their northern borders varies from 50 to over 700 miles.) For convenience in calculation, let us assume it to be 360 miles.*

A number of trucks moving in road convoy will travel, on the average, 15 miles per hour. Then the 360-mile trip will take 2 days if each truck and crew travel about 12 hours in a stretch. If the average truck carries 5 tons, then 400 to 800 trucks will be in the pipeline supplying our typical division.† The number of trucks will be even higher, perhaps 500 to 1000, if we include those that are down for repairs. Let us say, then, that on the average 750 trucks are engaged in supplying one division in combat, over a road that stretches 360 miles from a main supply base.

If the supply line must move cross-country, then the average speed of movement may be reduced to about 3 miles per hour and under the previous conditions a day's travel will cover about 36 miles, which is

---

* Actually, an army designed around ground mobility would probably not become so extended. There would be intermediate supply dumps as part of a massive buildup of supporting troops, a shorter distance from the forward combat area. However, supplies would still have to move from areas far in the rear to the forward zone; for the purposes of this example it does not matter whether there is an exchange of cargoes among vehicles somewhere along the way. This would, at most, slow the entire operation and require more vehicles than the example will show. It should also be noted that a fixed number of vehicles need not be kept available to supply each division in action, because not all of the divisions will be in the same combat condition. Vehicles will be reassigned among divisions as the exigencies of the military situation dictate. The relative amounts of different types of supplies needed will also require such shifts since, for example, a division in pursuit will use more fuel and less ammunition than one in defense, and both will require more supplies than one at rest. But we are concerned here with averages.

† It takes 100 to 200 trucks to carry each day's supplies; there are 2 days' supplies moving forward along the road, and the trucks that carried the previous 2 days' supplies are returning.

also about the distance a truck can go on a tank of gas in such operations. Then it will take each day's supplies approximately 10 days to cover the 360 miles, and we shall need five times as many trucks, or 3,750 on the average. In addition, we shall have to spend resources for more fuel and repair stations along the way, and to protect those stations against possible enemy action. Furthermore, since the vehicles are not designed for cross-country travel over sustained periods of time, their parts will wear more rapidly and the repair problem will be much more severe.

The need to build roads and bridges evidently becomes quite pressing. While the use of cross-country vehicles might reduce the expenditure of resources for fixed facilities, these vehicles are considerably more expensive than roadbound trucks. Resources will be spent in one way or the other. And the entire operation will be characterized by a massive building forward of the entire army, step by step, with thrust and consolidation, in order to move the ground line of supply ahead with the advancing combat units.

This seems to be contradicted by the fact that in World War II the Russians were able to mount massive drives that moved very rapidly over very large distances (100 or more miles per day). But these drives required a long period of preparation and buildup; large stores of supplies were carried to the troops beforehand and moved with them as they moved forward. This type of operation is compatible with a long war and the use of massed armies. We may note that Patton's drive through France bogged down after 7 weeks, simply because his highly mechanized forces ran out of gas.[5] The supply lines could not keep up with the speed of the combat forces. Furthermore, we have seen that the philosophy of massive armies making periodic drives over an area that is continental in scope, with long pauses for buildup between thrusts, is not compatible with the developing strategies of conventional limited war (or even general war).

## Resupply by Air

The map of Figure 6.2 [in Chapter 6] shows that the accessibility of areas with difficult terrain, and consequently freedom of maneuver, can be greatly extended by the use of aircraft.

Aircraft that can help free the Army from many fixed installations, the massive construction attending their preparation, and the need for troops to protect them, are currently in the military inventory. Helicopters, in various sizes that can carry up to 4 tons of military payload, are already used by the ground forces, and afford such independence for short-range missions. The Army's *Caribou* tactical transports need only a relatively smooth and hard dirt or sod surface about 1,000 feet long, and can carry military loads of 3 tons some hundreds of miles. The C-130 *Hercules,* standard tactical transport of the Air Force, can carry substantial loads for thousands of miles; it can also, with reduced load, operate out of a dirt strip not nearly as long as a standard air-base runway.

Within the next ten years or so, a new generation of transport aircraft will appear that will be able to carry similar loads over similar distances but will rise and land vertically without a ground run. These aircraft, operating like helicopters, would eliminate the need for airfields with runways in forward areas; they could complete a trend away from fixed air bases that might be initiated even with today's transports if the latter are used in conjunction with helicopters (which would very likely continue to meet certain needs uniquely).

Suppose it is desired to use current transport aircraft to resupply the division in the previous example. We shall assume that each aircraft operates 16 hours per day (approximately the same utilization that the domestic air lines currently achieve with their transport aircraft). If this time is divided evenly between flying and loading or unloading, each aircraft would be able to make four round trips per day, with the remaining time spent in maintenance and repair. For this operation, we would need about sixty aircraft to supply the division with 750 tons every day.

Procuring this air cargo capacity, if it is not already available, would be quite expensive. Assuming that the costs of military aircraft and vehicles are of the same order as their civilian counterparts of similar size and performance, we can estimate the first cost of these aircraft to be about $200 million, compared with a cost of about $20 million for the 750 trucks that would be needed for resupply over roads. But if the ground supply system must move cross-country, requiring about five times as many vehicles to carry the same daily load, or if the system is based on more expensive cross-country vehicles, the cost gap between vehicles and aircraft will be narrowed.

A similar trend characterizes the operating costs. The cost of delivering a ton of supplies over a mile distance is about 10 times as high for a large airplane as it is for a truck carrying the same load over a road. But when the truck or a more specialized vehicle must move cross-country, at slower speed and requiring more fuel and repairs, the operating cost for each ton-mile of cargo delivered approaches that of the aircraft. Although the ground vehicles are still likely to be cheaper than the aircraft to operate, the difference will not be as great as might at first glance be anticipated.

In the total picture, we can think in terms of supplying only part of the Army by air because of the high cost of expanding the aircraft fleet. The comparison for the division we have been examining might appear as shown in Table 13.1. These figures are far from exact — they are

TABLE 13.1

COMPARISON BETWEEN GROUND AND AIR
RESUPPLY SYSTEMS FOR A DIVISION

|  | Trucks Using Existing Road Net | Trucks, Cross-Country | Aircraft |
|---|---|---|---|
| Number Needed | 750 | 3750 | 60 |
| Average Load | 5 tons | 5 tons | 10 tons |
| Average Operating Time | 12 hours | 12 hours | 16 hours (8 flying) |
| Distance Covered | 180 miles per day, each | 36 miles per day, each | 4 round trips of 360 miles radius per day, each |
| First Cost | $20 million | $100 million | $200 million |
| Fleet Operating Cost | $20,000 per day | $150,000 per day | $200,000 per day |

"guesstimates," given simply to provide some sense of the relative numbers.

Suppose we are willing to pay the cost of achieving the greater mobility that the air logistic line of supply affords. Even after the necessary aircraft are procured, we shall have modified only the logistic mobility subsystem to take advantage of the greater mobility that aviation offers. The fighting part of the army will remain tied to the ground. Part of that army can be equipped with aircraft such as helicopters to let the combat forces take advantage of the greater long-range mobility afforded by the air logistics line. But the fighting units will in general be incompletely transformed, because their major combat equipment will be too heavy to be carried by the helicopters or other small aircraft that are used as combat vehicles. Still further changes in the equipment and organization of the ground forces will be necessary to assure that the combat and logistic mobility systems are matched.

## Transforming the Combat Forces

By giving up heavy armor and some of the heavier artillery pieces in favor of a number of lightly armored combat vehicles that are being developed,[6] a mechanized ground force can be created which can be transported in C-130 type aircraft. Suppose that, as a first step, major ground force elements are thus reconstituted. It would then be possible to move entire combat units, complete with all of their equipment when they land, to the combat area by air. This would represent a significant improvement over current capability. But such units would probably still be constrained to operate initially out of only a few large, well-prepared bases, because some of the heavier equipment, such as the armored combat vehicles, armored personnel carriers, and larger artillery pieces, will use the maximum weight-lifting capacity of the transport aircraft, requiring relatively large, well-prepared airfields.

The ability of air-transportable units to traverse difficult terrain in their tactical maneuvers can be improved through the addition of some heavy-lift, short-range helicopters — flying cranes — for such tasks as lifting heavy vehicles over deep ravines or wide rivers, and recovering disabled guns and vehicles that might otherwise have to be abandoned.

Such force modifications would lead to a considerable tactical and strategic advantage in moving to the battle area quickly, as well as to improved combat mobility on the ground in that area. The fundamental tactical employment of these ground forces in combat will, however, remain essentially unchanged. They will have some better ability to traverse terrain obstacles, and will be able to shift positions without the retarding effects of extremely heavy weapons and equipment. But their modes and speeds of maneuver will not change substantially from those typical of ground forces. The improvements will be of degree rather than kind.

How can we take better advantage of air mobility in the combat operations themselves? Assume that this can be done by making the helicopter (and, later, more advanced vertical-takeoff aircraft) the primary combat vehicle, in addition to using it exclusively for logistic support over short ranges. Then it is possible to conceive of a combat unit that has no surface vehicles, is completely air-mobile in the combat area, and is supported over long ranges by a flexible air line of supply.

Is such a unit feasible? What problems would be faced in creating it? Let us again follow through a simple example. Assume a battle group built around 200 aircraft: 30 helicopters able to lift 3 or 4 tons each for local logistics support and massed movement of men and equipment; and 170 smaller helicopters for tactical movement of squad-sized units, scouting, carrying weapons that can be fired from the machines, and so on.* By-passing for the moment the detailed problems of weaponry,

* A battle group is a unit of about 1500 men, similar in function to the World War II regiment. This is an arbitrarily selected mixture of aircraft and is not necessarily what would be needed for such a group; the optimum mix would have to be calculated. But the one suggested here is sufficient to illustrate the problem. The main conclusions will not be sensitive to changes in the aircraft mix provided the essential quality of total air mobility is preserved.

tactics and costs with the assumption that they can be solved, we can explore the impact of complete air mobility of this kind on the scope and character of military operations.

The assumed air-mobile battle group may be able to fly 50 to 100 miles from a temporary base without refueling. The temporary base might be shifted in a single move to a new location perhaps 100 or 200 miles away. Detailed examination of maps shows that suitable landing areas should be available within 100 miles of most militarily important areas, except in the most difficult terrain. The temporary base locations can be selected such that they can accommodate today's tactical transport airplanes; the latter can operate from a main support base as much as 300 or 400 miles to the rear of the temporary base.

If the temporary base is shifted every few days, then the enemy is vulnerable to surprise strikes anywhere within about a 500-mile radius of the main base. If critical ground can be held and defended by "dismounted" troops, it is also possible to consider linear movements reaching ever farther from the main base, with the possibility of using previous temporary bases, where some backlog of supplies can be built up, as intermediate points of support.

These changes in force structure and mode of operation would provide a highly mobile maneuvering force, much less constrained by terrain than even an air-supported ground force. It could engage the enemy with a great deal of tactical flexibility, selecting unexpected points of attack almost at will. With helicopter speeds on the order of 100 to 150 miles per hour, the group could move 100 miles in 2 or 3 hours, including all the times necessary to assemble and unload. The same maneuver might take perhaps 10 hours under good conditions for a group using ground vehicles; it could take days. Tactical strikes by the same air-mobile unit could be made at locations several hundred miles apart with delays of only a few days, whereas such maneuvers in difficult terrain by troops moving over land would take weeks (if the terrain could be traversed without enemy interference), or else different units would have to be deployed to the different locations.

Potentially, we can finally see the means to achieve the highly mobile operations necessary for rapid tactical decision by moderately sized forces in the difficult military and geographical environments where limited wars are most likely to take place. Military operations on land would assume much of the character of naval maneuvers at sea, with local applications of military strength against enemy strong points, areas of weakness, or strategic positions. The relatively small maneuvering groups would not be in continuous contact with the enemy, they would be harder for him to find, and their strikes would achieve the advantages of surprise while they exploit his weaknesses.

Like most schemes, unfortunately, this one has shortcomings with its advantages. It is not equally applicable in all kinds of warfare, and many problems remain to be solved before it can be even partically implemented. What must be done to create truly air-mobile forces, and what would be their inescapable limitations?

## Problems in the Transformation

*The Logistic System.* The nature of the supply problem will be vastly different for an air-mobile battle group than for the conventional one moving on the ground. Under average combat conditions the latter may need about 40 tons of supply per day, of which fuel and ammunition comprise about 80 percent. The air-mobile battle group may have to receive about 150 tons of supplies each day; most of the increase will be in fuel. A dozen transport aircraft, used as in the previous example of resupply for a division, could meet this need in terms of gross tonnages. But many of the transports will have to be converted into tankers (this would be required in the previous example as well).

Once the problem of transporting fuel is solved, we shall have to face that of keeping the helicopters in working order. The helicopter maintenance problem, associated in large part with the complex drive mechanism between the power plant and the rotor blades, is notoriously difficult. It has been a contributing factor in limiting helicopters' military and civil utility. Its consequences are felt in reduced useful operating time and an increase in the logistic problems of spare parts and repair. While the use of turbine engines, improvements in the design of high-speed rotating portions of the drive mechanism, and potential changes in basic rotor design[7] all offer promise of reducing this maintenance burden, it will probably remain more serious than comparable problems in surface vehicles.

The characteristic echelonment of maintenance — from simple repairs in the combat zones to major repairs in safe rear areas — will probably not be tolerable, however. The fluidity of the military situation in a large geographical region might be such that there would be long periods between returns to any particular base area. While logistic aircraft can deliver supplies to a forward temporary base, it will be difficult to return helicopters (and other major equipment) to a rear base for maintenance.

Instead of moving disabled machines to the rear, necessary spare parts would have to be flown forward to the temporary bases, where maintenance crews would be stationed. Since important repairs may be necessary at the farthest reaches of the helicopters' tactical movements, certain critical spares may always have to be carried on-board.

These changes will be felt elsewhere in the logistics system. The large buildup of many days' or weeks' reserve supplies of food, fuel, ammunition, spare parts, and other equipment in immediate proximity to combat areas, which characterizes ground-mobile operations, will not always be possible for air-mobile units. Spare parts and other supplies will have to be flown to the fighting units, on demand. Control over inventories must in such circumstances be extremely precise. Expert and timely coordination of activity at all points will be required. Automatic computation machinery for processing of inventory status reports and requests for materials will be needed, as will communications systems not susceptible to substantial delays. The form of the supply pipeline, with special "surge points" to fill gaps created when sections of the system are disrupted by enemy action or chance breakdowns, will become critically important. Finally field treatment of sick and wounded, with subsequent evacuation by air to main-base hospitals, will have to become a routine procedure.

Although current military logistic systems have all of these features to greater or lesser extent, they would have to be developed to extremes if major reliance were placed on air mobility.

*Giving the Group Fighting Power.* The heavy artillery and armed combat vehicles of the ground-mobile force constitute its substantive firepower; they give troops their fighting strength when they meet the enemy. If this heavy equipment cannot be carried by the air-mobile group, substitutes will have to be found. Several approaches can be taken; all will probably be necessary in some degree:

• Weapons can be mounted on the helicopters, to be fired in flight. Since it is difficult to build helicopters to take the shock of recoil of artillery-type weapons, these weapons will be limited to machine guns, guided and unguided rockets, recoilless rifles, anti-tank missiles, and the like. Special design problems in suiting such weapons for firing from helicopters may become severe enough to require a whole new family of weapons and fire-control systems for this purpose.

• The helicopters can be used as "prime movers" for conventional artillery pieces. Just as guns are now towed by trucks or tractors to firing positions, they would be lifted by the helicopters and carried to those positions. For this purpose lighter-weight guns than those now used, easier to carry and to manhandle on the ground, will be needed.

• The equivalent of very heavy firepower that cannot be carried by helicopters can be provided by tactical fighter-bombers. This will increase the need for tactical air-ground force cooperation much beyond that which exists today, so that the two can work together very closely much as the infantry-armor-artillery team does in current mechanized operations. Special radar and radio sets will have to be developed for this purpose. More tactical aircraft then we currently envisage, and changes in the Air Force structure, may be needed.

*Fighting at Night and in Bad Weather.* As Korea showed, an enemy who is placed at a serious disadvantage by our own use of aviation in daylight will choose darkness and inclement weather for his own operations. Further, many battles (such as the Battle of the Bulge in 1944) have hinged on the ability of one of the contestants to move in bad weather.[8] Extremes of wind, rain, blizzard, or dense fog can stop any military operations, air or ground. Of greater concern are the more frequent periods of poor visibility and low ceiling, or of darkness, when aircraft flights are restricted but surface movement is not.

In commercial operations and military operations outside a combat zone, instrument landing aids for bad weather can be installed at airfields, and radio aids to navigation scattered about the countryside. But these are time-consuming and expensive installations. In a war zone we could count on their existence only at large, friendly bases. If the enemy is sophisticated in electronic technology, he can jam radio devices used openly. Whether he is or not, they can be difficult to use in an austere countryside not under friendly control. In the extreme, setting a helicopter or aircraft down at night or in bad weather, in a landing zone that may come under enemy fire, is extraordinarily difficult.

These constraints require that external radio and radar aids to navigation and landing be portable and easily deployed in situations where they can be used, and that blind flying and landing systems be self-contained in the aircraft for use under the worst conditions. Devices to assist in finding the enemy would also be critically important; they would have to be simple and reliable to meet the logistic support requirements. Research and development in these areas would have to be accelerated if the full benefit of air mobility is to be achieved.

*Problems of People.* The changes in the organization and operating techniques of the ground forces implied by air mobility will affect the selection and training of troops as well as equipment and tactics. Expert mechanics and pilots will be needed in far greater numbers than currently. The added complication of automatic equipment for management of the logistic system will require a high order of technical skill. Inde-

168

pendent operations over long periods will place extensive command responsibilities on men relatively low in the organization.

All of this means that training periods will be extended. Length of service in air-mobile units may therefore have to be longer than in the other parts of the armed forces. Conceivably, units of this kind may come to be professional forces, not at all dependent on the draft for their manpower. Increased pay scales and a possible decrease in importance of the citizen army can be expected. This will simply accentuate current trends.

## Where and How Can They Fight?

It would be naive to think that air mobility would uniformly increase the military value of fighting forces in all kinds of warfare. The decision to modify a substantial part of the armed forces in this way must ultimately depend on this question of utility. What are its components?

*Air Mobility in Guerrilla War.* In the environments of unconventional warfare helicopters and airplanes allow a relatively small number of troops to use their strength in a large area of otherwise inaccessible terrain. It has become possible to react quickly when a guerrilla band is found or attacks suddenly at unpredictable locations. This situation permits some of the simplest and most immediate solutions to both the logistic and tactical problems of aircraftborne combat maneuvers, and has seen the first (and thus far only) application of such tactics to limited warfare. The operation of helicopterborne troops out of fixed bases scattered through the area of warfare was a tactic successfully developed and effectively used in Algeria. It is being used now with a fair measure of success in South Vietnam.

The reasons for the success of helicopter tactics in this kind of war are obvious. The guerrillas cannot do much to stop them. Experiences in Algeria and in South Vietnam have shown that helicopters can suffer a considerable number of hits by the weapons available to the guerrillas, without serious damage.[9] Losses can be cut further by air strikes to prevent the guerrillas from concentrating their fire. Major bases are available under the control of government forces who are largely immune to guerrilla attack, so that the logistic support problem is reduced to a minimum. It is possible to take advantage of air mobility in an environment where most of the problems are technical rather than tactical.

*Air Mobility in Conventional Warfare.* Against a formally organized enemy, one with more sophisticated weapons than the guerrilla and the ability to use them, conventional military doctrines assume far greater importance than they have in guerrilla war. Air-mobile troops in such situations are very likely to adopt maneuvering tactics similar to those of armored forces. Relative to armored forces, however, the scale of movement of air-mobile units using such tactics would be very much expanded. Attacks would start in friendly rear areas far from contact with the enemy and penetrate far beyond his forward positions. In the absence of massed artillery fire at the point of attack, heavy and continued attacks by tactical fighter-bombers would be indispensable to destroy enemy defenses there and along the route of approach to the attack. Air strikes would have to continue after landing, to inhibit enemy counterattacks. (These tactics have already been developed to a significant degree by the Marine Corps.)

Yet, no attack against enemy positions will be perfect; the enemy will always be left with some defenses against the passage or landing of the air-mobile troops. At the very least, they will have antiaircraft machine guns; they may well have radar-directed antiaircraft cannon and guided missiles. The helicopter is a very "soft" target which will be much more vulnerable to such weapons than to the guerrillas' meager weapons. Measures can be taken to reduce this vulnerability, but this can be expected to be a losing race as the enemy becomes better armed and his weapons become more sophisticated.

Therefore, against a strong enemy who fields a large, well-organized and well-equipped force, the use of air-mobile troops may have to be restricted to carrying troops and equipment behind our own lines, and to certain types of cavalry missions such as scouting, armed reconnaissance, and penetrations for harassment into poorly defended areas, while the main battle is fought by heavier forces on the ground. The pressures relegating air-mobile troops to a secondary role must increase as the strength, density, and sophistication of the defense increases — as we go from the non-European to the European conventional engagement. Clearly, if this role for air-mobile troops is the best that can be achieved in certain important military environments, then the presence of more conventional ground-mobile units will be indispensable, and the entire ground force structure will have to include some mixture of the two types of organization.

*A Summary of Tactical Utility.* Two factors become apparent from analysis of the tactical employment problems of air-mobile troops:

- Air supremacy in the area of operations is absolutely essential to the success of air logistic support and air mobile combat operations.

- There will be a scale of tactical utility that varies with kind of war, perhaps as in the following examples:

| Type of War | Probable Utility of Air Mobility |
|---|---|
| Guerrilla war ($E_3L_3$ element of limited-war matrix) | Troop movements, supply, rapid response to attack, hunting and attacking guerrillas |
| War against an unsophisticated but organized enemy ($E_2L_2$ matrix element) | Troop movements, supply, deep strikes into enemy rear, capturing important towns, disrupting enemy supply lines |
| War against a sophisticated, organized enemy ($E_1L_1$ matrix element) | Troop movements and supply as enemy air power permits, scouting and reconnaissance, harrassment |
| Incipient war | Early occupation of critical areas for deterrence (for example, British attempt to occupy Suez) |

## The Cost of Air Mobility

It must be clear at this point that this change in capability will not be inexpensive. A large-scale force modification might require hundreds or thousands of helicopters, and hundreds of transport aircraft. To their cost must be added that of the new weapons and equipment which will have to be developed to take full advantage of air mobility, the cost of creating and incorporating new organizations in the force structure, and the cost of expanded tactical air forces.

Commitment of a substantial portion of the ground forces to heavy reliance on air mobility can easily bring relatively small military units such as air-mobile battle groups, with all their necessary auxiliaries, into a cost region characteristic of entire groundborne divisions, POLARIS submarines, or attack aircraft carriers. It will be difficult if not impossible to make up these added costs by savings elsewhere. The difference in basic costs between ground vehicles and aircraft permits only a fraction of the added expense to be made up by reducing the numbers of vehicles in the ground forces. New weapons are likely to be more expensive than those they replace.

It is most likely that the military budget for the General Purpose Forces will have to increase, perhaps a substantial amount, to accommodate the revolution in military technology, organization, and tactics that extensive application of air mobility implies. Revolutionary changes in military capability made possible by technology have always led to more, rather than less, total expense. The addition of POLARIS submarines and ICBM's to the strategic forces, the development of supersonic tactical aircraft and the accompanying evolution of guided antiaircraft weapons, the redesign of naval ships to use guided missiles, all have led to greater total expenditure for a more sophisticated technology that vastly increased military capability. There is no reason to believe that another revolution in the structure and capability of the armed forces will not be just as costly.

In the long run, compensating gains are most likely to derive from the economy of force which the change can bring. By providing an opportunity to carry out military actions with decision and dispatch in many limited war situations, and by obviating the need for massive buildups of supplies and construction of transport facilities to meet enemy forces on their own ground, truly air-mobile forces of battle group or brigade size may become the equivalent of some larger number of divisions.

Unfortunately, there can be no certainty that these rewards will be reaped. Despite the positive value of maneuvers and exercises, the fighting power of air-mobile units cannot be tested precisely except in warfare. Therefore, the assessment of a military value for which a high cost must be incurred is faced with uncertainty that makes the decision extremely difficult.

# 14

## *Tactical Air Warfare: Some Critical Problems*

THE tactical air forces have four combat missions in limited war: to destroy enemy air power; to disrupt his rear-area supply and reinforcement operations by interdiction attacks; reconnaissance; and close air support — attacks on the enemy in forward areas to help troops engaged in combat with the enemy's ground forces.

In the first three of these missions, our own aviators must be equipped to overcome the most sophisticated defenses that a potential enemy can place in the field. Their aircraft must be able to fly several hundred miles over enemy territory. They must be able to fly high and fast to defeat the enemy's supersonic fighters. Darkness and inclement weather should interfere with their tasks as little as possible. In short, these requirements lead to the tactical fighter-bomber system that was described in Chapter 5.

The kind of aircraft required for close air support is not as easily specified. Deep penetration of enemy territory is not necessarily needed. The airplane should be readily available for emergency calls as the exigencies of the ground battle dictate. It should therefore be based close to the forward troop positions, and these bases should not be elaborate. The aircraft must be able to fly when it is needed, with little risk of being down for repairs. It should also be able to stay in the air near battle positions for a long time, ready to attack on a few minutes' notice. Close coordination of its attacks with ground troop activities is essential. But high-speed and high-altitude performance are not absolutely essential if the aircraft can be protected against enemy fighters by other means

173

(such as fighter escorts). The aircraft should, however, be highly maneuverable — able to make tight turns and sharp pullups — near the ground, in case repeated passes at a target are necessary.

The high-performance fighter-bomber can, to some perhaps considerable extent, do the close-air-support job. But the basic requirements of the mission might lead to a completely different kind of airplane. It could, for example, be a relatively small,* short-range subsonic aircraft, designed for easy maintenance in an austere environment. It would not need large airfields or concrete runways. It would need only a few elements of the complex electronic systems of the aircraft designed for deep interdiction and air combat.

Acquisition of an airplane of this type for close air support, as well as the very sophisticated aircraft for the other missions, would not be in keeping with the recent trend in the tactical air forces toward a single aircraft type for all missions. However, it is not absolutely necessary to have a single aircraft type. In fact, until recently, this was not possible simply because the technology of aircraft design required specialization for the separate missions. Aircraft that would fly fast and high for air combat could not fly far enough for interdiction; an aircraft that could carry a heavy load over a long distance could not maneuver as a fighter; and so on.

As a result, there are currently several types of combat aircraft in the tactical air force inventory. These include fast-climbing supersonic fighters for interception of enemy attackers, long-range fighters designed for escort duty and air battles deep over enemy territory, and bombers. Despite their specialization, the interceptors and long-range fighters are used in fighter-bomber versions for attacks against the ground and for reconnaissance as well. There has hardly ever been a fighter on which someone did not try to hang bombs or a camera.

The technology of aerodynamics, airplane structural design, and jet engine design have now advanced sufficiently to permit the creation of a single aircraft having the speed, range, and weight-carrying characteristics required by all the missions. The Air Force has seized upon these advances to reconstitute its tactical aircraft fleet. Aircraft such as the F-105, the F4C (a version of the Navy's Phantom II air superiority fighter) and the TFX (which is intended to enter the inventory near the end of this decade) are all designed for multiple-purpose operation. Eventually, a single aircraft of this type may make up the bulk of the Tactical Air Command's combat aircraft inventory.

---

* That is, its weight on takeoff, with bomb load, might be in the range of 10,000 to 30,000 pounds, compared with weights that could exceed 50,000 pounds for the supersonic fighter-bomber.

The Navy, however, continues to believe that, within its own force structure built around the aircraft carrier, airplanes that are specialized for their missions will do a better job in each mission than those designed to carry out all missions — that separate tools are ultimately better than a single, general-purpose tool. Separate aircraft designed for air combat, interdiction deep in enemy territory, reconnaissance, and attacks on ground targets in support of the ground battle are now in the Navy and Marine tactical aircraft fleet, and will probably continue to be in that fleet in the future.

But the really basic separation of tactical aircraft requirements today appears to be that between the close-air-support needs and the needs of the other missions. What are the pros and cons of this separation? What are the implications for tactical air force structure and their effects on the other branches of the armed forces?

## The Underlying Relationships in Aircraft Fleet Composition

As in previous cases, this problem can be approached through quantitative analysis of a hypothetical situation. While the details of such analysis are too involved and technical to present here, an outline of the variables of the problem and the kinds of results that may be expected can lead to useful insights regarding the nonquantifiable factors that must ultimately determine the structure of the tactical aircraft fleet.

The objectives of analysis might be to find the most economical fleet that can meet the tactical air mission requirements, when two types of fleet can be selected: (1) one comprised solely of general-purpose tactical fighter-bombers, or (2) a fleet including a mixture of the general-purpose aircraft and one designed exclusively for the close-air-support mission. Starting with our knowledge of the World War II and Korea experiences and adding estimates of the changes future war might bring, we can assume various reasonable values for the bomb tonnages that would have to be delivered in close-air-support operations each day. In the same way, we can assume values for the number of daily sorties that would be needed for other purposes. These daily operational requirements could cover a whole range of quantitative values, designed to express the needs of many different kinds and levels of limited war. They would be the primary variables of the analysis.

A number of other characteristics of the tactical aircraft system will also have to be considered as variables:

175

• The bomb load that can be carried by each type of aircraft and each specific aircraft design.

• The average effectiveness* of each type of aircraft in destroying targets.

• The number of sorties that each type of aircraft can fly each day (this depends on the airplane's ability to fly in darkness or bad weather, and on the amount of time that must be devoted to maintaining it, with all its subsystems, in satisfactory flying condition).

• The time spent, on the average, on each sortie. (This depends on what and where the targets are likely to be, on how far an airplane can fly, and how long it can stay in the air.)

• The average effectiveness of enemy air defenses against each type of aircraft.

• The number of aircraft that will be lost in normal, noncombat operation (for example, crashes on takeoff or landing).

• The costs of aircraft and their equipment, for systems designed to carry out individual missions.

All of these variables can be combined in calculations which show the required numbers of aircraft of each type, and the cost of fleets that can deliver various amounts of bombing ammunition in addition to flying various numbers of sorties for other purposes. These calculations would lead, first, to a set of graphs like those shown in Figure 14.1; there would be one figure like this for each combination of the variables describing system performance. These results can then be combined with the cost of various types of aircraft to show what it would take to buy a particular kind of fleet.

A typical set of cost curves is shown in Figure 14.2, which illustrates how marked the effects of changing the variables can be. Similar curves can be obtained for fleet operating costs. The combination of procurement and operating costs would give the total cost of purchasing and operating a fleet of airplanes for a specified time.

The effects of even a few of the variables on fleet cost can, as Figure 14.2 shows, shift the economic decision for type of fleet either way.

---

* Effectiveness can be defined, for attacks against ground targets, as the ratio between the amount of ammunition of any kind that actually destroys (or otherwise eliminates from action) a target, and the amount of ammunition that must be expended in attacking it because the delivery system accuracy is imperfect. For example, if one bomb of a certain size can destroy a bridge or a tank but 10 bombs of that size have to be delivered to *assure* their destruction, then the bombing effectiveness is 1/10. In a similar way, effectiveness in air combat could be the ratio of enemy aircraft destroyed to number of intercepts or air-to-air attacks attempted.

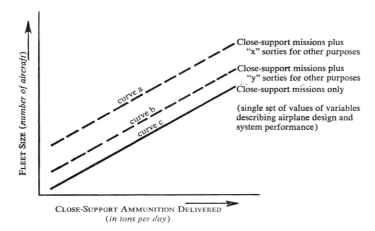

FIGURE 14.1 TYPICAL RESULTS OF FLEET SIZE CALCULATIONS
*Curves a and b show fleet size obtained by adding the aircraft needed for x or y other sorties to those needed for close air support (curve c).*

If the specialized close-air-support aircraft can carry the same bomb load as the general-purpose type but is not as expensive a system, then the dual-type fleet may be cheaper (left-hand pair of graphs). Moreover, the cost disparity can increase as more close-support aircraft are needed, because we benefit from the effects of the learning curve.

If the specialized aircraft is much smaller than the general-purpose type, many more of them will be needed to meet given mission requirements. The net result can then be a higher over-all cost for the mixed fleet than for the general-purpose fleet (right-hand pair of graphs). But if the smaller close-air-support aircraft is more effective (that is, can bomb more accurately) than the large, general-purpose aircraft, then a mixed fleet with many of the smaller aircraft can still cost less than a one-type fleet (upper-right and lower-left graphs) for a specified delivery capability.

Tradeoffs such as these will become even more numerous and complex when the effects of the other variables are introduced. Nevertheless, it would appear that the knowledgeable defense planner should be able, with the help of technical studies of airplane design and performance and with statements of operational requirements on the part of the Services and the Joint Chiefs, to estimate the values of the variables for a future aircraft fleet, and select the most economical one for the force structure.

The problem is not so simple, however. Estimates of the variables for future airplanes in unknown situations are highly uncertain. A host of

177

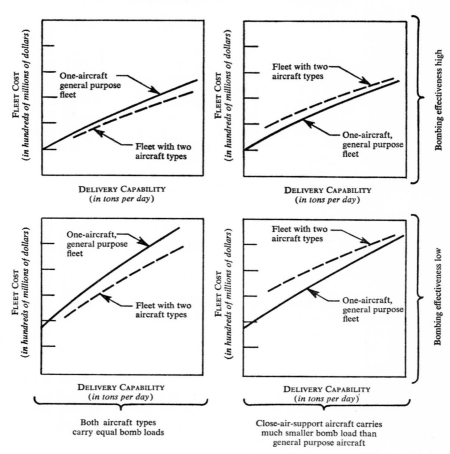

FIGURE 14.2  TYPICAL FLEET COST CURVES
FOR VARIOUS FLEET COMPOSITIONS

*Results are shown for a given number of sorties per day in air combat, interdiction, and reconnaissance, and for equal effectiveness of both aircraft types in the curves in one graph.*

intangible factors also acts to cloud the issues on which judgments must be made.

## Uncertainties and Intangibles in System Selection

*Effectiveness.* The bombing effectiveness of an airplane is extremely difficult to predict accurately enough for sound planning of fleet size and force structure. It is, in the first place, possible to make only rough estimates of what will be needed to destroy enemy weapons and installa-

178

tions that have not been observed closely and directly. To this uncertainty is added that of estimating the errors of the bombing system.

Bombing accuracies can be computed from error analyses of the aircraft approach to the target and the ballistic characteristics of the bombs themselves. They can be measured from tests on bombing ranges. But paper analysis and range tests under controlled conditions must of necessity omit consideration of the effects of the vagaries of battle, which are virtually impossible to quantify. Bombing accuracy in combat will be considerably degraded by the fact that the "live" targets are more difficult to see than a target on a firing or bombing range, and by the action of defenses that the pilot must be concerned to evade or penetrate as rapidly as possible during weapon delivery.

Detailed records describing the number of bombs delivered to destroy a tank or a bridge, the number of trucks damaged or the number of men in foxholes killed by a strafing run, or the net effect of air attacks on enemy operations over the long run, are exceedingly difficult to obtain in combat or afterwards. Furthermore, the opportunities to obtain such data have been relatively rare since World War II and Korea; air warfare has not played a major role in the large number of limited wars since then. And data obtained in the wars of the 1940's and early 1950's are losing validity with the rapid evolution of aircraft technology into regimes of speed, load-carrying capacity, and sophistication of weapon delivery systems that have never been tested in combat.

The proponents of one aircraft design philosophy might argue from range test data and error analysis that a relatively simple airplane moving at slow speed, and able to make the very tight turns possible only in low-speed flight, should be able to make attacks against targets on the ground more accurately than high-speed aircraft. On the other side, it might be argued that the technically advanced bomb delivery systems of the high-speed aircraft would overcome the accuracy-degrading effects of high speed. Neither side of the argument can be definitely proved, because we do not know for certain the effects of enemy defenses and other combat conditions on system performance.

*The Impact of Antiaircraft Defenses.* The potential presence of extremely effective antiaircraft defenses leads inexorably to an airplane that can overcome those defenses — an airplane expensive enough to demand a substantial fraction of the resources available for the tactical aircraft fleet. Since this aircraft can carry out the close-support mission to some degree, and little is left to obtain another aircraft specialized for that mission, the pressure toward a fleet composed of a single, general-purpose type of airplane is very strong. The close-support requirements tend to be ignored.

The close-support mission is a dangerous job of day-in and day-out bombing and strafing of troops, mobile weapons, and fixed positions close to our own troops. Many airplanes will be lost because of the necessary maneuvering at low altitude, even aside from the effects of the defenses. Then, since these maneuvers require prolonged exposure to the defenses at relatively low speed (unlike the strike-and-get-out tactics of interdiction), further losses may be expected.

Since relatively few of the very expensive general-purpose aircraft can be procured, there is a further countervailing pressure to reserve them for the vitally important missions that determined their design characteristics in the first place: interdiction, air superiority, and reconnaissance. Moreover, the use of the very expensive fighter-bomber will be especially justifiable on a cost-effectiveness basis, including the effects of potential combat losses, if it is used to deliver nuclear weapons.

The net result of relying exclusively on one type of aircraft for all missions therefore makes for planning in favor of nuclear limited war, and leads to reluctance to provide close air support to the ground forces. The implications for limited war capability and force structure are clear.

There must, however, be variations of defense effectiveness in the field. The most elaborate defense systems, requiring the greatest technical and logistic support, are likely to exist around relatively permanent facilities constituting strategic centers of a military complex (independently of possible location in rear areas or on permanent defense perimeters). The antiaircraft defenses in forward combat zones, where close support operations are needed and troop positions are expected to change frequently, are more likely to be simpler and by implication less effective. If this would be true in the case of an enemy with technological ability equivalent to our own, it may, perhaps, safely be assumed that against a less sophisticated enemy the defenses against close support attacks will be far from the most effective possible.

When the anatomy of the antiair defense structure is dissected, therefore, it begins to appear that the entire air combat fleet need not be designed to overcome the enemy's best defense technology. It begins to make sense to have a cheaper, less complex aircraft for the close-support mission, while the extremely expensive multiple-purpose plane is reserved for the times when it is needed beyond doubt. The pressure toward nuclear war would also be ameliorated if we could move in this direction.

But arguments such as these are difficult to quantify. Uncertainty about antiaircraft defenses makes for uncertainty in tactical aircraft fleet planning.

*Tactical Flexibility for Close Support.* If it is accepted that the defenses which may be encountered do not automatically preclude a rather simple aircraft for close air support, then there are many other arguments of a qualitative nature in favor of a mixed fleet. These arguments are concerned with questions of military utility, and can outweigh purely economic considerations.

First, if a large number of aircraft are available for assignment to the close-support mission there will be greater flexibility in tactical sortie assignments. More individual attacks could be carried out simultaneously without the need to wait for an aircraft to strike at one location before it can proceed to another. Also, if the forward defenses are about equally effective against both types, the total fleet may be hurt less by attrition of individual aircraft, in both cost and fraction of the fleet lost, if a large number of inexpensive machines are assigned to close support than if the task is done by a few that are very expensive.

Finally, a simple machine is likely to be easier to maintain at austere forward bases than a very complex one. It is therefore more likely to be available when needed, without demanding excessively large crews for maintenance and repairs. The logistic burden on the ground forces can thus be eased.

This is in keeping, too, with the realities of possible limited war engagements. The simple close-support aircraft would be more suitable for the armed forces of our allies in the underdeveloped areas of the world, for whom the maintenance and operation of the ever more sophisticated aircraft that will come to them from the U.S. tactical air fleet will become an increasingly insupportable burden. Since in these areas we can expect almost always to have to fight alongside indigenous forces, a relatively simple aircraft in our own forces could more easily be shared with our allies. Common usage of this airplane for air support of the land battle in the forward combat areas, while the more sophisticated U.S. aircraft assume the burdens of air superiority and deep strikes into the enemy rear, would offer obvious advantages in the greater contribution allied forces could make to prosecution of the war.

*Ammunition and Sortie Requirements.* The quantitative analysis leading to selection of the most economical tactical aircraft fleet was predicated on the assumption that average daily requirements for ammunition tonnages and combat sorties could be specified. It is not certain, however, that the mission requirements can be stated in this way.

In the course of any future war, it can be expected that the battle for air superiority will be joined, and will be crucial, at the beginning (if air supremacy for one side does not exist initially, as it did in Korea). It may appear that until air superiority has been gained little can be done to support the ground forces directly with tactical aviation. After we have defeated the enemy air forces, attention can be turned to the close-support and interdiction problems that may have a greater influence on the course of the ground war. Sortie and ammunition tonnage requirements will therefore vary markedly and unpredictably.

It is obvious, however, that the enemy will not always be so considerate as to allow our troops to operate easily without the close support, tactical reconnaissance, and interdiction they will need even as the air superiority battle goes on. There is thus a conflict in mission requirements, which can force us to take the offensive with only one of the combat arms at a time instead of all together from the start. It would appear that irreducible minima in close-support capability as well as in reconnaissance, interdiction, and air superiority sorties must be at the basis of force structure planning, if the forces are to be designed for an early military decision.

Unfortunately, the quantitative expression of these force level planning needs depends very much on anticipation of specific arrays of enemy military power, and on estimates of the direction, out of an almost infinite field of possibilities, that the engagement of this military power may take. The existence of a fleet of general-purpose aircraft offers the air commander great flexibility in adjusting his operations to the demands of unpredictable eventualities.

*Air and Ground Force Organization.* Much of the problem of tactical air fleet size and structure depends on the organization of the armed forces as we find it, and as we may expect it to exist for some time to come.

In the Marine Corps the ground commander, once he is ashore, exercises control over his tactical air support. The Marines can assign aircraft for close support, knowing that the Navy will provide for air superiority and operations deep over enemy territory.

In the Army-Air Force combination, however, the Air Force is assigned the tactical air support mission for the Army. The Army can make its requirements known, and the two can work together, but ultimately the Army must rely on Air Force judgment, and negotiation through a higher defense command, to have its needs fulfilled. Obviously, fears must arise that in this interplay the Air Force view will be influenced by its own important problems in both strategic and tactical aviation; that this view will influence the higher Defense Department planners; and that when a tactical fighter fleet is selected the very important close-support capability may be compromised in favor of the air superiority mission. The tactical air fleet size and composition may never appear adequate to the ground force planners, while the air planners believe they have met the national needs within the available resources, as they view them.

Further arguments arise as to who should plan and control the close-support fleet. The entire fleet selection problem, difficult enough to solve on its merits, becomes further confused in this "roles and missions" argument.

*The Tradeoffs, in Summary.* The entire question of structure and organization of the tactical air combat forces is seen to depend to a great extent on an uncertain view of aircraft requirements for a particular air warfare mission: that of close air support for troops on the ground. The effectiveness of air defenses and of tactical air strikes cannot be estimated precisely. Many intangible factors related to estimates of the military value of one kind of tactical aircraft fleet or another can outweigh purely economic arguments in selecting the best fleet to do a given job. And the job itself is not easy to specify, since it can be defined differently according to the ground and air forces' views of how a war will develop.

Moreover, the high cost of developing, procuring, and operating very sophisticated aircraft places a fleet composed of this type alone in a cost-effectiveness regime where the pressure to rely on nuclear weapons is great indeed; this is the most obvious way to make "efficient" use of the relatively small number of extremely valuable machines that would be available.

But if the strength of potential defenses in forward combat zones is overestimated, especially for situations outside Europe, then the resulting acceptance of extreme sophistication in all aircraft would again place American limited war forces in the position where they are designed to meet the ultimate threat, while undesirably compromised for use in situations which are much more likely to occur. A tactical air force structure based on a mixture of the two aircraft types would appear to lead to a distribution of capability better balanced to meet the needs of both European and non-European military action.

# *15*

## *Communications, Command, and Control*

It has always been important in warfare for fighting men in the field to be able to communicate with each other and with their commanders during a battle, and for the higher commanders to be able to communicate with their governments. Indeed, the outcomes of many crucial battles in the last several hundred years of history have depended on the ability of a Commander in Chief to receive information from and communicate instructions to his subordinate commanders distributed over the battlefield. In modern times, especially, the mainstay of military operations is the communication system that ties together the separate elements of a military force at all levels.

Communications on the modern battlefield depend on the organization and style of fighting — the tactical doctrines — of the armed forces. They are used to coordinate combat operations on the ground, to connect far-ranging tactical aircraft with the air operations center, to connect the air operations center with the ground units served by tactical air strikes, and to link combat elements with their logistic support systems. In the rear areas of a theatre of warfare, communications tie together the commanders of various major force elements spread over vast areas of territory. They also connect these commanders with the central theatre command and the latter with the Joint Staff, civilian Defense Department leaders, and the Commander in Chief at home. On occasion, as we noted in Chapter 5, a direct link may be needed between the extremes of this command chain.

All conceivable methods are used to make such connections. Messages may be carried by runners or liaison aircraft. Telephone and telegraph are used where forces are established long enough to emplace the needed wires and switching centers, or where a usable system exists. But radio communications have burgeoned during and since the two World Wars, growing into the largest and most complex communications net of the armed forces on the field of battle. Specialized radio sets vary from small ones having a range of a few thousand yards, by which adjacent groups of men talk with each other, to very large, permanent installations used for communicating around the world.

Military communications are made more difficult than the counterpart civilian systems by the need to incorporate two essential characteristics: (1) the ability to transmit large volumes of information in a very short time for a great variety of purposes, both independent and mutually supporting, without incurring undesirable delays, mutual interference among friendly sets, or interference from natural causes; and (2) security from enemy interception and interference.

To meet these requirements, military radio communications have come to use complex switching networks to permit ready access to individual communication lines or radio frequencies while connecting any pair of transmitting and receiving points uniquely. Military communications have come to use more and more of the available electromagnetic frequency spectrum, and especially those parts of the spectrum where the transmitting and receiving stations must be within sight of each other. When terrain and the curvature of the earth interpose barriers between the transmitting and receiving stations, various types of radio relay stations on the surface or in the air are mandatory, leading ultimately to the use of communications satellites as relays for long-distance communications.

Highly sophisticated circuitry makes possible various encoding and decoding schemes to deny information regarding the presence and content of radio-transmitted messages to the enemy. It assists avoidance of enemy jamming, and also makes possible the compression of large amounts of information into brief transmission times.

These trends have led to increasing size and complexity of radio sets and systems. At the same time, however, the trends of military force structure and tactics demand light weight — especially for radios designed to be used in aircraft or in the lower echelons of ground troop organization — and the ability to withstand the rigors of environmental extremes and military handling. The need to retain a high order of reliability and freedom from maintenance demands ruggedness that conflicts with weight reduction.

As in all the other areas of military operations we have examined, the stringency of the military requirements for communications equipment is especially influenced by the possibility of facing an enemy with technological capability of a high order. As always, this makes for the most complex and costly systems. Many possible solutions to the problems of designing these systems are offered by the extensive research and development efforts in modern radio technology, which have advanced the field of communications at least as rapidly as, if not more rapidly than, any other technical area. While mathematical information theory has shown how to achieve many of the functional objectives in new ways, advances in solid-state physics, leading to the transistor and like devices, have permitted important reductions in weight, volume, and failure rate of complex circuits. The scientific and engineering development of radio communications shows no tendency, yet, to reach a plateau but is proceeding at an extraordinary rate.

Unfortunately, this progress is faced by a Parkinsonian sort of development pattern that causes the demands on the communications system always to run ahead of the capability science and engineering provide. However many communications channels are available, and whatever the ease with which soldiers can speak over a distance of a few hundred yards or thousands of miles, there are always desires to send still more messages. This is not always the fault of the soldier, however. The inhibition of interpersonal interaction caused by dispersion of forces, and the greater strategic importance of individual weapons such as nuclear-armed missiles or tactical fighter-bombers that can devastate a city combine to increase the need for frequent communication and large amounts of information transfer.

Whenever the demand for communications channels approaches the number of channels available, there will be local delays in the transmission of information. These may be followed by occasional saturation or complete breakdown of portions of the system, sometimes for considerable periods of time.

To what might be called the technical delay is added that caused by the contraction of available channel capacity resulting from the competition for communication frequency allocations between the military and civilian users of the electromagnetic spectrum in peacetime. This may deny certain communications channels for military use at critical times before the outbreak of war, when the possibility of an outbreak hangs in the balance and delay caused by the shortcomings of machines can be as important as human factors in making the decision.

The intense interest in reducing communications delay, the ability to increase the information capacity of communications channels through improvements in communications technology, and the pressure of meeting the challenge of our most capable potential adversary, all make it easy to press for technical improvements in communications systems themselves, to the exclusion of other means of solving the problems. Preoccupation with technological advance can mask the fact that existing communications systems might be adequate if we could conceive of better ways to use them.

The approach to better usage must be made, not through technological development, but through reorganization of the basic command and control system which the communications are designed to serve. By implication, the structure of the armed forces may have to change, too.

It is well to remember that the communications system is simply a means for transferring information from the place where it is obtained to the place where it is used in decision making, and for transferring instructions from the decision center to the point of action. The information, its interpretation, and the actions it inspires are the crux of the operating military system.

Information is gathered by various means that include covert and overt intelligence, combat and reconnaissance reports. The information is stored and continuously brought up to date in a sort of huge library system with many centers and branches. Individuals from many decision centers have access to this "library," withdrawing items as needed for integration and interpretation. They may also make contributions themselves, much as scholars, students, and others both use and add to civilian libraries. The "libraries" as well as the decision makers have a part in the processing and transmission of the information. The decision makers must be alert for new "volumes" in areas of known importance; they may also occasionally overlook data that do not appear immediately relevant to their current purposes. This entire process is another source of error and delay, both of which can be reduced in proportion as the information processing and indexing procedures improve rates of access and incisiveness of interpretation.

All of this system exists to provide adequate control of military force for various military, political, and economic purposes by commanders from the President down. From the point of view of a commander at any level, if adequate intelligence exists and there are stated objectives which can be achieved or furthered by military action, it is his task to use his military forces to the extent necessary for success — no more, no less.

The timing of military responses or initiatives must follow some plan, rather than be merely rapid. Overreaction to an enemy move by application of too much force, too rapid application of force, or both, can cause undesired enemy actions and subsequent counterresponse which lead to uncontrolled escalation. Underreaction caused by excessive delays in intelligence gathering and interpretation, communications, or various inadequacies of the military force itself may lead to a response in which the objectives can never be achieved, though the drain on resources over a long period of time may be great.

The existence of nuclear weapons and the risks of escalation have created a need for extremes of precision in the control of military action which did not exist previously, when a difference between objectives and achievements might be corrected if enough time were available. The difference between victory for Israel and frustration for Britain and France in the Sinai-Suez crisis of 1956 was a matter of days; the events and risks of the Cuban quarantine and its resolution changed from day to day; the uncontrolled actions of a local commander in Berlin could conceivably trigger a nuclear war in a few hours.

With such changes in the demands for controlled responsiveness in the command and control system, and with the President directly responsible for the use of nuclear weapons, a trend toward centralization of the command function to higher and higher levels has been inevitable. This has created a parallel trend in which all communication lines and all information on the status and activity of field forces tend to be directed toward the center of decision. The size of the forces in the field, their widespread deployments, and the worldwide commitments for their potential use have created ever-increasing amounts of information to be transferred.

In short, the system design has tended to increase information flow and concentrate its arrival in a few terminals after passage through many steps on a command ladder. All of this tends to increase delay. At the same time the needs of the system have demanded a level of precision and timing of control of military forces which the communications delays can degrade unacceptably. The question is, then, whether this conflict can be resolved only through continuous technical improvement of the capacity of communications and information-processing systems, or whether changes in the command and control system can be made which will reduce the volume of information to be handled while preserving safety and precision.

One approach to resolution of this problem might shift the patterns of information flow away from the few central terminals of the network. Small, specialized units as well as integrated commands could be organized, much more than they are now, to transfer necessary information to each other and to take necessary action freely, in accordance with quite general orders, without the information having to move up and instructions back down the chain of command in all cases. In such a system, copies of messages would still have to be transmitted to higher commands to keep them informed and to request logistics and other support. But those commands would have to take control action, after the initial orders or plans were issued, only if necessary to change the direction of implementation. Infantry would coordinate its activities directly with artillery or missile commands; ground and air commanders would request and agree upon missions without the necessity to communicate through a theatre command; and combined arms commanders could coordinate major campaigns on their own initiative. A considerable amount of freedom would be allowed in the details of planning and tactics, the criteria for intercession from above being the detection of deviation of results from objectives or the settlement of disputes.

Actually, since the command and control function exists at many "echelons of command" with respect to many different military functions, the command and control system already combines the highly centralized and "parallel transfer" approaches under discussion (on the battlefield at least). Where and how the alternative parallel or centralized aspects of the system act at any particular time is determined by the scale of the action, the types of units involved, and the consequences of allowing subordinate commanders to pursue their tasks with loose control.

Certainly strong direction originating with the President may be essential during peacetime crises threatening war. But once the battle is joined, such direction may excessively inhibit forceful and decisive response to enemy military initiatives. The point to be emphasized here is that, while the freedom of the "parallel" system may exist currently among small, low-echelon units on the battlefield, the pressure towards more central control at higher levels tends to eliminate the "parallel" type of operation at the higher levels. If the system becomes more rigid at the top, that rigidity will gradually seep to lower levels. The future command structure can then look forward to losing much of its flexibility everywhere.

Greater stress on the "parallel" system in command and control would represent a return to earlier methods, which existed before communications system capacity permitted strong central control. The advantages of this system in terms of communications reduction come about because the vertical flow of messages is reduced in one direction, at least. Horizontal flow, or messages between commanders on the same level, would increase, but only adjacent or cooperating units would have to communicate, so that a net reduction in the total amount of information exchange may well result within the shifting communication patterns. Certainly communications delay as well as delay in control actions would be reduced because many intermediate processing and decision points would be eliminated in a number of situations, while decisions affecting local action would be made by those most intimately familiar with the local situation.

The disadvantages of such a system derive from this very flexibility and speed of response. Those monitoring operations at higher headquarters have a broader view of the entire conflict. Should they decide that a local action taken in a particular direction would not be in the best interests of the over-all needs or objectives of the war, they would have to intercede with extraordinary rapidity to change the action before it is under way. The inevitable delays in communication of plans and information, their evaluation, and decision would then create a high risk that intercession, when it comes, might be too late to stop operations that could cause undesired escalation or other unwanted effects.

This emphasizes, in fact, the critical tradeoff problem faced in constructing the command and control system: rigid, centralized control may inhibit the military system so that it cannot meet the needs, in conventional limited wars, of controlled response in short times; a loosening of control which could meet that problem in tactical situations increases the risk of losing strategic control.

It is probably true that once a war is in motion the exigencies of combat would force the loosening of an excessively centralized command and control system. The problem here is really with the transition period. For if war is to be kept limited, if long delays in adjusting to new situations are not to force a war to become long and severe, the military system must be able to act flexibly and decisively early in the action. If the command and control system is not built in advance to act this way, then regardless of the weapons in the force structure we are likely to face an undesirable expansion of conflict as we did in Korea.

Some of the potential changes in force structure which can vastly increase the effectiveness of a group of men of given size would appear to demand some loosening of centralized control. If, for example, the force structure includes a large number of air-mobile units with their tactical air support for combat and logistics, able to operate over tens or hundreds of miles in a matter of hours or a few days, such units could not avoid losing contact with headquarters, perhaps for long periods. This would be true as well under the various conceptions of a nuclear battlefield. Relatively small units must in all such situations operate as almost independent military forces, responsible to commanders of much higher rank than is usual in a closely organized, solidly occupied battlefield.

Local unit commanders would therefore have to understand thoroughly the general objectives of the operations and their strategic context, so that they could be assigned a relatively independent role. They would have to understand the problems and the methods of operation so well that they could judge accurately what parallel and higher commanders would be likely to do in given situations. They would have to understand the enemy's strategy, tactics, and military organization, and adjust to them on their own initiative according to the exigencies of battle. They would have to be kept informed of the over-all strategic situation and the status of available resources.

Lower-echelon commanders would therefore have to receive a much higher degree of training and responsibility for independent operations than they now do. A company or a battalion commander may be responsible for command functions and planning activities that in more conventional organizations are assigned to commanders of divisions and higher. These can be expected to include problems of "housekeeping," logistics, intelligence, transportation, control and manipulation of a variety of combat arms, and even military government. Traditional conceptions of rank and responsibility based on size of organization would have to give way to command doctrines based on function alone.

The degree of risk that can be accepted as a price for greater flexibility of response in tactical situations is clearly a matter of judgment at the highest executive level in the defense structure. Some way will have to be found, however, to achieve such flexibility while preserving the degree of control — and direct contact between the highest and lowest decision and implementation levels in times of crisis — that limited war in the nuclear age demands.

# 16

## Getting There: Strategic Response

THE ability to move substantial military units over long distances in a short time is an essential element in the creation of a limited war force structure. Such diverse historical experiences as the German response to the Normandy landings,[1] the U.S. response to the North Korean invasion, and the Suez intervention suggest that the effort required to win a war increases as the crucial opening battle in response to an enemy attack is delayed (if indeed the delay does not preclude response altogether). If the attacker can overwhelm the opposing forces and consolidate his strength in the positions he captures, he will be harder to defeat than if he is met and defeated before he consolidates. The more time he is given to build his defenses, the more it will take — in time, money, forces, casualties — to drive him out.

In this day of worldwide commitments, we cannot station forces powerful enough to stop a determined aggressor at all potential points of attack. We can and do build the strength of our allies to meet such attacks. If local war threatens, we try to move significant force into place in time for deterrence to act. To help with our own forces in the event of unanticipated aggression, we plan to move them rapidly into place after the attack.

This faces us, again, with a tradeoff problem in resource allocation. Airlift, sealift, and maintenance of foreign bases are easy to neglect in favor of the combat forces. They are all expensive. But so too are the equipment and support of the large forces that would be required to win if our military transport and logistic system is not adequate for a timely response to an invasion of an allied country.

The practical problems of rapid response can be highlighted by more detailed consideration of the strategic lift system and its mode of operation.

Given sufficient warning, it is possible to achieve tactical and strategic surprise by sending a Marine division-air wing team into action in a few hours or a day after they reach the scene of conflict by sea. Airborne operations and Composite Air Strike Force (CASF) deployments can also achieve such surprise. In either case, such forces can rapidly build up in the area after the enemy becomes aware of their presence because they have the initiative. If the maneuver is in response to an enemy initiative, however, then our own forces would have to accept days of delay in preparation and transport while the enemy presses his attack, days that would otherwise have been absorbed prior to the opening moves.

The fastest initial response might then be made by Air Force and airborne Army units on strategic alert. At roughly the same time additional, heavier forces, such as armored divisions, might start toward the combat area by sea. The first wave of airborne forces can, at best, carry with it a very few days' combat supplies. Some of the airlift that brought them to the area must therefore be used to support them in the field, while the remainder is used to bring in additional forces, and lower-priority support troops and equipment, until the airborne move is completed. At this point the airlift capacity assigned would be used to supply the active forces in combat until the seaborne reinforcements arrive. These would be followed by a seaborne "pipeline" that would assume the major portion of the logistic support operations. Part of the airlift would then be withdrawn into reserve, while the remainder would be used for appropriate logistic support to augment the main surface system.

Each of the major components of strategic lift can itself be considered to have several segments: movement to the embarkation point, loading, transit, unloading, and deployment into combat. These are illustrated schematically for airlift and sealift systems by the diagram in Figure 16.1, which shows typical durations for each segment of each type of system. The sum of loading and unloading time may be considered together as "turnaround time"; with this may be included the "dead time" of intermediate stops for fuel and repairs such as may be required of aircraft on a move exceeding their maximum cruising range. All of the times shown may vary widely, depending on distances between troop or supply depots and points of embarkation, distances from port or airfield of

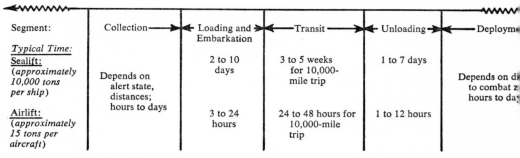

FIGURE 16.1  RANGE OF TIMES OCCUPIED IN VARIOUS
SEGMENTS OF STRATEGIC TRANSPORT SYSTEM

entry into a theatre to the combat zone, distance between embarkation and debarkation points, facilities available (especially in the theatre of engagement), nature of the load to be embarked (for example, combat troops and mobile equipment at one end, wounded and damaged equipment, or simply ballast, at the other), and state of prior preparedness and planning.

Speed in transit obviously has value only up to a point in the total operation. The average cargo ship may travel 10 to 15 knots, needing therefore on the order of 30 to 40 days to go from the United States to Southeast Asia or from Europe to India if the Suez Canal were not open. It may be possible to increase the speed of ships to perhaps 20 or 30 knots and so reduce this transit time to 2 or 3 weeks. While this would be a substantial improvement, it is clearly not adequate when responses in hours or a few days are necessary — this is the obvious reason for the use of airlift. Airlift itself can now move at 400 to 600 miles per hour; because it can take more-or-less direct routes, the distance it must traverse is likely to be shorter between two given points than for ships. It is possible to fly anywhere in the world from the continental United States in 36 hours or less, including in some circumstances an intermediate stop for refueling.

As Figure 16.1 shows, however, turnaround times can be at least as great as, if not greater than, times in transit. This is, then, a fruitful area in which to seek improvements in the over-all speed of strategic lift. It must be considered together with increases of speed in transit.

The economics of development of new aircraft and ships, and operation of mixed fleets, may in fact indicate that for certain applications resources might better be expended in reduction of turnaround times than for increased speed. It would be possible, for example, to spend billions to develop and procure a fleet of supersonic transport aircraft that could

194

cut in half, or even to a third, the flight time of overseas airlift. But if the total turnaround time of an aircraft is 2 days, the entire mission time may be reduced by only 20 per cent. This reduction could be achieved at far less cost by loading and unloading current aircraft more rapidly.

It is clearly important in the airlift problem to reduce turnaround time at the same time that aircraft speed is increased. It may further be argued on strategic grounds that if turnaround time can be reduced to the point where, with current aircraft speeds, a single aircraft can accomplish its entire mission in 24 hours, further increases in aircraft speed would not warrant the necessary expenditure of resources in that direction.

Systems for efficient packaging and rapid handling of aircraft cargo are coming into being. Loads are combined into standard packages; loading docks, conveyor belts, and specialized lifting equipment are designed to move them rapidly, in preplanned order, into the airplane cargo compartments. Cargo airplanes themselves are designed with fuselage floors at truck-bed height and built-in ramps to facilitate loading. All of these steps may be expected to reduce aircraft turnaround times to a few hours at most.[2]

One of the problems in application of these systems is to justify the cost of applying them universally, since the need for them varies through the system. The air logistics system is large and complex, with components in different parts of the force structure; it is intrinsically more difficult to modify the entire system than to provide high-speed aircraft alone. The changes become especially difficult away from major terminal bases, at the intermediate bases where the aircraft must be processed enroute to the theatre of military operations. When the need arises to transfer men and equipment between aircraft as they gather together from many sources for airborne operation into a combat area, the intermediate bases must be able to handle surges of transient aircraft by being prestocked with adequate amounts of fuel, maintenance, cargo-handling and parking facilities, much of which may not ordinarily be used. Most of the time these bases process much smaller average loads, so that the investment in peak-load facilities represents, in some sense, expenditure which may never be recovered by the military economic system. In the long-term view, however, this expense represents insurance that is needed desperately if it is needed at all. In the last analysis it holds one of the keys to rapid response.

The problem of ship turnaround time has many similar elements, but if it is to be overcome the effort required will most likely be substantially greater and more complex than it would be for the air logistic system. The gains to be made from an attack on this problem are obviously very great. Time in transit might be reduced from a month to a week by prepositioning of appropriate troops and supplies at strategic locations, or to 2 weeks by increasing ship speed. But if it must take 10 days to turn a ship around at its destination then much of the benefit gained at very high cost by the establishment of an advanced base or by increasing ship speed can be frittered away.

The technology of rapid cargo transfer, in terms of standardized shape, weight, and size of loads and automatic handling machinery, is available for ships as well as aircraft. Ship designs exist that permit mobile military equipment to roll on and off under its own power. Such design features can be incorporated in ships that will be much faster than those currently available. Thus it is possible to create an entirely new shipping system that will permit far more rapid surface movement of military equipment than is now generally possible.

The creation of such a system, however, would be an extremely expensive proposition. Much of our seaborne support comes from the Merchant Marine, which is made up in the main of World War II vintage ships, as is a large part of the military sea transport fleet.[3] These ships have neither the speed nor much of the built-in equipment needed for rapid turnaround. The ships themselves would therefore have to be modernized.

The economics and politics of merchant shipping also pose obstacles to modernization of commercial systems. The incorporation of new technology must inevitably lead to streamlining of the entire base of shore facilities, controlled (as is well known) by very powerful labor unions. Faced with possible unemployment as a result of automation, these unions, as those in other industries, have been reluctant to accept unreservedly a major revolution in the technology of handling ship cargo, even when the ships themselves are built for rapid loading. While changes have been made, they have been slow in coming and do not provide the vast improvement in capability that would be needed to make a significant change in the over-all agility of surface shipping.[4]

A further problem in the provision of adequate responsiveness for limited war forces is that of reserve readiness. In the callup of National Guard divisions in response to the Berlin Crisis of 1961, there was a delay of several weeks before these divisions were combat ready and the first troops arrived in Europe. Since such reserve units are rarely engaged in full-time training before callup, there must always be some delay in preparing them for full-time duty, and in enabling them to accept with ease the latest equipment and tactical doctrines. Part of the problem of strategic mobility is to assure the merging, without confusion, of regular and reserve forces, for smooth military response to a variety of contingencies that can be only dimly perceived in advance. The augmentation of the Army by two mechanized divisions, the transfer of three divisions from training to readiness status for the STRIKE COMMAND, as well as the proposals of the Secretary of Defense for modification of the National Guard to permit earlier deployment of reserve divisions,[5] have all been intended to improve responsiveness and reduce reaction time.

An often neglected factor in reserve readiness is the difficulty of moving men from a peacetime environment, even military encampments, in the United States into foreign areas where they are faced with the shock of sudden climatic changes, deterioration of sanitation conditions in the indigenous milieu, exposure to exotic diseases, and indigenous populations presenting unfamiliar language and social customs. Experience has shown[6] — and every foreign traveler has become aware — that sudden exposure to such environmental changes can present problems, such as intestinal disorder, heat prostration, and psychological shock, which can be debilitating enough to render a large group of men essentially ineffective for periods of days or weeks. While this might be tolerated if troops do not have to fight — if we are making a simple "show of force" for deterrence — it obviously adds to strategic delay time if active, open warfare is faced on arrival. It must extend the period of initial retreat, especially since the enemy's forces will have had weeks or months to prepare for their attack, with prior acclimatization.

This problem is much too severe to be remedied by simple inoculation programs, which in general anticipate only major disease threats such as cholera or yellow fever. Provision of the means and doctrines for strict sanitation discipline and prior acclimatization of reserve forces, and even regular troops, must affect training, research programs, and reserve callup policies in such a way that the maintenance of ready reserves can become more expensive than it has been in the past.

In addition to the changes that can be made in the strategic transport systems to reduce delay in responding, strategic needs for rapid deployment are met by forces stationed in friendly nations and by supplies prepositioned at various bases, so that both can be available closer to points of potential use. For airlift the benefit of long-term deployments overseas lies not so much in the reduction of transit time as in reduction of the need to move very large reserve supply tonnages, which would be beyond the capacity of available airlift, into ready position in supporting bases adjacent to the combat area. In one way or another, such supplies must be moved close to a theatre of warfare for distribution to military forces in that theatre. The logistic system would clearly be in a much better position to support a military operation if several weeks' or months' supply are in a base only a few hundred miles from the area of operations, and therefore much more accessible to the active combat forces, than if they must be moved from the United States after hostilities have begun. A simple calculation would show that perhaps a third as many aircraft would be able to supply a force in the field from a distance of a few hundred miles as from the United States.

Given the current configuration of the armed forces, much of whose necessary equipment and support must be moved by surface rather than air transport, the advantages of bases in close proximity to possible combat areas become obvious. The logistic as well as the combat advantage of Navy-Marine combat forces in worldwide deployment for ready action also becomes apparent.

In summary, we are faced with the problem of balancing various needs in creating strategic mobility for our limited war forces. Various demands on resources are made by the competing requirements for airlift, modernization of sealift, increase of speed in transit, reduction of turnaround time, provision of ready reserves, maintenance of overseas bases with prepositioned supplies, maintenance of base capacity to process infrequent surges of traffic rather than average levels of operation, and worldwide deployment of ready forces near potential conflict areas.

It is worth observing that, since strategic lift more than any other military capability presents possibilities for dual application to military as well as civil needs in the form of the Merchant Marine and the civilian air fleet, there may be attractive possibilities for applying the resources needed to meet some of these demands in the civilian sector of the economy.

Finally, it should be observed that the problems of strategic mobility can have a profound and far-reaching impact on force structure and the maintenance of combat readiness in ways not elaborated here. The previous discussions of battlefield mobility and tactical air warfare showed that one of the prices that will inevitably be paid for the achievement of economy of force through increased mobility and concentration of firepower will be a vast increase in required rates of logistic supply, and especially a huge rise in consumption of fuel for military vehicles, aircraft, and equipment. The surface fleet needed to provide this logistic support, which alone can carry the necessary huge amounts of fuel across the oceans, becomes an even more critical link in the entire force structure than it was in the past. At the same time, the Soviet and other Communist submarine fleets, far larger than the U-boat fleets of World War II,[7] pose an extremely serious threat to this line of supply. It would be dangerous to assume that the strategic value of an attack against it, as our combat forces come to depend on it ever more heavily, would be neglected even in a limited war.

The most obvious counter to this threat is to increase the ability of the surface and undersea combat fleets to meet it — to concentrate ever more heavily on antisubmarine warfare. More subtle approaches may permit circumvention. Fuel can be carried in nuclear tanker submarines (as suggested by President Eisenhower[8]) which would be much less vulnerable to the threat. In the far future, nuclear power in the theatre of warfare may be found useful in many applications now demanding petroleum fuel. Much of the logistic load devoted to transfer of major equipment, maintenance materials, and replacement troops might be shifted to airlift.

But any or all of these steps would require major changes in force structure. In the long run, then, the combat and logistic forces will have to evolve together, and the major problem for the defense planner will be to keep this evolution balanced between the two. Since the combat arms tend in general to have first call on resources, there is a great risk that they will reach a condition where they may be extremely effective in combat, but the means of strategic mobility cannot take and support them where they are needed when they are needed. Such an imbalance could so seriously degrade the over-all effectiveness of our limited war or general-purpose forces that we would find ourselves in a worse position militarily than existed before some of the major force structure changes were undertaken.

## PART V

# UNCONVENTIONAL WARFARE: SOME SPECIAL PROBLEMS

# *Introductory Note*

*If the Communist-dominated "war of liberation" is a new type of threat to the Western world, but recently recognized in the United States as a major military and political challenge to the free world's existence, it is obviously not new to the Communists. Preached by Lenin, applied successfully by the Chinese Communists, it has given Communism a 30- to 40-year head start in the tactics and strategy of aggression by subversion.*

*Conventional armed forces and conventional warfare as we have known them in the last century cannot meet this challenge. In the nuclear age it is dangerous for them to try, and they are in any case inappropriate.*

*How, then, is the threat to be met? We shall try, in the following chapters, to reach some answers to this question. Entirely new and different political, economic, and military approaches to warfare are needed. Their impact on the armed forces, and indeed on the organization and operation of our government, can be profound.*

# 17

## *Working with Allies*

UNCONVENTIONAL warfare represents an indirect attack by the Communists on the main sources of Western power: the United States and NATO countries. Many of the nations of Africa, Asia, and Latin America, with their underdeveloped economies, physical environments appropriate for guerrilla warfare, geographical positions in command of natural resources, and newly formed political structures rising out of the dissolution of the pre-World War II colonial empires are particularly vulnerable to subversion. If independent and able to maintain economic and political ties with the West, they are, with NATO, a source of world strength against Communist expansion. If Communist and hostile to the West, they can contribute to an inexorable decline of Western power.

Short of an obviously improbable subversive attack on the United States itself, it is apparent that we will never engage alone in defense against subversion. It is highly unlikely that we will ever fight in an unconventional war as a primary belligerent. Rather, we can expect always to be helping a third party who is under attack by this form of "internal aggression."

In the past, we have tried to build and support military strength in nations that are obvious targets of overt attack, because, in the words of the Draper Report

The nations of [the free world's far flung defense perimeter], without our help, cannot defend it. Together we do have the strength. . . . If strong and

203

well armed forces hold these perimeter positions, then, in the event of local aggression, our friends, our allies, and we ourselves gain time for reinforcement, and . . . political action. . . . Also, the capacity of these forward allied forces to meet limited attack . . . provides another and much more acceptable alternative than surrender or resort to atomic warfare.[1]

But the Communist unconventional warfare tactics are obviously designed specifically to bypass such defenses. Experience has shown that nations whose military forces have been equipped and trained to meet organized external aggression have not been able to defend themselves against the unconventional warfare threat, so that we (and our European Allies) have of necessity become involved in such wars.

No matter how we become involved, it is clear that our purpose is not to win a military engagement of our own with our own forces but to help another country win its battle against a threat which is apparently internal and often has a good measure of right and reason on its side. Must the United States engage in this complex battle alone, without the aid, advice, and cooperation of its major European allies who have an equal stake in preventing the success of the Communist challenge and threat? The answer to this question must probably be yes.

First, the United States is, by virtue of its military and economic power, the leader of the free world. We have established a worldwide system of alliances and commitments, many interlocking with international commitments on the part of our major European allies. All demand our participation in the anti-Communist struggle, precisely because our position of leadership has left for us no alternatives but participation or surrender to Communist expansion.

Second, in addition to our position of worldwide power and leadership, we are the only ones of the major NATO powers who have not engaged in extensive colonial empire building; we can proffer assistance without the psychological barriers that must inevitably exist between a major power and its former vassals. This situation forces us many times and in almost all areas (including Latin America, where, although the European and colonial tradition has had virtually no impact for over a hundred years, we have been the major external power to exert political and economic influence) to take the initiative in providing assistance against Communist attack.

Even though our tradition of freedom at home and avoidance of colonial empires in general makes this role a more or less natural one for us, it is not necessarily an easy role to assume. In unconventional wars not involving the Communists, we have faced the dilemma of wishing to sympathize with and perhaps actively help the indigenous populations seeking freedom, while at the same time not outwardly supporting such movements because we have had to avoid severe strains within the NATO alliance whose powers have controlled the areas in revolutionary ferment. This has placed us in a position of appearing at times to work against the interests of our NATO allies, weakening that alliance. At the same time, because we do not actively support the revolutionary movements, we become identified with the colonial powers, making it more difficult for us to intervene in apparent good faith when the Communists begin to participate. Given that we can intervene, the previous identification with the colonial powers gives the Communists an issue which they can exploit in seeking the support of the local population. American economic aid and investment interests are interpreted in Communist propaganda as neocolonialism or economic imperialism; to the extent that the charge is credible locally (regardless of its validity), our task becomes still more difficult.

The colonial (or ex-colonial) powers in NATO are Britain, France, the Netherlands, Belgium, and Portugal. Of these, only France and Britain can be seriously considered as potential Western allies in unconventional war.

The Netherlands did not have the power to withstand the pressure of the Indonesians for independence after World War II. Further, however unsatisfactory they felt the final arrangement to be, they permitted American mediation in the dispute over West New Guinea, with the result that they could withdraw from that area and its economic burden[2] on terms which met the minimum acceptable conditions of principle and prestige. Belgium withdrew from its African possessions without war, leaving the problem for the United Nations to resolve. Portugal is now facing, in Angola, Mozambique, and Timor, the same problem that the French faced in Algeria and Indochina — a colonization so thorough that they must consider an essentially alien area, with a basically suppressed non-Portuguese population, as a province of Portugal proper, while that population demands independence. Portugal's problems in its colonies or "overseas provinces" threaten to face us with the same difficulties that were posed by the Algerian war; the problem is how we can help resolve the conflict between our NATO interests and our desire to help colonies achieve independence, not how Portugal can help us fight subversion elsewhere.

France found in Indochina and Algeria that the close "family" relationship could not be maintained. In Indochina, they lost to the Communists, who spearheaded the attack against French rule and inhibited any moves towards non-Communist independence. The French lost in Algeria because they would not (until the proper conditions were created, too late, by de Gaulle) accept the idea of political separation and independence with some economic interdependence. How successful the final withdrawal of the French from Algeria, with some preservation of economic ties and lack of Communist influence, will be, remains to be seen. In their other African possessions, where the French took a more flexible attitude and withdrew in time, they may well have avoided unconventional warfare while retaining the ability to aid in the economic and political development of these areas.

With its checkered history, France is hardly in a position to assume a large share of the expensive and politically burdensome struggle against Communist "internal aggression." If Communist-stimulated unconventional war breaks out in former French Africa, the French may be in a psychological position where they can enter the contest. But the outlook of the French armed forces after defeat in Indochina and Algeria would not be encouraging as to their willingness to participate. Nor would the potential economic burden of participation, for a country undertaking to build an atomic deterrent force for Europe, appear to be politically acceptable or economically feasible. The French and British reluctance to respond to American pressure for coordinated SEATO military action in Laos is perhaps indicative.[3]

Great Britain has probably been most successful in withdrawing from her empire while leaving a residue of friendliness, along with economic and political ties through the Commonwealth. She has granted independence without the spur of unconventional warfare where this was possible — for example, India, Burma, Ghana, Nigeria, Tanganyika — and where she fought in unconventional wars, she fought, apparently, on the assumption that independence would be granted, but for the purpose of creating a situation most favorable for future political and economic ties, as in Cyprus and Malaya. (Even this favorable picture has, however, not been one of complete success. The British failed in Egypt due to the rise of Nasser, in Palestine they left a severe problem in the hands of the United Nations, and the resolution of the Cyprus situation has not proven to be lasting.) Great Britain is now in the process of attempting to disengage from the remainder of her African empire in the same manner, but with uncertain prospects of success. She is faced with possible drains on her resources by threats of unconventional warfare in Aden and Malaysia.

The British and French experience with this type of war has been so extensive that, even if in new outbreaks they could not share a great deal of the economic and military burden, and even if their overt presence in an area were not welcomed by the local government, it would appear obvious that we should benefit from their advice and knowledge, both positive and negative. But in relation to future engagements, there is an important hiatus in their experience; their historical positions were not analogous to ours of the present and future.

We have not the close "family ties" that the French have had in key parts of their colonial empire, with the attendant emotional involvement and willingness of our population to support a heavy military investment in such areas. Nor do we have the central political command which permitted firm control of the interplay between military and civil activities that attended the British colonial governments' operations in areas under attack. We are also without the ability to grant independence, which was perhaps the greatest inducement to a satisfactory settlement the British, or the French when they chose or were able to use it, could offer.

The utility of such active support and assistance as Britain and France can give will depend critically on the political relationships and residue of local attitudes about them, which exist differently in different areas. Moreover, the United States has long been virtually the only major power to exert substantial influence in most of Latin America; political, military and economic problems in this area must therefore be resolved between the United States and its neighbors to the south.

Taking together all these crosscurrents of history, current international positions and attitudes, and demands of free world leadership, it appears that we are to a very great extent forced to make our own way in areas threatened by Communist infiltration and wars of subversion. Unconventional warfare in these areas faces us as an essentially new problem that is in many ways more complex and difficult for us than it was for our Western allies.

The case of the war against the ELAS Communists in Greece during the late 1940's is instructive on the problem of aiding allies under guerrilla attack. In that war the Communists tried to overwhelm a country whose people, while living in a state of poor economic development, accepted by and large the essential ideas of Western thought, democracy, and economics. There was a basic sympathy between our own objectives and those of the Greek government. We faced, nevertheless, difficult problems of building on this already favorable base with economic aid, and of giving military aid in an area where there was already a tradition of fighting of the kind necessary to win. Even under the existing favorable conditions, the war lasted over four years. In the end, the Western victory depended critically on the closing of the Yugoslav border after Tito's falling-out with Stalin, which forced the Communists into a premature attempt to organize themselves into a formal military structure.[4]

In contrast to the generally favorable situation that we faced in Greece, we must now extend our assistance in unconventional warfare to locations where the political, cultural, and economic orientations are vastly different from ours. The difficulties are compounded by the need to change military patterns not suitable to meet the problems of unconventional warfare, which we ourselves created by building armies for protection against overt invasion. We must also overcome tendencies to use armies as instruments of prestige and politics rather than effective military forces.

Further, although the objectives of economic growth and industrialization under a democratic order may appear to exist, the economic base in these areas is not as high as it was even in Greece, making the growth more difficult to initiate. The governing elites may have different objectives in achieving economic growth, and their interest in encouraging the existence of free societies as we understand them is not necessarily as strong as our own. Hans Morganthau expressed the problem as follows: ". . . the beneficiaries of both the economic and political *status quo* are the typical recipients of foreign aid given for the purpose of changing the *status quo*. To ask them to use foreign aid for this purpose is to require a readiness for self sacrifice and a sense of social responsibility which few ruling groups have shown throughout history."[5]

# *18*

# *Force Ratios and Organization*

How is it that a few hundred poorly armed, ill-disciplined bandits cannot be suppressed or eliminated by thousands of well-trained troops with modern equipment? Is something wrong? Or do we have to accept this anomaly and live with it? These questions are among the most puzzling and frustrating that have faced Western military men since Communist revolutionary warfare infiltrated the world scene after World War II.

In conventional war there can be a military victory for one side though the opposing military forces are approximately equal in total numbers (see Figure 18.1). To be sure, the side that ultimately achieves a preponderance of force including superiority of men, equipment, and tactics is more likely to win. But that side is as likely to gain victory in an offensive by achieving superiority in a local area, winning a battle, and then exploiting the resulting shock and disorganization of the loser as by sheer weight of numbers. There are times when the less numerous side can win by such tactics. The Germans defeated the Allied forces in France in 1940 with a numerically inferior force whose tanks were outnumbered almost 2 to 1.[1]

It appears to be generally accepted that in an attack against well-defended positions a local superiority of forces by the attacker of something like 3 to 1 or better is necessary to win.[2] The expressed NATO requirement for 30 divisions in Western Europe is based in part on this consideration.[3] Thus we can conceive that in conventional military

209

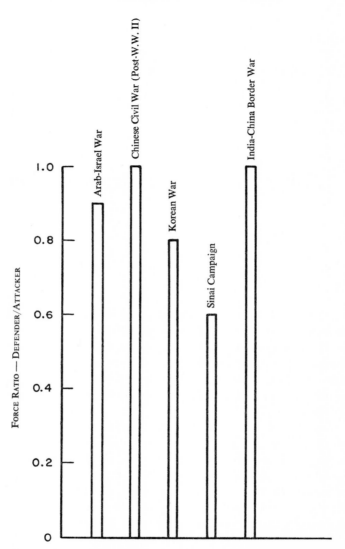

FIGURE 18.1 ESTIMATED FORCE RATIOS IN CONVENTIONAL
LIMITED WARS SINCE WORLD WAR II

actions force ratios can become unbalanced by a factor of 2 or 3 with the issue still remaining in doubt and victory by either side, or stalemate, possible.

In unconventional warfare quite a different picture has been found to be true. In Malaya, the British had a total of 175,000 troops to suppress an attack by 10,000 guerrillas. In Algeria, the revolutionary armies did not number much over 40,000, yet a French force of approximately half a million men, with a full complement of modern equipment and all the resources of a wealthy nation behind them, using a vigorous "offensive defense," could not suppress the guerrilla attack. In South Vietnam an estimated 20,000 to 25,000 "hard-core" guerrillas are attacking a nation with a 200,000-man army and additional quasi-military forces numbering approximately 100,000. That nation is aided by over 15,000 men of the most powerful military nation on earth. Yet the result hangs in the balance. It appears from these and other data in Figure 18.2[4] that in any unconventional war in which the defenders are to be successful the force ratios must favor the defender by factors varying from 5 to almost 20 to 1. (It is of interest to note in this connection a news item[5] to the effect that the Castro government in Cuba, which may be said to understand the problem, committed 25,000 troops to the suppression of a guerrilla force estimated at 600 men.)

Part of this disadvantage for the defenders comes from the fact that all of the troops are not always engaged on both sides. If they were, the regulars with their greatly superior numbers and equipment would have no severe problem. But it will be remembered that the very nature of the guerrilla's attack is based on the presumption that few of his men will ever be engaged at any particular time, and engagement with the bulk of the defender's force is to be avoided.

The ubiquitous and stealthy nature of the guerrilla attack almost invariably leads the defender to fragment his forces at first, for even in underdeveloped areas there are many hundreds of points to defend against an outbreak of terrorism. The wide dispersion of the defense plays naturally into the guerrillas' scheme of things by allowing them to follow the sound military principle of attacking only where the enemy is weak, with a corresponding certainty of winning in the local engagement, and helping them arm themselves in the process. The initial deployments for defense therefore tend to give the guerrillas a free hand in building their strength and weakening that of the government. A few men supported by the population can do a lot of damage if they have little interference.

Only after the guerrillas gain in strength and their attacks become more damaging is it realized that the police and a few units of the armed forces will not be able to suppress them. Then the further steps of military sweeps against them and, perhaps, guerrillalike forays into their territory may be undertaken. Since the guerrillas are by that time stronger then they were in the beginning, and the fixed military positions, the population and economy have still to be protected, the offensive

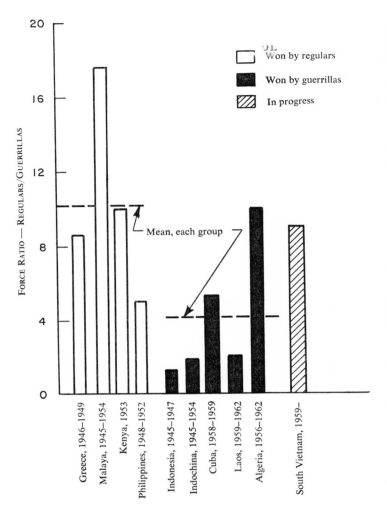

FIGURE 18.2 ESTIMATED FORCE RATIOS IN SOME
GUERRILLA WARS SINCE WORLD WAR II

government forces can often only be added to those already committed
to defense.

The military counterguerrilla activities can therefore come to include patrolling in strength in guerrilla territory; guerrillalike attacks
on guerrilla strongholds; defense of critical facilities and population
centers; police/intelligence activities; and the maintenance of civil self-

defense units to guard thousands of villages distributed outside the major population centers. The regular forces of the government need, also, a significant number of troops for logistic support, while the guerrillas live in and off the population. A much greater allocation of resources and military strength is clearly required on the part of the government than on the part of the guerrilla insurgents.

The disparity in resources required is compounded if there is a need to keep large regular forces available to meet a threat of invasion from outside. While they would be counted in any over-all estimation of the ratio between the forces of the defender and those of the insurgents, most of the defender's forces might never become involved in the fight. (In areas contiguous to the Communist borders, we can therefore expect the Communists to maintain, as part of their strategy, the continuing latent threat of overt aggression.)

The demands on the government forces become even greater in the last stage of the unconventional war when the insurgents form regular units. These formations operate in conjunction with continued guerrilla activity.[6] The government, while still forced to carry out the dispersed activities described above against the remaining guerrillas, is then faced with the additional need to put a large army in the field, and to fight an intensive conventional war. This obviously constitutes a still greater drain on the government's resources, and explains in part why an unconventional war which has entered the last stage is so much more difficult for the defender to win.

And so it must be accepted that in this type of war the over-all ratio of forces between defender and attacker will be far larger than has been found necessary in conventional warfare. The government forces needed to meet a guerrilla attack will not necessarily have to be larger than would be needed to meet overt military aggression. *The critical point is that even though the aggressor's forces in unconventional warfare may be quite small in comparison the government will still need its full military strength to win.*

Nevertheless, there are ways of reducing the force ratio, making it less of a burden to the defender, and improving thereby his chances of success.

An obvious step would be appropriate choice of tactics and equipment. If the defenders can use highly effective weapons combined with a vast improvement in tactical mobility as discussed in Chapter 13, then a small force should be able to defend a large area more effectively than can conventional infantry. This is simply extending the principle of mobile defense as it has been developed in armored warfare.

Furthermore, the counterguerrilla forces who operate as guerrillas in guerrilla territory need not be large. The special British jungle forces in Malaya numbered less than 10 per cent of the total British force. The raiding forces in Greece numbered about 3,000, and represented only about 1 per cent of the entire Greek military force arrayed against 28,000 guerrillas. The forces that Magsaysay took into the field against the Hukbalahap in the Philippines numbered only a few thousand against over 5,000 Communist forces. The insurgents are, after all, faced with similar problems when attacked by "guerrillas," and they do not have the resources to engage in all the other counterguerrilla activities of an economic and social nature such as building schools and providing medical care, which the Government can undertake.

As a further step, the defender can — in fact, he must — change his military organization to suit the conditions of unconventional warfare. He needs to be organized, not in regular divisions as for conventional warfare, but in smaller units that can be scattered over the entire area under attack. These units must be able to move fast and far while retaining communications with central headquarters. The command and control system must be so organized that forces can be moved rapidly to meet continuously shifting tactical contingencies. At the same time, it must allow a considerable amount of local freedom of action to meet the more loosely controlled, decentralized guerrilla attack, or to take initiatives rapidly as opportunities are presented by the guerrillas. In addition, there must be, in the villages, better-trained civil guards and police forces capable of effective defense and even pursuit of unsuccessful attackers.

All of these organizational needs compete for manpower with the regular army, which is designed to meet external threats. The training required is very different from that which is given to the regular army. Therefore greater risks must probably be incurred by the United States and its allies in reducing indigenous regular military forces while the United States, perhaps NATO, or even the United Nations assume greater responsibility for guarantees against external aggression.

This view of the necessary modification of U.S. alliance policy may not be as extreme as it seems at first glance. First, in the underdeveloped areas the Communist powers in general outweigh their neighbors in military strength,[7] so that active intervention on the part of the United States and others to meet external aggression would probably be needed in any case. This is the point of our alliances and international commitments. Second, the American strategic and conventional limited war forces are designed to deter just such attacks, so that the risks of escalation would appear, for the overt aggressor, to be credible and great.

In the military sphere alone, the necessary changes of organization would, ideally, call for training and preparation for counterguerrilla warfare *before* the initial terrorist and guerrilla attacks, so that the first ones can be met effectively. This is particularly true for the police, civil guard, and village self-defense forces. It is much more difficult to organize them for the defense while under attack; the time taken gives the guerrillas the opportunity to build to the point where they are harder to defeat, making the problem of meeting a guerrilla attack an uphill fight all the way. It follows that we must anticipate where guerrilla attack may be likely (even though it has not yet started and may at a given time and place *seem* improbable) and somehow persuade the local authorities and population to organize for defense against it.

All of the preceding means a change in outlook with respect to our own efforts in military assistance, a change that could be very difficult to effect at home and transmit abroad since it would require undoing policies and attitudes we have worked long and hard to create.

It means, for example, that in areas where there is great prestige attached to large armed forces with modern U.S. equipment (which may be difficult or impossible to use) we must discourage the acquisition of such status symbols in favor of counterguerrilla forces that are far less glamorous and must be based to a much greater extent on the participation of all the people. It means above all that the indigenous government and population must believe in and support such efforts and want to undertake them. Concomitantly, our own military assistance organization must thoroughly understand the problem in terms of local conditions, and be able to persuade the local authorities and population to take steps which may run counter to their traditional outlook and which, on the surface, are not necessarily in keeping with the local interests. Local governments may prefer to build military power as a means for *controlling* the population and making the presence of the government obvious if not necessarily popular; such aims are clearly inconsistent with the diffusion of military power *through* the population.

To accomplish such changes America and its allies must take the unconventional war threat seriously enough to base major military planning, training, research, development, and procurement efforts on it. They must, further, integrate these military activities with the efforts by the military and civil authorities here and abroad to effect the political, social, and economic transformations necessary to make unconventional warfare much more difficult for the Communists to undertake or to win.

To appreciate how difficult this may be, we need only contemplate

215

the slowness with which the United States has been able to persuade several Latin American countries to close their doors to Cuban travel and arms traffic and to undertake the reforms of the Alliance for Progress — this despite the appearance of terrorism in Venezuela and obvious Communist preparation for it in Brazil.

# 19

## Military Assistance and Specialization

THE Military Assistance Program (MAP) began in 1951, spurred by the Korean War. It was designed to give free nations American support in strengthening their defenses against the then obvious threat of overt Communist aggression.

Two aspects of the program must be differentiated: that devoted to the more advanced nations of NATO and a few others, such as Japan or Nationalist China, having the ability to manage modern armed forces and to make a contribution to their own defense through scientific research and development of modern weapons; and that devoted to the training, maintenance, and equipment of regular armed forces in under-developed or new nations, who do not have this capacity. After the surge of arms support for the European-NATO area in 1953–1954, the second aspect of MAP, which is the one primarily related to U.S. world-wide limited-war strategy, has absorbed half, or more, of all military assistance funds.[1]

For military aid in response to both sets of needs, the equipment and organizational know-how have the same source: the American defense forces. It would not be accurate to say that MAP has been used as a "dumping ground" for obsolete U.S. equipment. (In fact, a 1956 directive of the Secretary of Defense (No. 2110.23 3-9-56) says that "Planning for the Military Assistance Program must exclude . . . using that program simply as an outlet for excess inventories or obsolescent items."[2]) Nevertheless, the equipment given to recipient nations outside

NATO has most often been that which is no longer the most modern available to U.S. forces and is surplus to their needs. From a large pool of existing equipment we have tried to match the needs of the various countries receiving aid and to make distribution accordingly. The military organizations and operational doctrines built around this equipment have, as might be anticipated, largely been modeled after those of the American armed forces.

This procedure has shortcomings for military aid to underdeveloped nations. The equipment is designed for use by Americans who have a background of technological sophistication and long-term training paralleling the evolutionary introduction of the equipment. It is tailored to American military methodology and is designed to fit our own conceptions of military organization and logistics.

The imposition on indigenous forces of a maintenance and logistic support burden which strains even our own forces is likely at best to deprive their forces of the high mobility and sustained fighting power demanded by modern warfare, and at worst to paralyze their military operations. Choosing equipment for them that is simple and rugged enough to permit easy training and effective use presents problems in the underdeveloped areas that do not exist in areas such as NATO Europe.[3]

Indigenous personnel may be able to learn "first echelon maintenance" of complex equipment such as aircraft, modern combat vehicles with automatic transmissions, or radios — changing electronic tubes or spark plugs is a straightforward procedure. But without a cultural background based on technological and industrial development, troubleshooting that requires sophisticated diagnosis along with complete dismantling and rebuilding of equipment may present insurmountable difficulties to troops who have rarely handled a machine more complex than a plough. Moreover, since the equipment is old, the manufacturing lines are closed and spare parts may not be readily available. The useful life of equipment in indigenous hands in such circumstances can be expected to be much shorter than would be experienced in American usage.

In addition, such equipment is designed to be compatible with and supported by a logistic system representing, fundamentally, a carry-over of the highly complex distribution and supply system associated with our own industrial society. Such a system is impossible for a non-industrial society to match because there is no equivalent model to emulate or indigenous experience on which to base the teaching of pertinent methodology. Nor, in an area where most of the population is of necessity devoted to agricultural pursuits, can we expect the manpower for a complex military maintenance and supply system to be readily available.

Beyond this general problem, specific environmental variations may demand special solutions to weapon and equipment needs that may simply not be readily available in the American military inventory. Several examples can be cited:

• For cross-country operation in areas where there are few roads, we may have to develop military vehicles and trucks far less complicated and expensive than those our forces use. If we insist on giving allies road-bound trucks, then logically we or they must assume a much larger burden of road building.

• We may have to develop new airplanes especially suited for "bush" operations by technologically primitive people. Modern transports and jet fighters are of little use to those who have few airfields and little skill in "keeping them flying."

• We may have to develop or adapt weapons, more suitable than our own military small arms, for use under primitive conditions by irregular troops. Lightweight rifles, shotguns, rugged submachine guns, all may require procurement outside our own military channels.

• We may have to apply our science and technology of food processing to development of new, concentrated, spoil-resistant packaged foods, analogous to the dried-beef *biltong* of the Boer Afrikaaner or the pemmican of the American Indian, for troops whose culture restricts available foods and who are reluctant to accept new types of rations.

It may be argued, with some justification, that the Communists do not use specialized tools of warfare in their "wars of liberation" — they use whatever standard military equipment is given to them or they can capture, and manufacture such crude devices as their resources permit. If they can fight this way, why cannot our allies? Is not the question one of motivation?

This is, in part, true. We must remember, however, that the Communists are the aggressors. They have the advantages of surprise that accrue to the side with the military initiative; and they have strong motivations, whatever they are, that led them to take up arms in the first place. For either conventional or guerrilla warfare they also have the advantages in motivation wrought by the ceaseless indoctrination that is the mark of a Communist society. They do not avoid all the compromises forced upon them by the need to use available military equipment. Rather, they accept these compromises, and rely on their ability to adapt to local difficulties to mitigate their effects. This is, indeed, a characteristic of guerrilla fighters anywhere.

But there is no need, on our part, to emulate the Communists in this respect. There is no reason why we should not help our allies in every way possible. To the extent that we can furnish them with equipment better suited to their specific situations, they will have a useful advantage over their adversaries in this desperate struggle. To the extent that this happens, the *élan* and motivation of their forces should increase.

The need for specialized weapon development in MAP was recognized in the Draper Report, which said that

The weapons systems being developed for United States forces in the foreseeable future are increasingly complex and costly. Not all of these weapons will be essential or even suitable for all free world countries exposed to Communist attack. A number of nations presently lack the level of training and technical skills required to operate and maintain highly sophisticated systems. If they are to have such systems, they must be taught the necessary skills or else the weapons must be installed and operated by the United States. . . . One of the impacts of technology upon military assistance is that there will be a need to develop, and to produce either in the United States or through offshore procurement, simple, less expensive, modern weapons tailored to the particular needs and capabilities of the various recipient countries. Such weapons should be made available wherever more sophisticated weapons are inappropriate.[4]

Unfortunately, even though weapons and equipment may be "simple, less expensive," they still require resources to develop and procure. The provision of weapons and equipment is the province of our military Services, who through tradition and experience are in the best position to understand military requirements and their translation into hardware. It is understandable that they would view expenditures to develop hardware designed for others as an unacceptable diversion of resources from the job of building U.S. forces to meet more severe threats, such as that posed by the Soviet Union in Europe. It would clearly be considered a more economical procedure to search existing inventories for military equipment that can be adapted somehow to special allied needs, especially when those inventories include equipment, still usable, that becomes surplus under the continuous pressure of U.S. force modernization.

Adaptation of equipment designed for the use of U.S. forces requires, in addition to the use of highly sophisticated hardware, the use of hardware which is rarely specialized for particular military situations.

American weapons systems are usually designed with the most difficult military situation in view, but with a general-purpose outlook that intends adaptation to meet almost any other situations that might arise. But as the *creators* of the military capability represented by the equipment we develop, *we* have the best understanding of its form and function and are therefore in the best position to adapt it to new needs. This is much more difficult for troops and military organizations who do not have this background.

This is not to say that we do not have any specialized military systems; we do. Some are designed especially for operation in arctic, jungle, or mountain areas, or for use by organizations like the Special Forces. But these items are still designed for use by American forces.

Yet we cannot forget that our primary task in most limited war is to help allies fight and win, on terms and under conditions basic to their situation and not ours. Their victory is in our interest as well as theirs. It follows that the development of specialized military equipment, organizations, and tactics which can be used only by foreign personnel on their home grounds is a problem that the United States faces as a part of building what amounts to its own limited war capability. To ignore this problem or to evade it is to abdicate an important responsibility for our own security.

It is worth observing that in carrying out such a program we would not always be serving uniquely the needs of foreign nations, even in the immediate area of equipment development. Many of the attributes of military hardware that are considered necessary to meet the problems of our allies — light weight, ease of maintenance, small logistic burden, appropriateness to the environment, and independence of fixed facilities — are also desirable for American equipment. We cannot always assume that American equipment does not work well in primitive environments because indigenous troops do not know how to use it. Many items inappropriate for indigenous use, such as trucks in rice-paddy land, will also be inappropriate should American forces become involved in active war.

A military equipment program specialized for MAP, which may appear to cater solely to foreign needs and to be only remotely related to the main U.S. problems in conventional limited war, could become a major source of necessary American equipment for such war.

221

# 20

## *The Human Problems of Unconventional War*

SOLUTIONS to the problems of military operational techniques, reduction of force ratios, organization for counterguerrilla offense and defense, and specialization in MAP (Military Assistance Program) are necessary but far from sufficient for success in unconventional war. Any efforts we may make can contribute to success only as they are translated into action by those most vitally concerned, the indigenous population with their civil and military leaders.

The implication is that of a close working relationship, in which we may provide resources and guidance but in which essential action of any significance must be taken by our partners. Therefore our own efforts stand or fall in proportion to others' willingness and success in implementation.

It will not always be expedient or correct, in the larger scheme of things, for us to be extremely responsive to our allies' expressed demands, nor will they always wish to accept our guidance, though we may believe such acceptance imperative. These potential conflicts open a wholly new area of endeavor, requiring that we look to human problems far greater in scope than those of military organization and hardware. Only if we are successful in the entire effort can the necessary *and* sufficient conditions for winning be established.

This point has been central to all the preceding discussion of unconventional warfare, in this and previous chapters. It will be of interest to reinforce it still further by examining in some detail a technical problem crucial to counterguerrilla operations: that of finding the guerrillas.

Guerrillas are, in the main, people moving through and living in the countryside. They give few clues by which they can be traced, since they use no vehicles, have no heavy equipment, and use little radio communications. They disguise themselves well, taking expert advantage of their physical environment, which may include heavy vegetation, caves, mountains, or other natural features. They often merge with and become part of the general population when not actually engaged in hostile actions. There are, as in all military operations, two sets of circumstances in which they must be detected: when they are attacking, and when they are being hunted or attacked.

The first presents a somewhat easier problem if there is a fixed position, such as a village, which must be protected. There are many electrical, acoustic, or optical devices that can be used in a signal and alarm ring about the village. Traps, mines, and obstacles such as barbed wire fences or vegetation barriers can be used to make attack more difficult. All of these devices have a certain utility and each has weaknesses or deficiencies, so that all are more effective when used in combination than when used alone. Many of them cannot be used because they depend, for proper operation, on the existence of technological sophistication that simply cannot be found in the villages.

If it is assumed that combinations of detection and alarm devices, traps and obstacles can be installed, with simple radios to call for reinforcements, and that the cost is accepted for thousands of villages, how effective are they likely to be? Probably, the cost and complexity required of the system will go down and its effectiveness will increase as the villagers are willing to use it to defend themselves. Probably no system, however elaborate, will be very effective if a village is infested with guerrilla sympathizers who can subvert the defenses from within. The critical problem is one of identification, of separating friend from foe when both look alike and live together.

It is even more difficult to trace guerrillas in the field, where warning of ambush is needed or guerrillas are being chased. In relatively open country, visual observation or photography from the air may show signs of enemy activity or even groups of enemy men. Scout parties can be sent out to search an area. But experience in many unconventional wars, such as the one taking place in South Vietnam today, shows that if guerrillas are hiding in wooded or swampy areas or in other features of rugged terrain, they are almost impossible to find by such means even if their location is known approximately. Individual tracks can be followed, perhaps with the assistance of dogs. Great effort can be devoted to development of machine aids to following or locating people.

But individual tracking, even if aided in some ways, is a slow and arduous task. It is not possible to track all individuals. Improvement of detection devices and establishment of detection networks would undoubtedly make life more difficult for the guerrillas. But if they take care to disperse into small groups, combining only for action, then the payoff may be relatively small for a large expenditure. And even a small amount of cooperation with the guerrillas by a sympathetic population can vitiate the effects of tracking and identification systems. Stern repressive penalties may discourage such help, but it is also likely to discourage a favorable attitude toward the government. In the absence of such an attitude, all the measures just outlined may simply absorb extensive resources for what must in the long run be marginally useful military operations.

There is another class of solutions that can be and always is used in combination with the military-technological approaches to the problem. A police intelligence system, if effective, will lead to information permitting anticipation of guerrilla moves and countermoves. Guerrillas can then be attacked in known locations and in vulnerable condition. This requires, as is well known, careful, lengthy, painstaking work, building day after day for long periods on previous information and results. Population movements, even of individuals, must be observed and controlled through curfews, travel permits, identity cards. The attending police work includes questioning of many individuals who may be culprits or innocent citizens, following of clues, maintaining dossiers in particular cases. There is a need also to use clandestine informers, and to have friends in the citizenry who must be able to give information about guerrilla activity without fear of severe reprisals; protection as well as search is part of the problem. (Here, again, there are temptations to seek solution in hardware. For example, the use of lie detectors to achieve more rapid and certain results in questioning might appear attractive. But if we suggest the use of such devices, we do so in an environment where we know little of their utility — where lying may have different connotations, such as pleasing the questioner by telling him what he wants to hear, than in our own culture. At best, even in our society, such devices are used only as an adjunct of uncertain utility in the entire spectrum of police activities.)

The efficacy and acceptability of the police effort depends in great measure on its relationship to the population and its aims. Certainly it has been used to great effect for suppressive purposes in Communist and Fascist societies. In a free society, it is accepted by the population as a means of *preserving* the individual's rights, and the scope of police activities is circumscribed by law. Used in a repressive sense, without such circumscription, the police may well perform the desired task at the cost of destroying the freedom that is the objective. Used to preserve freedom, police work can succeed only with the active cooperation of the general populace. If circumscribed in accordance with the demands of freedom but without that cooperation and acceptance of its purposes, it can only be ineffectual. (Our own experience with the attempt to enforce prohibition is instructive on this point.)

If the populace in a country torn by subversive war is to support the police and their intelligence efforts willingly, they must have the feeling that they are identifying themselves with the winning side, that they can do so safely, and that they want that side to win. This is precisely the feeling that both sides try to develop within the population, each with respect to itself. It is in fact the core of the entire unconventional warfare conflict.

The application of hardware and strictly military techniques to this "combat intelligence" problem can obviously be of great assistance, but it is equally obvious that it cannot offer the entire solution. The technical parts of the problem emerge as ancillary elements of the entire process of societal revolution that reflects itself in the outbreak of subversion and guerrilla war.

Let us assume that we can identify and express the various objectives of the local population, the local government, and the United States — modernization, improved economic conditions, orderly control of the processes of political conflict and evolution in a climate of freedom — and bring them into consonance with each other. We would still face the major task of obtaining a real as well as a verbal commitment to these objectives on the part of the ruling classes or "power elite." This is an extraordinarily difficult problem. The elite must obviously fear that if, during economic growth and modernization, they allow the proliferation of conflicting ideas and political opposition, they may be overthrown. On the other hand, if they do not accept this risk they, and we with them, may be forced into the position of restraining the pressures for change, failing to hold the support of the population, and, in a degradation of high objectives to a struggle for sheer retention of power, working to stifle the dynamic evolution of the economy and the body politic.

If the local government and military cannot, with our help, relinquish strong central control sufficiently to carry out the necessary tasks of unconventional warfare, but if at the same time we help them improve the police and military intelligence methods that are a part of the un-

225

conventional war battle, then we will have succeeded in giving an unpopular or inept government better techniques for population control and more power to resist the necessary reforms.

We would simply have contributed to the continuation of the undesirable, rigid conditions that led to insurrection in the first place, and would have defeated our own objectives as well as those of the local population. We then would face inescapable, unpleasant alternatives: (1) having to continue to support a group that probably cannot win, negating the very principles and objectives for which the United States became involved in the war; (2) having to encourage dissident, possibly clandestine opposition movements in a three-way conflict which would be hard to control and which might ultimately destroy the small and educated group that must oversee orderly growth; or (3) abandoning the field to the Communists, with disastrous consequences at home and abroad.

Two examples, illustrating the positive and negative aspects of the problem, stand out unambiguously. In the Philippine Hukbalahap insurrection, Magsaysay arose as a popular hero through democratic processes that the United States encouraged. He effected a revolution in relations between the government and the population, which in great measure won the war against the Communists.[1] In South Vietnam, during the time of the Diem regime, we committed ourselves to support a government exerting tight central control over all military, social, and economic activities, one that lived in fear of a coup by other non-Communist nationalist groups.[2] That government is gone, victim at least in part of its poor relationship with its people. And the war remains to be won.

The problem is not, moreover, simply one of turning our best efforts, by unanimous agreement at home, to the persuasion of indigenous elites and populations that a social revolution in *their* society is necessary to fend off the unconventional war threat. There are too many special interests and shades of opinion in our own country for ready agreement on the steps necessary to defeat Communism.

Economic objectives of various U.S. groups are not necessarily in consonance with those of the "revolution of rising expectations." It will be remembered that there was substantial support for Trujillo while he ruled the Dominican Republic, because of his anti-Communist stand, even though all that he stood for as a dictator ran counter to our stated objectives for the democratic evolution of Latin America. We might also contemplate the conflicting economic pressures that have been working through American private economic leadership and the Congress in such questions as stabilization of coffee prices, restriction of textile imports from Japan (whom we nevertheless wish to prevent from trading with Communist China), and restriction of oil imports from Venezuela. For the future, we might imagine the difficulties that would be faced by an American administration that found it desirable or necessary, in the larger scheme of things, to acquiesce in expropriation of American oil holdings by a Latin American country. Thus we face the difficult problems of influencing opinion and effecting action simultaneously at home *and* abroad.

Assuming that our leadership at home can influence the public and private outlook in a favorable direction, how would we accomplish the task abroad? We must first understand the traditional societal structure and the impact of modern Western civilization on it so that, whether we accept them or not, we know the system of constraints within which we must work. We must understand, for example, the role, in economic assistance, of such phenomena as bribery, which to us is corruption, but which in the local society may not be so considered. (In Imperial China a certain amount of such activity was considered to be proper compensation for leadership responsibility, in positions which were filled by examinations selecting the most intelligent and able individuals from the population.[3]) We must understand the role of the military in the local power structure, and the opportunities for working with the military in economic activities which in our own country are rarely a part of the military task. We must know how the United States and its military representatives appear, and what is expected of us, in the eyes and esteem of both the local elite and general population. Without this broad comprehension of the situation we have entered in support of an ally's unconventional war effort, it may well be impossible for us to establish the necessary rapport with the key individuals and their many sources of power, or even to formulate a common set of concrete objectives.

While the state of our knowledge and the pressures of world events require that we gain understanding in the doing, we shall clearly progress more rapidly if there is a deliberate and orderly effort to increase our knowledge and learning rate to support our efforts in the field. An obvious way to do this is to increase pertinent research efforts in military, political, social, and economic science. The research should not be esoteric or theoretical, as much research in the pertinent areas of the social sciences has been in the past. It should be designed to tell us very specifically what we have to know about particular countries where we face the problems of unconventional warfare. It must also tell us how well we are doing in those countries.

Attention to those problems also has long-term implications for military manpower policy. It is possible in conventional warfare to make a clear distinction between the task of the professional military man who does a military job and that of the political leader who uses the results of military success to press for the political objectives of the war. This separation is not easy to make or even desirable in unconventional war. The political-military relationships in this type of war call for an outlook, professional training, and skill on the part of the military people quite different from those with which we have heretofore been familiar.

It is accepted in the military establishment that various specialties require directed and intensive training, and that military careers continue in these areas of specialty. It is recognized also that all men are not equally qualified for all jobs. Within the very broad professional areas of land, air, or sea warfare some men find themselves better able to exercise operational command, while others specialize in various aspects of military science and technology, such as aerial reconnaissance, chemical warfare, communications, artillery, or logistic support.

So, too, unconventional warfare is an area of specialty requiring career concentration. The special skills needed include those applicable to the military aspects of guerrilla and counterguerrilla warfare, police methods, the economics of development, and the politics of government in a wide assortment of cultures. They may also include engineering knowledge for development of roads and of power and communication networks; knowledge of the role of the local military in government and economic life in specific countries; knowledge of traditions and cultures in local areas of operation; facility with languages; and diplomatic finesse in dealing with representatives of local government and people as well as with our own economic and diplomatic missions.

Clearly, men having only the conventional military skills are likely to be ill equipped for the unconventional warfare task. A military policy of two- or three-year rotation, where a man may be assigned to a "counterinsurgency" task or a MAAG with only a brief prior training period, and then move on to new assignments having to do with conventional warfare, would not do justice to the job or the man. Rather, this area, as the others, requires full-time professional careers, founded on basic military training in the ground, air, or sea aspects of warfare, the additional skills called for by the military as well as the nonmilitary aspects of unconventional warfare, and uninterrupted continuity of service.

A base exists on which a military corps for unconventional war can be built. Selection for MAAG's (Military Assistance Advisory Groups) is not haphazard, and the Army Special Forces (with their counterparts in the other Services) do provide full career opportunities with specialized training in the military aspects of unconventional warfare and some brief training in the other aspects. We must build on this base to provide the full capability necessary, as it is clarified by our heightened understanding of the threat and the anatomy of this type of war.

The building of a much more extensive specialized force than currently exists will probably have to be accomplished over a considerable period of time, during which personnel selection and training programs are more highly developed and the underlying basis of knowledge is built from operational experience and research in this area. At the start, we could take advantage of the many experts to be found outside the military sphere in diverse fields from languages and anthropology to industrial development and business management, whose experience in underdeveloped areas could augment the available resources for research and training.

It might be possible, in fact, to attract such people into the unconventional warfare field on a permanent basis, much as other elements of the population have been attracted into the conventional defense and space fields. Aside from building a national commitment and capability that is now largely lacking, this would provide a much stronger focus than currently exists on the threat as a problem of national concern.

# *21*

## *Who's in Charge?*

IN the previous chapter the assumption was made that the military has a necessary role in all sorts of activities not included within the traditional scope of military affairs. The question should properly be asked, whether this is a valid assumption.

It could be argued that it is not. The Country Team in a specific nation is made up of specialists assigned by various U.S. agencies, in political affairs, economic development, cultural exchange, and military problems. Should not the military members of the Team deal only with military affairs, in an effort coordinated with those of the other specialists by the leader of the Country Team, the Ambassador? This is the current state of affairs; any change requires a different definition of the role of the military and demands valid arguments in favor of redefinition.

These arguments do, however, exist. The military, during the normal course of its operations, has many contacts with the local population at many levels of authority and social strata. The local military are highly important and influential in the governments as well as the armed forces of underdeveloped countries. Since our own military personnel must be in contact with them on many levels and for many reasons, it follows that they deal continuously with those at the center of political power, both military and, by extension of routine contacts, nonmilitary. This intercourse, both social and official in nature, affords many opportunities to carry on the political as well as the military work of the Country Team, opportunities which, if the military members of the Team are properly trained and oriented by responsibility, could be used in a more carefully planned and controlled manner than is possible otherwise.

Further, since military assistance represents a large part of our foreign aid in most underdeveloped areas, the American military has control over the distribution of substantial sums and enters the area in large numbers to exercise this control. The Defense Department, acting at home and through its military representatives abroad, has resources of a magnitude that may far exceed those available to other departments. These can be applied in many ways, including research in the pertinent sciences; development of weapons and equipment; training of indigenous personnel in their use, with relevant extensions to more general, vitally necessary technical training; economic development such as construction of public works, health, and sanitation facilities; and much more. Involvement of the military in such activities can place them on a footing with the indigenous elite and population far different from that, giving the appearance of an army of occupation, which may be inevitable if they remain apart from the mainstream of civic life.

Consideration of all these factors makes it apparent that both sets of arguments have validity, that the pros and cons of an expanded role for the U.S. military in nonmilitary affairs do not cancel each other but are complementary.

The entire job of military training and economic development could obviously not be given to the military, nor should this be done. For they could not possibly be effective in all areas. There is no reason to discontinue the present basic system of dividing responsibility among various specialists, from various government departments, under a single director. There will inevitably be variations in competence, so that some Teams will work together better than others; many will make mistakes or even be ineffective. This is not a reason for changing the system, any more than most failures in military operations cause more than a change of command.

But if we are to improve our over-all effectiveness in unconventional warfare, and if our military is to assume the expanded role that the situations and opportunities seem to justify and even demand, then there must be changes in the patterns of operation and responsibility. Two kinds of distribution of responsibility are affected: interdepartmental, within the Country Team; and inter-Service, within the military part of the Team.

In the first area there is, at least, a responsibility on the part of the military to be informed. There can certainly be no objection to having all personnel of the Country Team *understand* the local cultures, problems, power structure, and images that the local military and political

231

leaders have of themselves and of the Americans; nor can there be any objection to efforts on the part of all agencies involved toward improving their programs of personnel selection and training for unconventional warfare operations. Does the military have a responsibility to carry its efforts further?

The type of activity they would carry out is most closely described by the JCS definition of psychological operations, which include

Psychological Activities—those activities conducted in peacetime or in areas outside of active military theatres of war which are planned and conducted to influence the emotions, attitudes, or behavior of foreign groups in ways favorable to the accomplishment of U.S. policies and objectives.

and Psychological Warfare, which provides for similar activities in a theatre of active military conflict. This definition is general enough to include all of the types of activity outside of the purely military sphere that have been discussed. What is required of the military is a shift of traditional emphasis, in planning and training, from psychological *warfare* — the activities associated with inducing the enemy to surrender — to peacetime operations that are much broader in scope.

Responsibilities in these areas, in both research and operations, are currently assigned to many different agencies. Surveys of opinion and of the influence of news media, as well as the distribution of information, are the responsibility of the United States Information Agency. Construction of transportation facilities such as dams, roads, and bridges, as well as other economic developments, are the responsibility of the Agency for International Development and other groups concerned with economic and technical assistance. Political negotiations for tax and land reforms, such as the conditions for aid under the Alliance for Progress, are problems within the scope of State Department responsibility.

But all of these things are involved in the prevention or fighting of unconventional warfare. The assignment of responsibility must be flexible, depending in practical operations on the state of development of the country in which the Team is working and on the imminence of the unconventional warfare threat. If the threat is immediate, or if the guerrilla phase of the war is actually in progress, then the role of the military will probably come to the fore; they will have primary responsibility for winning, and for using all necessary means, with the assistance and cooperation of other members of the Team. If the threat is more remote, or if it cannot be established that the unconventional war is even in its opening phase of clandestine preparation, then the peacetime activities of the other agencies — Department of State, United States Information Agency, Agency for International Development, Peace Corps — will be paramount.

But even in that case the military will have an important part to play. This will include MAP (Military Assistance Program) activities, training and organization for conventional defense, and preparation to meet the threat of unconventional war, which we must assume can in some circumstances appear in virtually any newly developing area.

In addition, because of the special place the local military has as a relatively better-educated segment of the population in underdeveloped countries, our military will have to assume at least part of the load of general technical training, through military schools and perhaps in civil schools as well. In areas where the local military plays an important role in government, our military could usefully work with them in civil programs of construction and resource management. (They do in fact have this mission, under the heading of "civic action.") They will also have to advise and cooperate with the other U.S. agencies in their tasks of guiding modernization and growth, in negotiations for the implementation of political and economic plans. This will allow the Ambassador to take full advantage of the close rapport which (we hope) is likely to exist between the two military groups.

The boundaries of responsibility between the military and other members of the Country Team would therefore be obscure. The flexibility called for might well require an order of cooperation, selflessness, dedication, and magnanimity on the part of the various members of the Country Team, and leadership and diplomacy on the part of the Ambassador with respect to the group, that may in the natural order of things be more than we have a right to expect as a matter of routine. However, we are concerned here with what needs to be done. Our success in warding off or defeating Communist insurgency will probably be measured by the closeness with which we can approach the ideal, and our failure by the schisms which develop within the over-all organization.

Undoubtedly, effectiveness in practical field operations will be aided by careful staff work in the United States, detailed definition of tasks tailored to each specific area of operations (with continuous modification according to the dictates of experience in these areas), and clear, unambiguous instructions and assignment of responsibility to the Team elements* by the Defense Department, State Department, and the other agencies concerned. Required also will be these agencies' effective cooperation, in the United States, in comprehensive planning and research involving all of the pertinent areas of effort.

Thus it appears that there are both a need and an opportunity for redistribution and sharing of responsibility in this area, crossing strictly

---

* As used here, a Team element refers to all the members of a Team from one department.

defined departmental lines. Most important of all, rivalry regarding responsibility, which can prevent those able and willing to do the work from doing it, and can thereby cause the necessary output to be lost "between the cracks," must be avoided; the approach must obviously be aimed at getting the job done, with a reasonable assignment of responsibility on a cooperative basis, regardless of traditional doctrinal orientations.

And the Congress and the American people must recognize the problem in all its scope. They must be willing to supply the resources, whatever they are, and to permit the changes in government structure that are essential to ward off this insidious and deadly threat to our survival.

The Defense Department itself faces the same sort of problem with respect to *inter-Service* responsibility. This is best illustrated by the Air Force initiation of its air commando program for warfare against guerrillas. In the announcement describing the program[2] no mention was made of other Service activities in this area, or of inter-Service cooperation or complementary activity. It was not long before the Army objected that the Air Force was usurping its assigned mission in unconventional warfare.[3]

The difficulty was obvious, that in this area there can be no purely Army or Air Force effort. Operations by the two Services are very closely related; Air Force aircraft are needed in support of Army-guided tactical strikes and logistic movements, while the Air Force cannot act alone to disrupt guerrilla operations decisively without the support of ground troops. And in such activities as combat intelligence there may hardly be any difference between the necessary activities and needs of the two Services.

Arguments regarding Service responsibility in this area can be resolved in three ways:

1. The Services can cooperate closely while acting along traditional lines of responsibility for land, air, and sea warfare.

2. Primary responsibility can be assigned to a single Service whose required role is dominant, while the others are given supporting responsibilities.

3. A separate command, reporting directly to the Secretary of Defense or the JCS, can be established for all unconventional warfare.

The last would be an extreme approach as difficult to implement as has been the unification of the Armed Forces in the areas of conventional limited war and strategic warfare. The second approach would have the disadvantage, again often demonstrated in the history of the Defense Department, that the Services given the supporting roles would tend to

234

consider those roles secondary, and so do less than their utmost to meet their responsibilities. This would lead the Service having primary responsibility to initiate programs designed to fill the gaps, causing the others to claim that their roles and missions were being usurped or encroached upon.

Thus each alternative has its advantages, problems, and disadvantages. Probably, the more extreme measures are necessary only in proportion to the failure of effective cooperation within the present structure. The point to be emphasized here is simply that the joint nature of operational requirements, and therefore responsibility, in unconventional warfare requires joint action.

In this as in the interdepartmental area, the framework of responsibilities exists that would enable each element of the national force to carry out its component of the task. The problems are those of adjustment, cooperative action, and especially, depth of commitment to a difficult task whose magnitude has not been easily recognized or freely admitted.

# 22

# *What About a Turnabout?*

THUS far we have dealt with "first things first"; we have been concerned with the problems of defending free nations from the professed Communist threat of unconventional warfare. It has become obvious that the techniques of unconventional warfare are extremely effective against an organized society which, though it may have extensive military forces, also has weaknesses that encourage subversion and violent revolution.

If this technique of warfare is so effective why not turn it on our Communist enemies? Why not, for example, instead of fighting a de-defensive action against the Viet Cong under difficult circumstances in South Vietnam, use guerrilla war to destroy the North Vietnamese source of support for the Viet Cong attack? Why not use the techniques of unconventional warfare, which won Cuba for Castro, to overthrow him? Why not use them to free the European satellites from their Soviet masters?[1] It will be of interest to explore the possibilities, without necessarily advocating a course of action.

A counteroffensive of this kind may well be possible. But just as the conditions making it possible exist in the non-Communist part of the world, so they must exist and be cultivated in the areas where we would encourage such operations.

There, the Communist control over all facets of the population's activities presents severe obstacles. Tight military and police control of the population's movements, the political indoctrination of the armed forces, the ubiquitous presence of the Communist Party in all sections of daily life, government control over all the necessities of life — food, housing, clothing, communications, transportation, trade, and all means of expressing opinion and spreading information — make the necessary penetration of cultural, economic, and political activity extraordinarily difficult. As long as these controls exist, untempered by human values except the most materialistic, and exerted with fanatical dedication, it would appear to be virtually impossible for cadres of organizers to penetrate the Communist-controlled societies. And encouragement of spontaneous revolution, if not underpinned by a broad base of trained and capable leadership with external material support, is insufficient to stand against the massive military suppression that the Communists are capable of and willing to exert, as demonstrated in Hungary and Tibet.

The offensive and defensive aspects of the problem in the real-world situation are simply not symmetrical. While the Communists are aided in carrying out unconventional warfare by the open character of most non-Communist societies, we are inhibited by their closed societies. In many areas of the free or uncommitted world, for example, Communist Party activities are permitted and carried out openly. Penetration of all aspects of daily life is relatively easy. This opportunity would certainly not exist for a "Freedom Party" in Communist societies.

This does not mean that penetration of Communist-controlled areas is impossible. But we would have to choose the right conditions and the appropriate time.

All parts of all Communist countries are not impenetrable, if only because the border areas of these countries cannot be guarded with uniform effectiveness everywhere. Many parts of the Communist empire are remote from centers of control, rugged in terrain, and peopled by inhabitants who have not been easily accessible to the Communists themselves. These areas might be fruitful places to start political penetration and preparation for guerrilla war, perhaps through training of refugees or individuals deliberately withdrawn for this purpose.

Ultimately, however, we would have to reach the more populous centers where contact of the population with the regime is the greatest and where (perhaps for this reason) the most important potential base of support lies. But here the tight control of the dictatorial regime is obviously strongest, more carefully built and guarded. We can only take the same, patient approach as that taken by the Communists in initiating unconventional warfare and probe any weaknesses that may exist or develop after a period of Communist rule.

It is most likely that such weaknesses will exist either immediately after the Communists have assumed control, while they have not yet had time to consolidate their position (the Guatemala countercoup against the pro-Communist Arbenz regime in 1954 succeeded in these circumstances), or after a long period of rule when the difficulties of governing and building the economy have created tensions which make control more difficult.

Probably the period between these extremes is the least attractive for initiation of the clandestine activities of unconventional warfare. At such times the rulers, having succeeded after years of struggle in establishing themselves by these very methods, are likely to be especially sensitive to such threats. They will therefore be on their guard, the secret police can be expected to be most active, and repressive measures against a perhaps still unaccepting general population strongest. Infiltration may be possible, but action difficult.

If we are to take advantage of the later period, that of relaxation or deterioration of control, we obviously face a long wait. But there is much to do in preparation while waiting. If strong dictatorial controls relax, it may be that beneficial transformations of the society are taking place, and we can take advantage of this to try to detach the country in question from the central Communist sphere by open political maneuvers. Our policy toward Poland and Yugoslavia has followed this approach.[2] Unconventional warfare would hardly be necessary in these circumstances.

But if Communist controls deteriorate because the population has become restive under continuing repressive rule, the opportunity may exist to begin exploitation of the internal situation. This is still a difficult task. Action must be clandestine, automatically making it more difficult, and we would have to devise ways of assisting penetration by continuous, overt political and economic warfare.

If we wish to plan for such operations, we must face certain unpleasant prospects.

While we are waiting for and doing our best by nonmilitary methods to encourage the proper conditions for penetration, we must continue the unpopular policy of "containment" to prevent the further expansion of Communism. We must carry the economic and military load of large deterrent forces and concentrate on defensive unconventional warfare in areas under Communist attack. Moreover, in planning to take the offensive we cannot announce what we are doing.

The long, arduous, expensive work of setting up and supporting guerrilla action does not lead to dramatic results, until perhaps the very end. This goes against the American character and makes it hard for any Administration to commit itself and win national and Congressional support. The 5 to 10 years that may elapse before visible results appear involve one to three Presidential elections, two to five Congressional elections, five to ten budget hearings, two to five rotations of military tours by people doing the job. There is bound to be much political sniping about too much, or too little, or the wrong kind of action. Secrecy will be impossible to preserve, and it may be difficult to identify U.S. interests with those of a bunch of "bandits" in a remote corner of the world.

If we approach close to the Soviet heartland — in Eastern Europe, for example — we shall assume added risks. American success may lead the Soviets to feel that massive retaliation is the only way out. Any relaxation of tensions between the United States and the Soviet Union must probably be based on a mutual recognition that neither side should threaten areas close to the other's heartland. If such a tacit *detente* is more valuable to us than an uncertain offensive with a high risk of escalation, then we shall have to proscribe unconventional warfare in such areas as Eastern Europe. This further restricts the scope of a "turnabout" strategy. We would have to accede to a perpetuation of Communist control in many countries and hope for its beneficent evolution — again, an unpopular course.

In situations where we do opt for an offensive unconventional warfare strategy, all the pressures attending apparent inaction can lead us to act precipitately. This is likely to end in disastrous failure.

The example of Cuba is pertinent here. As the Bay of Pigs story is currently understood, a small group of Cuban refugees was trained for the invasion. It was apparently intended that they would establish a beachhead and declare the existence of a government that we could openly support[3] or, failing this, that they would reach a relatively inaccessible area on the island and carry on guerrilla warfare from that base.[4] It was apparently believed that support (not necessarily open rebellion[5]) by the population would materialize after the landing took place.[6] The United States was not openly involved, nor was overt military support intended.[7]

If this was considered to be an attack according to the precepts of unconventional warfare, then it did not appear to follow these precepts in almost any particular. It is not known that there was any long-term preparation of a base of support within the population in advance of military operations; it simply appeared to be assumed, on the basis of intelligence estimates, that such support would exist. To have gained it with high probability would have required the training of cadres and their infiltration in small groups over a long period of time so that they could organize a guerrilla attack from within. For such a move to succeed the men would, ideally, have had to be *of* the population with which they would have had to work. These men were not. They would have had to work with peasantry and laborers where Castro's main support exists; but they came from the middle class that was excluded from the revolution. They could not in any case have been assured of support by the peasant and labor classes had they claimed it.

Then, since a movement of over a thousand men is difficult to hide, neither the fact of the invasion plan nor the location of the intended landing could be kept secret. This gave Castro the opportunity to mass his defensive forces in advance and to arrest those individuals who might have represented sources of uprising and support for the landing party. A worse effect of this inability to hide the operation was that the U.S. hand in it was bound to become obvious, even though American forces were excluded from the landing operation for precisely this reason. By making our part in the operation apparent we gave up one of the main advantages of unconventional warfare, that is, that we do not wish the leadership of the anti-Communist revolutionaries to be attributable to the United States in any positive manner. Any other course would give the opponents of the revolutionary group the opportunity to claim, with some credibility, that the revolutionaries are U.S. puppets rather than a true popular movement arising from within the Cuban population.

It has been argued[3] that since we were not able to hide our part in preparing and encouraging the landing, we would have done better to give more massive military support openly, particularly by committing our air power to help the landing succeed. There are valid reasons why this would not have been a wise course of action.

First, there was no assurance that, once ashore, the group would be able to hold the beachhead long enough for U.S. action on the world scene to take effect, or to make its way to an area where it could hide, gain popular support, and carry on a lengthy guerrilla attack against the organized authorities. Therefore, even if the *landing* had succeeded, the entire operation might still have died a slow death. (Although this is an obvious risk in any military operation, it would appear to have been a far greater risk than we should have accepted in this case.)

Second, and much more important, obvious military intervention by the United States would touch an area of great sensitivity in other Latin American countries, especially the larger ones such as Brazil and Mexico. They have shown that even now, despite the outright Communist form Cuba's government has assumed, they are particularly sensitive to the prospect of "North American" military action. Although this sensitivity is giving way to practical necessity in the face of the Cuban and Soviet/Chinese subversive threat, such "intervention" *at that time* may well have set our relationships with the Latin American countries back to their condition in the early part of the twentieth century. Even if this had not cost us a severe loss of influence with the Latin American governments in hemisphere affairs, it may have made American programs like the Alliance for Progress, difficult enough to implement even under current circumstances, virtually impossible to initiate and carry out. In the long run this could have made Communist penetration of Latin America much easier. Some such damage was done in any case;[9] only the fortuitous circumstance of a long Soviet strategic gamble has helped us overcome it.

Not the least of the lessons to be gained from this, which appears to have been America's first attempt at offensive anti-Communist unconventional warfare, is that if we wish to use this strategy we have much to learn about applying the technique against its modern-day originators. We need especially, the patience to nurture its long, slow development, along with infinitely more subtlety than we displayed on that occasion.

# 23

## *Legality and Morality*

ALTHOUGH the problems of defense and offense in unconventional war are extremely difficult there is no doubt that, if we recognize their difficulty and make the necessary changes in our own programs and operations, they can be overcome. Strong commitment to success can, however, only exist nationally if it is founded on a strong base of favorable public opinion. But public opinion is torn by a dilemma, which we cannot evade, posed by the legal and moral questions unconventional warfare raises. If not resolved, this conflict makes the problems of engaging in such warfare far more difficult by engendering confusion about motives, policies, and actions to an extent that can hobble the freedom of action of our government and very likely lead to disaster.

Obviously if we can use our influence in the underdeveloped nations to create a hostile climate to guerrilla attack, we have a much better chance to prevent its initiation or, if it does begin, to prevent its growth into the much more dangerous stage of organized civil war. This means, of course, that the actions we take in peacetime are the most important in the long run.

But if there is no evident attack against local national leadership and its ability to exercise control in its country, then the urgency of needed internal change is hard to demonstrate. Therefore, political and economic maneuvers on our part to overcome evasion of painful decisions and resistance to change, maneuvers that in an objective view amount to coercion, will undoubtedly be required. Without the military pressure of an insurgent attack, moral persuasion alone can hardly be expected to move an inflexible government ruling over a repressed or indifferent society. Even with such pressure the task is difficult, as we found in South Vietnam.

The policy of resisting Communist encroachment on the non-Communist world through unconventional warfare would thus seem to entail unavoidable interference in the national affairs of other nations and peoples.

If this is true in the defensive case, it is even more so for offensive unconventional warfare. For then we would much more clearly be fomenting rebellion, arming revolutionaries secretly, and preparing for the violent overthrow of what, over a period of years, will have become a legally constituted government.

Strictly speaking such activities, whether overt or covert, run counter to our ideas of law and morality. American law states that

Whoever, within the United States, knowingly begins or sets on foot or provides or prepares a means for or furnishes the money for, or takes part in, any military or naval expedition or enterprise to be carried on from thence against the territory or domination of any foreign prince or state, or of any colony, district, or people with whom the United States is at peace, shall be fined not more than $3,000 or imprisoned for not more than three years, or both.[1]

The United Nations draft Declaration of Rights and Duties of States, Article 4, which was adopted without opposition by the United Nations International Law Commission, reads

Every state has the duty to refrain from fomenting civil strife in the territory of another state, and to prevent the organization within its territory of activities calculated to foment such civil strife.

Our Constitution has been designed to prohibit the President from committing the United States to a state of war with another nation without the approval of the Congress. Furthermore, the principles upon which our government is based include our respect for the right of self-determination by all states. Our objectives in support of self-determination were clearly stated in an address by Walt W. Rostow to the Army Special Warfare Center Graduating Class on June 28, 1961:

We seek two results: first, that truly independent nations shall emerge on the world scene; and second, that each nation will be permitted to fashion out of its own culture and its own ambitions the kind of modern society it wants. The same religious and philosophical beliefs which decree that we respect the uniqueness of each individual make it natural that we respect the uniqueness of each national society.

We believe, moreover, that this policy will be to our advantage in the end:

> ... we Americans are confident that, if the independence of this process can be maintained over the coming years and decades, these societies will choose their own version of what we would recognize as a democratic open society.

There are additional practical arguments for following the path of legality. We stand for a world rule of law and adherence of all nations to legal principles. This is our reason for supporting and trying to build the strength of the United Nations. We fall back on the principles of law and morality in opposing Communist moves; for example, we supported U.N. resolutions condemning Communist action and interference in Greece, Hungary, and Tibet. If we then violate these principles by fomenting rebellion or apply massive pressure for change in directions we dictate in countries under Communist domination or attack, our position becomes completely vulnerable to Communist counterattacks in the political arena. How can we expect the international community to condone our violation of principles and law to which we profess, and demand, adherence?

Even if the Communists are completely cynical in using this argument, they can apply it effectively to discredit us with nations who are especially sensitive on the issue of intervention. Further, the more obvious the pressures we apply, and the more obvious our hand in encouraging unconventional warfare that is lengthy and ambiguous in decision, the more likely it will be that domestic opposition to this course will arise in the United States.[2]

There is also the moral consideration, which we experienced painfully after the Hungarian Rebellion in 1956, that if we assume (or appear to assume) responsibility for revolution in Communist-dominated areas, and if this is followed by the military disasters that must occasionally occur, we shall be placed in a position where the risk of escalation to much more dangerous levels of warfare is the only alternative to withdrawal. Having encouraged resistance that ends in failure, we may then be forced to abandon the local population to its fate, regardless of the words with which we cloak such actions.

Thus, the dilemma: if we prosecute unconventional warfare in the ways that are necessary for success, then we are likely to violate the laws and principles which we are pledged to uphold, and on which all our policy is based; if we do not violate these laws and principles, it will be almost impossible to take the steps necessary for success. If we assume the reponsibility without pressing for success with all available means, then we put our policy, our prestige, and ultimately our future in grave jeopardy.

The argument over this dilemma burst into public view after the Bay of Pigs disaster. Stewart Alsop, in a column printed in *The Washington Post,* May 3, 1961, said:

... the Communists are at liberty to arm, supply and support by all means short of actual invasion any Communist guerrilla movement on non-Communist territory, but any attempt by our side to support a resistance movement in Communist territory is an act of war and must be ruled out.

Surely, it is clear that we cannot possibly win the game under such rules, and indeed that we must lose the game in the end. Must we play under such rules?

The answer depends in part on the peculiar nature of guerrilla warfare. . . . Where the press is free and the opposition vocal, it is a very tricky business to support a resistance movement in a foreign country. And it is above all difficult for a democratic government to provide a foreign resistance movement with . . . certainty of victory. . . . [But] if the rules are not changed, we shall lose the game in the end.

Walter Lippmann expressed the other side of this argument in a column in *The Washington Post* on the previous day, saying that to support the rebellion in Cuba, we would have had to violate our treaties with the other American states as well as our own laws, which prohibit the preparation of foreign military expeditions in the United States. An even stronger statement of the latter view was given by Arthur Larson in the *Saturday Review,* May 13, 1961:

We do not build a world of law by flaunting law when it gets in the way of our sympathies, no matter how strong and well founded those sympathies may be.

In the view of those upholding the latter side of the argument, what options are open to us in countering the Communist subversion threat? To quote Larson again,

... we can give our help by operating through the channels of the OAS, the UN and the various treaties and declarations aimed at collective action against such subversion.

We may note also that the Eisenhower Doctrine, pledging American aid against indirect Communist aggression in the Middle East, contained the condition that we would not interfere in any country except on request of the government of that country.[3]

But suppose there is a subversive threat which for various reasons of politics and pride the local government wishes to ignore or discount. Suppose, for example, we had not been asked by Lebanon, in 1958, to intervene in the crisis in that country. The landing would not have taken place, nor, assuming that it had some strong influence in stabilizing the entire Middle Eastern area, would we have reaped its benefits. We may well suppose that the United States government applied pressure, *sub rosa,* to assure that the landing would be requested. If so, would not this, by itself, constitute intervention of the same kind that the writers just quoted have declared to be illegal? Can we afford not to intervene in this way? If such a request is left solely to the discretion of the local government, and is delayed until the country under attack cannot avoid recognizing that its survival is at stake, if perhaps the subversive war against it has entered its last phase, then we would find successful intervention to be a much more formidable if not impossible task. The example of South Vietnam makes this clear.

In any case, the idea of intervention for legal or illegal, selfish or altruistic reasons, is an ambiguous one. Rostow has said that the basis of our policy is simply the following:

. . . It will permit American society to continue to develop along the old humane lines which go back to our birth as a Nation—and which reach deeper into history than that—back to the Mediterranean roots of Western life. We are struggling to maintain an environment on the world scene which will permit our open society to survive and to flourish.[4]

In this statement there is no condition calling for our actions to take account of the basic interests of the other nations involved. By implication, what is good for us — the preservation of a free, open society — is in their best interest as well. In a sense, quite aside from the threat of Communism, our military and economic aid programs can easily be interpreted as intervention in the affairs of others. In the Alliance for Progress, we have demanded certain reforms as a condition for assistance. The possibility that such reforms would be jeopardized lay behind the temporary halt of our economic aid program when a military government assumed power in Peru.[5]

This is an age of "peaceful invasion." Probably at no other time in Western history have there been, without military occupation or colonization, so many military and civil representatives of the major powers in other nations less advanced materially. This presence is surely not for completely altruistic purposes, yet it is commonly accepted. This means that the principle of noninterference in nations' internal affairs is undergoing evolution and reinterpretation. The strong presence of one nation in another offers an opening already used by all sides in the cold war.

The opportunities and the reasons for expanding this opening have been expressed as follows by Admiral Arleigh Burke:

Power might be said to be the capacity to induce others to behave according to patterns in one's own mind. . . . Pure and unrestricted choice seldom occurs in real life; pure persuasion is very infrequent. . . . The term "influence" connotes the forms of power between pure force and pure persuasion. Behavior is neither forced, nor is it determined by dispassionate persuasion. Rather, the power that exercises the influence obtains the desired behavior by controlling the choices available to the "influenced." . . . For in every case the choice is left to the "influenced" party. Only the conditions of choice are controlled. . . . Yet there are those who believe that the human race has moved to a new capacity for peace based solely on the power of persuasion. . . . We have been unwilling to intervene in the domestic affairs of foreign countries on which the Communists seek to impose their power. . . . Yet in the midst of the ideological struggle, non-alignment is a meaningless posture. The Communist movement intervenes in ways unknown to traditional international law. Against this challenge, U.S. policy has responded with countermoves carefully measured to the whimsies of the new nations. . . . The principles of a nation's responsibility for its actions must be invoked, and, if necessary, enforced. Whenever American interests are violated, wherever the peace is broken . . . the United States must impose penalties. . . . Conversely, cooperation and a realistic search for economic stability must be rewarded . . . countries which have cooperated with the United States should be made to flourish. . . . Such a policy, let it be understood, is not a policy of direct intervention. It is simply an insistence that no one shall escape the logical consequences of his choice. The new states must face the fact that no one is absolutely sovereign, that cooperation is the price of responsible independence. *We must make it clear that U.S. power will be used to control the course of events. . . .*[6] [Author's italics.]

The burden of Rostow's and Burke's arguments is simply this: that vital national interest must take precedence over abstract moral considerations. There is ample historical evidence that it always has: in the use of the atom bomb, the Mexican war, war with Spain over Cuba, the destruction of American Indian tribal society, failure to support the Hungarian rebellion, and so on. We were able to rationalize our moral problems, which were real and recognized, because the political and economic problems were greater and more urgent. Moreover, our own interests and course of action were clear and obvious to us.

The point is we must be able to recognize and express the nature and extent of genuine and vital American interest that would be given widespread public and political support.

The implications of Rostow's statements of policy are that we equate the welfare of the emerging nations with our own; that we do not intend to sit on the fence; that it is our policy to support American welfare by means of our actions in the rest of the world; that we hope our objectives and those of the other nations can be achieved in the normal course of political and economic evolution; but that it would be to our detriment, and therefore unacceptable, to allow evolution to move in the Communist direction.

And yet, there is the question of how to do it. There are limits to the efficacy of direct application of power. The ultimate historical fact is that no nation, however strong, has ever been able to support indefinitely its influence in the world solely through the naked use of its power without the consent of those whom it attempts to influence. We cannot, like the Communists, sit outside the world and rationalize our attempts to mold it in a direction favorable to our narrow national interests. We must, somehow, make ourselves a part of everyone's struggle for a better deal.

The entire question would appear to hinge, in fact, on the meaning and implications of "consent." What is considered pressure or intervention is actually so only if there is no consent, or if acquiescence is obviously forced because there is no other choice. The same actions or proposals for action become acceptable and legally proper if they are accepted by everyone because the inner necessity is recognized and they are desired.

It may well be that the key to the problem lies in the idea expressed by Burke, of autonomous but *interdependent* states. The example of Britain and the British Commonwealth indicates that there are many ways of exerting influence when events and people cannot be controlled directly. Among these are the creation of economic systems in which there is unavoidable *mutual* dependence; control of the means of communication and affecting public opinion, even indirectly through the formal education system; as well as, in carefully selected situations of urgent necessity, recourse to hidden diplomatic pressures reinforced by the potential use of economic and military power.

The British Commonwealth arises out of British colonial experience, and is not necessarily a valid model for American emulation. But we must devise ways to achieve similar effects. Certainly we have been able, with but one exception (the Civil War), to reconcile bitter political differences at home. We have long recognized that to achieve stability, law, and order rather than anarchy, the letter of the law must be interpreted in terms of the public welfare. And conceptions of the public welfare are also subject to orderly change. If we could adapt this approach to the international scene, we could achieve our ends without any reasonable objections as to violation of law and morality.

248

# CONCLUSION

## *Where Do We Stand?*

LET us now hark to President Kennedy's call for a strengthening of our military forces for limited war, quoted in the Introduction to this book. We have examined a few of the issues that must be resolved, and the alternatives available, to bring our military capability into consonance with our foreign policy commitments. What choices are we making?

Time has not stood still since President Kennedy spoke; his words have been followed by action. By the middle of 1963 a great number of steps had been taken to enlarge and transform the armed forces so that they would be better able to meet the challenge of limited war that is the natural outgrowth of a nuclear standoff between East and West.

The Army was expanded from fourteen to sixteen divisions; the sixteen were made fully combat-ready, compared with only eleven that were in that state previously.[1] This growth was accelerated by the Berlin crisis of 1961, for which two National Guard divisions were called into service and remained until the two new divisions were activated and brought up to strength. The original three divisions of the Strategic Army Corps, ready reserve for deployment to any overseas theatres of warfare, were augmented by five divisions.[2] It was united with the tactical air forces in the new U.S. STRIKE COMMAND (STRICOM). This assured necessary airlift and tactical air combat support for the ground forces and laid the foundation for more closely coordinated planning of combined operations.

Even before this, steps were taken to increase the strategic airlift capacity by purchasing a large number of newly developed jet transports to "better assure the ability of our conventional forces to respond, with

249

discrimination and speed . . . to . . . any deliberate effort to avoid or divert our forces by starting limited wars in widely scattered parts of the globe."[3]

Later improvements in strategic sealift were planned for the general cargo fleet.

We propose to build a *Comet* roll-on/roll-off vessel each year for a number of years, beginning in 1963. . . The roll-on/roll-off type of ship greatly reduces loading and unloading times for vehicles. The new ships . . . will give us a capability to move one whole armored division overseas and get it into action considerably sooner than if the vehicles had to be hoisted in and out of the holds of conventional cargo ships. Furthermore, these ships eliminate the need for special booms and cranes and enable heavy tanks and other vehicles to be put ashore at relatively primitive port facilities.[4]

Two other steps were taken that will substantially affect the structure of the conventional limited-war forces. An "Army Tactical Mobility Requirements Board," under the chairmanship of Lieutenant General Hamilton Howze, ground force commander of STRICOM, made sweeping recommendations to the Secretary of Defense for increases in Army reliance on air mobility. It called for organization of "air assault divisions and air cavalry brigades" having large numbers of appropriate types of Army aircraft and helicopters.[5] Although this idea has met with resistance by the Air Force[6] and some members of the Congress[7] on the grounds that the Army would be "taking over the Air Force's mission," steps are being taken to organize an air assault division on a trial basis.[8] Pending the success of these trials, the renewal of ground force equipment continues in more conventional directions. Substantial sums were allotted, in the 1963 budget, for the new M-60 tank, self-propelled artillery, battlefield missiles, and over 36,000 trucks of various sizes.[9]

The problem of combat air support for limited-war operations has also been taken up, but the direction of its resolution appears at this point to be somewhat ambiguous. The major steps towards improving the combat power of the tactical air forces have included plans to procure a ground attack version of the Navy's Phantom II (F4C) supersonic air superiority fighter,[10] and development of the new TFX aircraft. The latter, in a program which will cost in excess of $6 billion for something over a thousand aircraft,

should be capable of very high speeds at altitude, as well as low-level bombing operations. This fighter should be highly efficient in all the tactical and air defense missions for either limited or general war. . . .[11]

In other words, the philosophy of a general-purpose, highly sophisticated aircraft for tactical air operations continues to predominate.

There are, however, reports that in the Army view

... the close troop support aircraft [should] be designed for relatively low speed operation, leaving the role of defeating enemy fighters to air superiority fighters overhead.[12]

A "considerable number" of A4D-5(A4-E) light attack aircraft are being procured for the Navy and Marine Corps, as are quantities of the A2F-1(A6-A), the "new, all-weather close support attack and electronic reconnaissance aircraft." There are plans for development of a "new . . . Triservice close-support aircraft," whose configuration has not yet been fully described.[13] The Army, in the meantime, has, with the approval of the Secretary of Defense, been experimenting with its low-performance MOHAWK observation aircraft for a close support role.[14]

Thus the intended evolution of the systems for air support of ground operations remains obscure. But it appears that, if all these plans are implemented, there will be a mixture of very high performance, general-purpose fighter-bombers for tactical air warfare, with more specialized, less expensive attack aircraft for close air support of troops on the ground.

All of these moves to improve the nonnuclear fighting capability of our "general-purpose forces" have been taken against the background of growing debate regarding the problems of limited war in Europe, described in Chapter 3. But probably the greatest change in orientation and planning for the limited war forces has occurred in the unconventional warfare area.

Awareness of the threat and the problems has been heightened by our increasing involvement in such wars — in Laos, Vietnam, and Cuba. The simultaneous occurrence of near disaster in Laos and a marked increase of the intensity of the Communist attack in South Vietnam led to our entry into the latter conflict. The Cuban debacle increased our realization of the difficulty of such engagements. For the first time, this was treated in the Defense Secretary's planning as a major area of endeavor:

There has come into prominence, in the last year or two, a kind of war which Mr. Khrushchev calls "wars of national liberation" or "popular revolts," but which we know as insurrection, subversion and covert armed aggression. I refer here to the kind of war which we have seen in Laos and which is now going on in South Vietnam. . . . Actually it is not a new Communist technique. We have seen it in many other parts of the world since the end of World War II. . . . We have a long way to go in devising and implementing

251

effective countermeasures against these Communist techniques. But this is a challenge we must meet if we are to defeat the Communists in this third kind of war. *It is quite possible that in the decade of the 1960's, the decisive struggle will take place in this arena.*[15] [Author's italics.]

At the same time, the nature of such war has also been recognized. In the same presentation, Secretary McNamara said

. . . to meet successfully this type of threat will take much more than military means alone. It will require a comprehensive effort involving political, economic, and ideological measures as well as military.

In a much more detailed discussion of the dimensions of this struggle, Walt Rostow, Chairman of the State Department's policy planning staff, said, in part:

The victory we seek will see no ticker tape parades down Broadway—no climactic battles nor great American celebrations of victory which will take many years and decades of hard work and dedication—by many peoples—to bring about. This will not be a victory of the United States over the Soviet Union. . . .

.  .  .  .  .  .  .  .  .  .

I do not need to tell you that the primary responsibility for dealing with guerrilla warfare in the underdeveloped areas cannot be American. There are many ways in which we can help—and we are searching our minds and our imaginations to learn better how to help; but a guerrilla war must be fought primarily by those on the spot. This is so for a quite particular reason. A guerrilla war is an intimate affair, fought not merely with weapons but fought in the minds of the men who live in the villages and in the hills; fought by the spirit and policy of those who run the local government. An outsider cannot by himself win a guerrilla war; he can help create conditions in which it can be won; and he can directly assist those prepared to fight for their independence. . . .

.  .  .  .  .  .  .  .  .  .

My point is that we are up against a form of warfare which is powerful and effective only when we do not put our minds clearly to work on how to deal with it. I, for one, believe that with purposeful efforts most nations which might now be susceptible to guerrilla warfare could handle their border areas in ways which would make them very unattractive to the initiation of this ugly game. We can learn to prevent the emergence of the famous sea in which Mao Tse-tung taught his men to swim. This requires, of course, not merely a proper military program of deterrence, but programs of village development, communications, and indoctrination. The best way to fight a guerrilla war is to prevent it from happening.[16]

President Kennedy reiterated these ideas in a still different form in his 1962 address to the West Point graduating class,[17] and stressed the multifaceted nature of the military man's training and career that this type of war demands.

To put this new philosophy into action, a number of steps have been taken beyond our direct involvement in South Vietnam. The size of the Army Special Forces was increased nearly fourfold since early 1961.[18] Their mission, and the Army's, have been expanded to include "civic action" in the economic and social development fields. Training in guerrilla-counterguerrilla warfare has been introduced into the curriculum of many Service schools whose primary mission is in the area of conventional, organized warfare.[19] The guerrilla warfare school in Panama has undertaken to train Latin American military officers in unconventional warfare techniques.[20] The Air Force has initiated the air commando program, to which we referred earlier (Chapter 5), for use in "counterinsurgency," and the Navy has stressed development of its unconventional warfare units. Tentative steps have been taken in the Service research and development programs toward development of equipment specialized for allied use in unconventional warfare — a "COIN airplane," for example. (COIN is an abbreviation for "Counterinsurgency," or unconventional warfare.)[21]

Finally, a special group at the highest level of government reportedly has been assigned the problem of coordinating the activities of all the government agencies and Departments — State, Defense, Agency for International Development, Central Intelligence Agency, United States Information Agency — who are concerned with this type of warfare.[22] The group is said to include the heads of the Departments and agencies or their designated representatives, as well as the Chairman of the Joint Chiefs of Staff and the Attorney General. It is supposed to make certain that critical tasks get done and that nothing falls "between the cracks" of responsibility or suffers from intergroup rivalry.

The Communist enemy has not, however, been idle. The daily press dispatches from South Vietnam indicate that the war there hangs in the balance, between the guerrilla and organized warfare stages. The critical base area of Laos remains under strong Communist pressure, under an uneasy agreement for neutrality. Signs of Communist cadre activity have appeared in Thailand, and attempts are being made to counter them. Communist terror raids and incipient guerrilla action mount in Venezuela. Caches of arms from Cuba have been found in Brazil, and Communist agitation in that country's northeast provinces is rife.[23] It is certainly too early to say whether our own long-delayed actions to meet this threat will be successful against the long Communist headstart.

All of the picture I have sketched out, for conventional as well as

253

unconventional warfare, does not indicate, by any means, that the defense planning problems for limited war have all been met or that the solutions are in hand. Even though the Kennedy Administration recognized the limited-war problem and took steps, continued since, to cope with it, we do not know if Congress and the public fully support these steps. And critical issues of armed force structure remain to be resolved.

But we have at last come to grips with these problems.

# Notes

## Introduction

[1] We are not going to explore here the moral problem of right and wrong in the use of warfare, or the very difficult question of what is to replace it in dealings between societies. We simply accept the fact that warfare is being used. For an excellent discussion of the intricacies of the problem of discarding warfare as an instrument of policy, see Walter Millis, "The Peace Game," *Saturday Review,* Vol. 43 (September 24, 1960), pp. 13 ff.

[2] Cf. Richardson, Lewis F., *Statistics of Deadly Quarrels,* edited by Quincy Wright and C. C. Lienau, The Boxwood Press, Pittsburgh, 1960, and Quadrangle Books, Inc., Chicago, 1960, Chapter 2. Richardson shows approximately one war per year over a 400-year period, and over the last hundred years. Following Richardson's definition for wars of magnitude 3 and higher, the data of Chapter 1, to follow, show one and five-eighths wars per year since World War II.

[3] The term "fringe" war, used to connote the "death of a thousand cuts. Each cut to itself . . . relatively harmless" as compared with the "single, quick, incisive blow of the executioner's axe" was used by H. B. Slim in "The Navy and 'Fringe' War," *U.S. Naval Institute Proceedings,* Vol. 77 (1951), p. 835. The term "brush-fire" had gained currency and was used seriously in, for example, *Army–Navy–Air Force Register,* Vol. 79 (May 24, 1958), p. 1; it was used, with "fire brigade," by J. G. Norris in the *Army–Navy–Air Force Register,* Vol. 77 (October 6, 1956), p. 1.

[4] Leckie, Robert, *Conflict: The History of the Korean War,* G. P. Putnam's Sons, New York, 1963, pp. 59–60.

[5] Dulles, John Foster, "The Evolution of Foreign Policy," *Department of State Bulletin,* Vol. 30 (January 25, 1954), p. 108.

[6] Taylor, Maxwell D., *The Uncertain Trumpet,* Harper & Brothers, New York, 1960, pp. 7–9, 59, 62–63.

[7] Composite Report of the President's Committee to Study the United States Military Assistance Program, W. H. Draper, Chairman, August 17, 1959, Vol. I.

[8] *Ibid.,* p. 145.

[9] Cf. Halperin, Morton H., "Limited War, An Essay on the Development of the Theory and An Annotated Bibliography," Harvard University Center for International Affairs, Occasional Papers in International Affairs, No. 3 (May, 1962).

[10] Annual Message to the Congress on the State of the Union, January 30, 1961, in *Public Papers of the Presidents, John F. Kennedy, 1961,* U.S. Government Printing Office, Washington, D.C., 1962, p. 24.

[11] *Ibid.,* p. 401.

[12] *Ibid.,* p. 24.

[13] Hearings before the Subcommittee of the Committee on Appropriations, House of Representatives, 80th Congress, 2nd Session, on the Military Functions, National Military Establishment, Appropriation Bill for 1949, Part 1, p. 2.

[14] Statement of Secretary of Defense Robert S. McNamara before the House Armed Services Committee, The Fiscal Year 1964–1968 Defense Program and 1964 Defense Budget, January 30, 1963, Mimeographed release, Table 7.

[15] *Ibid.*

[16] *Ibid.*

## PART I

### Chapter 1

[1] All of the data on recent limited wars in Tables 1.1–1.5, and in much of the following discussion, have been taken from the following references:

Appleman, Roy E., *United States Army in the Korean War: South to the Naktong, North to the Yalu, June–November, 1950,* Office of the Chief of Military History, Department of the Army, Washington, D. C., 1961.

Braestrup, P., "Limited Wars and the Lessons of Lebanon," *The Reporter,* Vol. 20 (April 30, 1959), pp. 25–27.

Contemporary newspaper accounts (primarily from *The New York Times* and *The Washington Post*).

*Current Biography* (1952), "Ramon Magsaysay," H. W. Wilson Company, New York, 1953, pp. 391–393.

"Deployment to Lebanon," *Army-Navy-Air Force Register,* Vol. 79 (May 24, 1958) pp. 1, 3, 23.

Eden, Anthony, *Full Circle, The Memoirs of Anthony Eden,* Houghton Mifflin Company, Boston, 1960.

*Encyclopaedia Britannica* (1959), Vol. 12, "Indonesian Independence," p. 266.

Fall, Bernard B., *Street Without Joy,* The Telegraph Press, Harrisburg, Pa., 1961.

"The Front Lines of Asia," *The Reporter,* Vol. 26 (June 7, 1962), two articles: Marshall, S. L. A., "An Exposed Flank in South Vietnam," pp. 26–29. Warner, Denis, "Two-Headed Pennies in Laos," pp. 21–23.

Halpern, A. M., and H. B. Fredman, "Communist Strategy in Laos," U.S. Air Force Project RAND Research Memorandum, RM 2561, June 14, 1960.

Henriques, Robert, *A Hundred Hours to Suez: An Account of Israel's Campaign in the Sinai Peninsula,* The Viking Press, New York, 1957.

"Historical Survey of the Origins and Growth of Mau Mau," Her Majesty's Stationery Office, London, 1960.

Leckie, Robert, *Conflict: The History of the Korean War,* G. P. Putnam's Sons, New York, 1963.

Lorch, Netanel, *The Edge of the Sword: Israel's War of Independence, 1947–1949,* G. P. Putnam's Sons, New York, 1961.

Marshall, S. L. A., *Sinai Victory,* William Morrow and Company, New York, 1958.

Meyer, Karl E., and Tad Szulc, *The Cuban Invasion,* Frederick A. Praeger, New York, 1962.

Murray, Col. J. C., "The Anti-Bandit War," *Marine Corps Gazette,* Vol. 38 (January–May, 1954).

O'Ballance, Edgar, *The Arab-Israeli War 1948,* Frederick A. Praeger, New York, 1957.

—— *The Sinai Campaign of 1956,* Frederick A. Praeger, New York, 1960.

Osgood, R. E., *Limited War: The Challenge to American Strategy,* The University of Chicago Press, Chicago, 1957.

*Problems of Freedom, South Vietnam Since Independence,* edited by Wesley R. Fishel; contributors: Joseph Buttinger, John C. Donnell, John T. Dorsey, Jr., Wesley R. Fishel, William Henderson, John B. Hendry, Wolf Ladejinsky, Craig S. Litchenwalner, M.D., Tran Ngoc Lien, Robert R. Nathan, Edgar N. Pike, Vu Van Thai, The Free Press of Glencoe, Inc., New York, 1961.

Pye, Lucian W., *Guerrilla Communism in Malaya,* Princeton University Press, Princeton, N.J., 1956.

Reynolds, J. A. C., "Terrorist Activity in Malaya," *Marine Corps Gazette,* Vol. 45 (November, 1961), pp. 56–58.

Rivero, N., *Castro's Cuba: An American Dilemma,* Robert B. Luce, Inc. (David McKay Co., Inc., New York), 1962.

Romulo, C. P., *Crusade in Asia: Philippine Victory,* John Day Company, New York, 1955.

"The Security of the Nation," Publication of the Association of the U.S. Army, p. 7.

Shepley, James, "How Dulles Averted War," *Life,* Vol. 28 (January 30, 1956), pp. 70–79.

Strandberg, Carl, "Philippine Marines," *Marine Corps Gazette,* Vol. 45 (November, 1961), pp. 54–55.

Sulzberger, C. L., *The Test: De Gaulle and Algeria,* Harcourt, Brace and World, Inc., New York, 1962.

Tanham, G. K., *Communist Revolutionary Warfare: The Vietminh in Indochina,* Frederick A. Praeger, New York, 1961.

Testimony of General Maxwell Taylor, Department of Defense Appropriations for 1960, Hearings before the Subcommittee of the Committee on Appropriations, House of Representatives, Part 1, Policy Statements, p. 298.

Valeriano, Col. N. D., and Lt. Col. C. T. R. Bohannon, *Counter-Guerrilla Operations: The Philippine Experience,* Frederick A. Praeger, New York, 1962.

2 It is of interest to note that since the time of writing there was a revolt in the British territory of Brunei, which was put down by force; Indonesia has undertaken guerrilla war on the borders of Malaysia; Communist terrorists and guerrilla bands have begun operations in the Lake Maracaibo, Caracas, and mountain hinterland regions of Venezuela. With respect to the latter, cf. Press Association Reports, *The Washington Post,* February 2, February 7, February 8, February 9, February 13, April 3, April 4, April 5, April 8, April 26, 1963. Guerrilla war has continued in Yemen, and sporadic fighting in Laos never ceases. There was also a military flareup on the Morocco-Algerian border, and conflict on Cyprus has been renewed.

3 Gruson, S., *The New York Times,* October 28, 1961, p. 1.

4 Crum, B. C., *Behind the Silken Curtain,* Simon & Schuster, Inc., New York, 1947, pp. 148–158.

5 Marshall S. L. A., *op. cit.,* Robert Henriques, *op. cit.,* Anthony Eden, *op. cit.*

6 Eden, *op. cit.,* pp. 584–588.

7 *Ibid.,* pp. 597, 625.

8 Aron, Raymond, *On War,* translated from the French by Terence Kilmartin, *Doubleday Anchor Books,* Doubleday & Company, Inc., Garden City, N.Y., 1958.

## Chapter 2

1 Aron, Raymond, *On War,* translated from the French by Terence Kilmartin, *Doubleday Anchor Books,* Doubleday & Company, Inc., New York, 1958, pp. 66–67. Copyright © 1958 by Martin Secker & Warburg, Ltd. Reprinted by permission of Doubleday & Company, Inc.

2 Garthoff, Raymond L., "Unconventional Warfare in Communist Strategy," *Foreign Affairs,* Vol. 40 (July, 1962), pp. 566–575; Bjelajac, Slavko N., "Unconventional Warfare in the Nuclear Era," *ORBIS,* Vol. 4 (Fall, 1960), pp. 323–337.

3 "Two Communist Manifestos," Texts of Statement Issued in the Name of World Communist Leaders Meeting in November of 1960 and of an Address by Premier Khrushchev on January 6, 1961, The Washington Center of Foreign Policy Research Affiliated with the School of Advanced International Studies, The Johns Hopkins University, 1961, pp. 51–52.

4 "The Differences Between Comrade Togliatti and Us," editorial in the *Peking People's Daily,* December 31, 1962. Reprinted in English in *The Washington Post,* January 3, 1963.

5 Department of Defense Appropriations for 1963, Hearings before a Subcommittee of the Committee on Appropriations, House of Representatives, 87th Congress, 2nd Session, Part 2, p. 49.

6 Harriman, W. Averell, "What We are Doing in Southeast Asia," *The New York Times Magazine,* May 27, 1962, p. 7.

7 "A Threat to the Peace—North Vietnam's Effort to Conquer South Vietnam," Part II, Appendices, Department of State Publication 7308, December, 1961.

8 Cf. Dispatch by Robert Trumbull, *The New York Times,* April 28, 1963, p. 3; also dispatch in *The Washington Post,* March 25, 1963, by Richard Hughes.

9 General Vo Nguyen Giap, *People's War People's Army,* Foreign Languages Publishing House, Hanoi, Vietnam, 1961, pp. 106, 159.

10 Cf. discussion of this possibility by John G. Norris, *The Washington Post,* May 16, 1962, p. A-7.

*Chapter 3*

1 Taylor, Maxwell D., *The Uncertain Trumpet,* Harper and Brothers, New York, 1960, p. 138.

2 Halperin, Morton H., "Nuclear Weapons and Limited War," *Conflict Resolution,* Vol. 2 (June, 1961), pp. 146–166.

3 Strachey, John, "Reversing NATO Strategy," *Encounter,* Vol. 18 (April, 1962), p. 14.

4 Quoted in F. O. Miksche, *Atomic Weapons and Armies,* Frederick A. Praeger, New York, 1955, pp. 105–106.

5 Morton Halperin in his bibliography (Footnote 9 of Introduction) cites over 100 items, out of 328, dealing with the problems of limited nuclear war; as his bibliographical notes suggest, many points of view on nuclear-weapons use are represented.

6 Talensky, N., "On the Character of Modern Warfare," *International Affairs* (Moscow) (October, 1960), pp. 23–27; also B. Teplinsky, "The Strategic Concepts of U.S. Aggressive Policy," *International Affairs* (December, 1960), pp. 36–41; see also Soviet Commentary on the Doctrine of Limited Nuclear Wars, translated from the Russian by Leon Gouré, RAND Paper T-82, March 5, 1958.

7 Statement of Secretary of Defense McNamara before the House Armed Services Committee, The Fiscal Year 1964–1968 Defense Program and 1964 Defense Budget (January 30, 1963), Mimeographed Release.

8 *Ibid.*

9 "The Communist Bloc and the Western Allies—The Military Balance, 1962–63," Publication of the Institute for Strategic Studies.

10 *Public Papers of the Presidents, John F. Kennedy, 1961,* U.S. Government Printing Office, Washington, D. C., 1962, p. 538. See also Winston Churchill, *Triumph and Tragedy,* Houghton Mifflin Company, Boston, 1953, p. 492.

11 Kissinger, H. A., "NATO's Nuclear Dilemma," *The Reporter,* Vol. 28

(March 28, 1963), pp. 23–37. See also B. Brodie, "What Price Conventional Capabilities in Europe," *The Reporter*, Vol. 28 (May 23, 1963), pp. 25–33.

[12] Press Conference Statement of President De Gaulle, January 14, 1963; discussed at length by L. J. Halle, "Why De Gaulle Cannot Win," *The New York Times Magazine*, June 2, 1963, p. 9.

[13] Aron, Raymond, *On War*, translated from the French by Terence Kilmartin, *Doubleday Anchor Books*, Doubleday & Company, Inc., Garden City, N.Y., 1958.

[14] *The New York Times*, August 16, 1959, p. 69.

[15] Garthoff, Raymond L., *Soviet Strategy in the Nuclear Age*, Frederick A. Praeger, New York, 1958, pp. 87–89. This view continues, in general; see V. D. Sokolovskii, ed., *Soviet Military Strategy*, translated by H. Dinerstein, L. Gouré, T. W. Wolfe, Prentice-Hall, Inc., Englewood Cliffs, New Jersey, pp. 46, 337, 404, 405. For expression of the opposite view held in the U.S., see B. Brodie, *Strategy in the Missile Age*, Princeton University Press, Princeton, New Jersey, 1959, pp. 165–172, 252–253.

## Chapter 4

[1] Norris, J. G., Report on Anglo–U.S. Air Defense Aid for India, *The Washington Post*, April 11, 1963, p. A-8.

## PART II

## Chapter 5

[1] The descriptions of the armed forces summarized in Table 5.1 and the following discussion are contained in more detailed form in: Marvin L. Worley, Jr., *A Digest of New Developments in Army Weapons, Tactics, Organization and Equipment*, The Stackpole Company, Harrisburg, Pa., 1959; "This Is a Look at the New Atomic Army . . . ," *U.S. News and World Report*, Vol. 42 (January 25, 1957), pp. 50–53; "Organizing and Deploying our Forces," *Army Information Digest*, Vol. 13 (June, 1958), pp. 21–30; H. P. Viccellio, "Composite Air Strike Force," *Air University Quarterly Review*, Vol. 9 (Winter, 1956–1957), pp. 27–38; Maxwell Taylor, *The Uncertain Trumpet*, Harper and Brothers, New York, 1960; Department of Defense Appropriations for 1962, Hearings before the Subcommittee of the Committee on Appropriations, House of Representatives, 87th Congress, 1st Session, Part 2, p. 55; "The Communist Bloc and the Western Alliances, The Military Balance, 1962–1963," The Institute for Strategic Studies, 18 Adam Street, London, November, 1962; also Trade Journals as *Aviation Week and Space Technology, Ordnance, Armor, Naval Institute Proceedings*, and so on.

[2] See, for example, the JCS order to General MacArthur to carry out the "destruction of the North Korean Armed Forces." Robert Leckie, *Conflict: The History of the Korean War*, G. P. Putnam's Sons, New York, 1963, p. 153.

[3] National Security Act of 1947, PL 253, 80th Congress, July 26, 1947. Amended through December 31, 1958, Title I, Sec. 101, 102, Title II, Sec. 212.

[4] Map from *The New York Times*, Sunday, July 8, 1962, p. E-3; © 1962 by the New York Times Company. Reprinted by permission.

[5] Dobson, Charles A., Special Forces, *Army*, VII N 011, pp. 44–52. Also, United States Army, Special Warfare Center brochure entitled *Special Warfare*, published by 1st PSYWAR Bn (B&L), Fort Bragg, N.C.

[6] Announcement by General LeMay, *The New York Times*, April 28, 1963, p. 10, col. 1.

[7] For a detailed description of tactical fighter systems, see C. Brownlow, "F-105D's Limited-War Capability Boosted," *Aviation Week and Space Technology*, Vol. 78 (February 25, 1963), pp. 105–111. See also typical description in Republic

Aviation Corporation advertisement, *Aviation Week and Space Technology,* Vol. 78 (April 1, 1963), p. 17.

### Chapter 6

1 The data which follow have been obtained from:

*The American Oxford Atlas,* Brig. Sir Clinton Lewis, Col. J. D. Campbell, eds., Oxford University Press, New York, 1951.

*Atlas Mira* (World Atlas)—Glavnoy Uprovlenye Goedezzii Kartografyi, MVD, U.S.S.R., Moscow, 1954.

Cressey, G. B., *Asia's Lands and Peoples,* 2nd edition, McGraw-Hill Book Co., New York, 1951.

*The Oxford Economic Atlas of the World,* 2nd edition, Oxford University Press, New York, 1959.

They have been summarized in S. J. Deitchman's "Classification and Quantitative Description of Large Geographic Areas to Define Transport System Requirements," presented at the Symposium on Quantitative Terrain Studies, Annual Meeting of the American Association for the Advancement of Science, Chicago, December 26, 1959.

2 Cf. Northrop, Filmer S. C., *Philosophical Anthropology and Practical Politics,* Macmillan Company, New York, 1960, pp. 123–296.

### Chapter 7

1 See for example:

Dupuy, T. M., "Can America Fight a Limited Nuclear War," ORBIS, Vol. 5 (Spring, 1961), pp. 31–42.

Gavin, J. M., "Cavalry, and I Don't Mean Horses," *Harper's Magazine,* Vol. 208 (April, 1954), pp. 54–60.

———— "Why Limited War?" *Ordnance,* Vol. 42 (March–April, 1958), pp. 809–813.

Kintner, W. R., and G. C. Reinhardt, *Atomic Weapons in Land Combat,* Military Service Publishing Co., Harrisburg, Pa., 2nd edition, 1954.

Lapp, R., *The New Force,* Harper and Brothers, New York, 1953.

Miksche, F. O., *Atomic Weapons and Armies,* Frederick A. Praeger, New York, 1955.

Mataxis, Col. T. C., and Lt. Col. S. L. Goldberg, *Nuclear Tactics, Weapons and Firepower in the Pentomic Division, Battle Group and Company,* The Military Service Publishing Company, Harrisburg, Pa., 1958.

Patton, Capt. George S., "Operation Crusader," *Armor,* Vol. 67 (May–June, 1958), pp. 6–19.

Watson, Mark S., "Can We Limit an 'A-War', The Lessons of Sagebrush", *Nation,* Vol. 181 (December 24, 1955), pp. 550–551.

2 Ruppenthal, R. G., *U.S. Army in World War II, The European Theatre of Operations, Logistical Support of the Armies,* Vol. I, U.S. Government Printing Office, Washington, D. C., 1953, pp. 490–491.

3 Miksche, *op. cit.,* pp. 110–116.

4 Patton, *op. cit.*

5 The author is indebted to Mr. Douglas B. Dahm of Cornell Aeronautical Laboratory, Inc., Buffalo, New York, for his suggestion of this concept of a nuclear land war.

6 *Soviet Military Strategy,* edited by V. D. Sokolovskii, translated by H. Dinerstein, L. Gouré, T. W. Wolfe, Prentice-Hall, Inc., Englewood Cliffs, N.J., pp. 343–344, 410–417.

7 See, for example, J. Davison, "Tank Killers are Getting Deadlier," *NATO Journal,* Vol. 3 (October, 1962), p. 28.

## NOTES

### Chapter 9

### PART III

[1] Stanley, Timothy W., *American Defense and National Security,* Public Affairs Press, Washington, D. C., 1956, pp. 38–60.

[2] Based on a comprehensive organization chart showing the organization for "Science and Technology in the Federal Government," published by National Science Foundation and Official Federal Government Organization Documents, distributed by the Committee on Government Operations, U.S. Senate, April 1, 1963.

[3] The extraordinarily complex process of providing weapons systems is described in Merton J. Peck and Frederic M. Scherer, *The Weapons Acquisition Process: An Economic Analysis,* Division of Research Graduate School of Business Administration, Harvard University, Boston, 1962.

[4] Department of Defense Appropriations for 1962, Hearings before the Subcommittee of the Committee on Appropriations, 87th Congress, 1st Session, Part 3, p. 201.

[5] *Ibid.,* Part 4, pp. 200–202.

[6] Hitch, C. J., and R. N. McKean, *The Economics of Defense in the Nuclear Age,* Harvard University Press, Cambridge, Mass., 1960, is an excellent example.

[7] See, for example, *ibid.,* Chapter 9; Charles Hitch, "Uncertainties in Operations Research," *Operations Research,* The Journal of the Operations Research Society of America, Vol. 8 (July–August, 1960), pp. 437–445; Douglas L. Brooks, "Choice of Pay-offs for Military Operations of the Future," *Operations Research,* The Journal of the Operations Research Society of America, Vol. 8 (March–April, 1960), pp. 159–168; E. S. Quade, The RAND Corporation, "Pitfalls in Military Systems Analysis," presented at Symposium on the Methodology of Weapons Systems Decisions, November 26, 1962, Meeting of the Electronic Industries Association, San Francisco, California.

[8] Address of Asst. Secretary of Defense Charles J. Hitch before the 22nd National Meeting of the Operations Research Society of America, Philadelphia, November 7, 1962.

[9] Malcolm, D. G., J. H. Roseboom, C. E. Clark, W. Fazar, "Application of a Technique for Research and Development Program Evaluation," *Operations Research,* The Journal of the Operations Research Society of America, Vol. 7 (September–October, 1959), pp. 646–669.

[10] Hitch and McKean, *op. cit.,* p. 56; also address by Hitch before 22nd National Meeting of the Operations Research Society of America, Philadelphia, November 7, 1962.

### Chapter 10

[1] From statement by Secretary of Defense McNamara on the 1964 Budget, before the House Armed Services Committee, The Fiscal Year 1964–1968 Defense Program and 1964 Defense Budget, January 30, 1963, Mimeographed release, Tables 6 and 7.

[2] Ramo, S., R. W. Porter, E. P. Wheaton, A. R. Kantrowitz, "What the Future Holds," a panel discussion in *Space Technology,* edited by H. S. Seifert, John Wiley & Sons, Inc., New York, 1959, Chapter 33, pp. 33–01, 33–19.

### Chapter 11

[1] Department of Defense Appropriations for 1962, Hearings before the Subcommittee of The Committee on Appropriations, 87th Congress, 1st Session, Part 3, pp. 196–197.

2 Statement by Secretary of Defense McNamara on the 1964 budget before the House Armed Services Committee, The Fiscal Year 1964–1968 Defense Program and 1964 Defense Budget, January 30, 1963, Mimeographed release, p. 63.

3 General Maxwell Taylor, in "Security Will Not Wait," *Foreign Affairs,* Vol. 39 (January, 1961), p. 179, states that the Army at that time was still largely equipped with World War II equipment.

4 von Karman, T., "What Price Speed? Specific Power Required for Propulsion of Vehicles," with G. Gabrielli, *Collected Works of Theodore von Karman,* Academic Press, New York, 1956, Vol. IV—1940–1951, pp. 399–413.

5 Churchill, Winston, *The Grand Alliance,* Houghton Mifflin Company, Boston, 1951, pp. 616, 653–654.

6 Morison, E. E., "A Case Study in Innovation," printed in *Frontiers in Science,* edited by E. Hutchings, Jr., Basic Books, New York, 1958, p. 333.

7 *Ibid,* pp. 329–338.

## Chapter 12

1 Department of Defense Appropriations for 1962, Hearings before the Subcommittee of the Committee on Appropriations, 87th Congress, 1st Session, Part 3, pp. 211–219.

2 *Ibid,* p. 214.

## Chapter 13

1 Ruppenthal, R. G., *U.S. Army in World War II, The European Theatre of Operations, Logistical Support of the Armies,* Vol. I, U.S. Government Printing Office, Washington, D. C., 1953, pp. 305–327.

2 Progress in this drive is summarized by Ruppenthal, *ibid.,* pp. 475–481.

3 Patton, Capt. George S., "Operation Crusader," *Armor,* Vol. 67 (May–June, 1958), pp. 6–19.

4 Department of Defense Appropriations for 1963, Hearings before a Subcommittee of the Committee on Appropriations, House of Representatives, 87th Congress, 2nd Session, Part 2, p. 64.

5 Ruppenthal, *op. cit.,* p. 515.

6 Department of Defense Appropriations for 1962, Hearings before the Subcommittee of the Committee on Appropriations, 87th Congress, 1st Session, Part 4, p. 113; Marvin L. Worley, Jr., *A Digest of New Developments in Army Weapons, Tactics, Organization and Equipment,* The Stackpole Company, Harrisburg, Pa., 1959, pp. 142–147.

7 Hibbard, H. L., and R. R. Heppe, "Concept and Development of a Simple, Stable and Economical VTOL Vehicle," *Aerospace Engineering,* Vol. 21 (February, 1962), pp. 16–23.

8 Merriam, Robert E., *Battle of the Bulge,* Ballantine Books, Inc., New York, pp. 102–147.

9 News reports of the fighting in South Vietnam for the period January 1, 1962, to December 31, 1963, indicate that of approximately twenty-six helicopters hit by enemy fire, seven were forced down, and of those it is indicated that three were wrecked and could not be recovered.

## Chapter 16

1 See Ryan, Cornelius, *The Longest Day,* Simon and Schuster, Inc., New York, 1959.

2 Hendricks, James D., "463L System Integrates Cargo Handling," *Aviation Week and Space Technology,* Vol. 77 (July 11, 1962), pp. 56–64.

3 The Role of the U.S. Merchant Marine in National Security, Project WALRUS

Report by the Panel on Wartime Use of the U.S. Merchant Marine, National Academy of Sciences—National Research Council Publication 748, Washington, D. C., 1959, pp. 10, 36–40.

4 *Ibid.,* pp. 16–21.

5 Department of Defense Appropriations for 1963, Hearings before a Subcommittee of the Committee on Appropriations, House of Representatives, 87th Congress, 2nd Session, Part 2, pp. 53, 59, 151.

6 See, for example, the experience of seasoned men, *Merrill's Marauders, February–May, 1944,* Military Intelligence Division, U.S. War Department, June 4, 1945, p. 114.

7 "The Communist Bloc and the Western Alliances, The Military Balance, 1962–1963," The Institute for Strategic Studies, London, November, 1962, p. 26.

8 White House Announcement, August 8, 1958, printed in *The New York Times,* August 9, 1958, p. 7.


## PART V

### Chapter 17

1 Composite Report of the President's Committee to Study the United States Military Assistance Program, W. H. Draper, Chairman, August 17, 1959, Vol. I, pp. 8–9.

2 Scofield, J., "Netherlands New Guinea," *National Geographic Magazine,* Vol. 121 (May, 1962), p. 587.

3 Sulzberger, C. L., *The New York Times,* January 4, 1961, p. 32, and February 11, 1962, p. 22.

4 Murray, Col. J. C., "The Anti-Bandit War," *Marine Corps Gazette,* Vol. 38 (January–May, 1954), especially May, 1954.

5 Morgenthau, Hans, "A Political Theory of Foreign Aid," *The American Political Science Review,* Vol. 56 (June, 1962), pp. 301–309.


### Chapter 18

1 Guderian, General Heinz, *Panzer Leader* (abridged), translated by Constantine Fitzgibbon, Ballantine Books, New York, 1957, p. 72.

2 Quoted in F. O. Miksche, *Atomic Weapons and Armies,* Frederick A. Praeger, New York, 1955.

3 Strachey, John, "Reversing NATO Strategy," *Encounter,* Vol. 18 (April, 1962), pp. 8–19.

4 Reproduced from S. Deitchman, "A Lanchester Model of Guerrilla Warfare," *Operations Research,* Vol. 10 (November–December, 1962), p. 821.

5 UPI dispatch in *The Washington Post,* July 2, 1962.

6 General Vo Nguyen Giap, *People's War People's Army,* Foreign Languages Publishing House, Hanoi, Vietnam, 1961, p. 159.

7 Cf. "The Communist Bloc and the Western Alliance, The Military Balance, 1962–1963," The Institute for Strategic Studies, London, November, 1962, p. 26.


### Chapter 19

1 Composite Report of the President's Committee to Study the United States Military Assistance Program, W. H. Draper, Chairman, August 17, 1959, Vol. I, pp. 151–152.

2 Quoted in *ibid.,* p. 170.

3 Report to the Congress of the United States, Summary of Reviews of the Maintenance and Supply Support of Army Equipment Furnished to Far East

NOTES

Countries under the Military Assistance Program, by the Comptroller General of the United States, August, 1962, pp. 3–8.
[4] Draper Report, *op. cit.,* p. 158.

### Chapter 20

[1] Romulo, C. P., *Crusade in Asia: Philippine Victory,* John Day Company, New York, 1955, pp. 148–155.
[2] Bigart, H., article describing problems of Diem Government, its relations with its own people and the United States, *The New York Times,* July 25, 1962, p. 1.
[3] Linton, Ralph, *The Tree of Culture,* Alfred A. Knopf, Inc., New York, 1955, pp. 564–566.

### Chapter 21

[1] *Dictionary of United States Military Terms for Joint Usage,* Joint Chiefs of Staff, JCS Pub. 1, February 1, 1962, Amended July 2, 1962.
[2] Announcement by General LeMay, *The New York Times,* April 28, 1962, p. 10.
[3] *Army-Navy-Air Force Journal and Register,* Vol. 49 (July, 1962), p. 1.

### Chapter 22

[1] See, for example, Slavko Bjelajac, "Unconventional Warfare in the Nuclear Era," *ORBIS,* Vol. 4 (Fall, 1960), pp. 323–337.
[2] Fisher, J., "Yugoslavia's Flirtation with Free Enterprise," *Harper's Magazine,* Vol. 223 (August, 1961), pp. 11–18.
[3] Meyer, Karl E., and Tad Szulc, *The Cuban Invasion,* Frederick A. Praeger, New York, 1962, p. 107.
[4] Alsop, S., "The Lessons of the Cuban Disaster," *The Saturday Evening Post,* Vol. 234 (June 24, 1961), pp. 26, 68–70.
[5] Dulles, A., "The Craft of Intelligence," *Harper's Magazine,* Vol. 226 (April, 1963), p. 168.
[6] Meyer and Szulc, *op. cit.,* pp. 118–132; Rivero, N., *Castro's Cuba: An American Dilemma,* Robert B. Luce, Inc. (David McKay Co., Inc., New York), 1962, pp. 189, 192.
[7] Kraslow, D., interview with Robert Kennedy, published in *The Washington Post,* January 21, 1963, p. A-1.
[8] Alsop, *op. cit.,* p. 70.
[9] Carroll, W., *The New York Times,* April 21, 1961, p. 1.

### Chapter 23

[1] 18, United States Code, Annotated Section 960.
[2] The Mansfield Report on U.S. Aid to S.E. Asia stated that, after $5 billion in aid over 7 years, the situation in the area remained substantially unchanged, and questioned whether the aid should be continued beyond the earliest possible cut-off date.
[3] Documents on American Foreign Relations, 1957, published for Council on Foreign Relations by Harper & Brothers, New York, 1958, pp. 205, 235.
[4] Rostow, W., Address to the Graduating Class, U.S. Army Special Warfare Center, June 28, 1961, printed in Congressional Record, Vol. 108, August 6, 1962, p. A-6013.
[5] Kurzman, D., Discussion of U.S. relations with Peru Junta, *The Washington Post,* January 10, 1963, p. A-15.

264

6 Burke, A., "Power and Peace," *ORBIS,* (a quarterly journal of world affairs published by the Foreign Policy Research Institute of the University of Pennsylvania) Vol. 6 (Summer, 1962), pp. 187–204.

*Conclusion*

1 President Kennedy, statement at press conference, April 3, 1963.
2 Article on expansion of Strategic Army Corps, by E. C. Fay, AP, *The Washington Post,* February 23, 1962; see also Note 5, Chapter 16.
3 *Public Papers of the Presidents, John F. Kennedy, 1961,* U.S. Government Printing Office, Washington, D. C., p. 24.
4 Department of Defense Appropriations for 1963, Hearing before the Subcommittee of the Committee on Appropriations, House of Representatives, 87th Congress, 2nd Session, Part 2, p. 108.
5 Booda, L., "Report on DOD order to Army establishing the Howze Board," *Aviation Week and Space Technology,* Vol. 77 (June 25, 1962), pp. 26–27.
6 Norris, J. G., "Report on Army Air Mobility," *The Washington Post,* October 28, 1962, p. E-3; also W. MacDougall, *The Washington Post,* February 6, 1963, p. A-6, on Air Force objections. See also, *Aviation Week and Space Technology,* Vol. 78 (May 27, 1963), pp. 30–31, on the dispute.
7 AP Dispatch, *The Washington Post,* February 7, 1963, p. A-5.
8 Statement of Secretary McNamara on the 1964 budget before the House Armed Services Committee, The Fiscal Year 1964–1968 Defense Program and 1964 Defense Budget, January 30, 1963, Mimeographed release, pp. 56–58.
9 Department of Defense Appropriations, 1963, *op. cit.,* Part 2, pp. 63–64.
10 *Ibid.,* p. 74.
11 *Ibid.*
12 From a discussion of Tactical Support Aircraft in *Aviation Week and Space Technology.*
13 McLucas, John L., "What's Needed in Tactical Warfare," address before the National Rocket Club, Washington, D. C., April 16, 1963, Mimeographed copy, pp. 3–5.
14 "Aviation Roundup," *Aviation Week and Space Technology,* Vol. 77 (August 6, 1962), p. 25.
15 Department of Defense Appropriations for 1963, *op. cit.,* Part 2, pp. 49–50.
16 Rostow, W. Address to the Graduating Class, U.S. Army Special Warfare Center, June 28, 1961, printed in Congressional Record, Vol. 108, August 6, 1962, p. A-6013.
17 President's Address to the Graduating Class at U.S. Military Academy, June 6, 1962.
18 Remarks of Secretary of Defense Robert S. McNamara at the Annual George C. Marshall Memorial Dinner, Association of the United States Army, Oct. 10, 1962.
19 MacDougall, W. L., *The Washington Post,* May 17, 1962.
20 UPI Dispatch in *The Washington Post,* February 17, 1963, p. A-19.
21 McLucas, *op. cit.,* p. 5.
22 *Wall Street Journal,* Vol. 161 (June 27, 1963), p. 1.
23 Brant, J., UPI dispatch in *The Washington Post,* January 13, 1963; see also, N. Rivero, *Castro's Cuba: An American Dilemma,* Robert B. Luce, Inc. (David McKay Co., New York), 1962, pp. 110–142.

# *Index*

Africa, U.S. military commitment in, 56, 57n
Agency for International Development, 232
Air commando program, 234, 253
Air Force, U.S.: air commando program, 234, 253; inter-Service cooperation, 234–235; limited-war force structure, 68ff; logistics role, 161ff; planning responsibilities, 111ff; *see also* Aircraft, tactical, Airlift
Air-mobile battle groups, 163–172; conventional war use, 169–171; costs of, 171–172; guerrilla battle use, 169, 171
Aircraft, tactical: air-mobile battle groups, 163–172; bombing effectiveness, 179; *Caribou,* 162; command control and fleet composition, 182–183; cost variable in fleet composition, 176–178; fleet composition determinants, 175–183; *Hercules,* 162; logistics role, 161ff; *Mohawk,* 251; nuclear battle role, 91, 93, 95; present fleet composition, 250–251; SSM comparison with, 152–157
Airlift, for strategic response, 72, 193–194, 197, 249–250; *see also* Logistics
Algerian Rebellion, 27, 35, 40, 59, 205–206; belligerents, issues, and resolutions, 17, 22; FLN military objectives, 37–38; force ratios in, 211; "Third Power" involvement, 25
Alliance for Progress, 216, 232, 241
Alliances, U.S. military, 14; outline of, 56, 57n; *see also* NATO
Alsop, Stewart, on unconventional war, 245
Ambush, guerrilla tactic, 100–102
Ammunition, for close-support operations, 181; *see also* Bombing
Angolan Rebellion, 205; belligerents, issues, and scope, 17, 23; "Third Power" involvement, 26.
Antiaircraft defenses, aircraft fleet selection, 179–180; effectiveness, 97–98; *see also* Radar
Antitank weapons, in nonnuclear battle, 98–99
Aqaba, Gulf of, 21, 29
Arab-Israeli conflict, 59; issues and scope, 16, 20; progress, 27–30; "Third Power" involvement, 24; *see also* Israel
Arbenz, Jacob, 238
Armed forces, U.S.: *see* various Services
Army, inter-Service cooperation, 234–235; limited-war force structure, 68ff; planning role, 111ff; technological innovations affect, 77–78; 98–99; *see also* Special Forces
"Army Tactical Mobility Requirements Board," 250
Aron, Raymond, on unconventional war, 32
Assassination, guerrilla tactic, 36

Bases, U.S. overseas: map of, 75; for strategic mobility, 72, 74, 197–198
Bay of Pigs, 17, 23, 239; *see also* Cuba
Belgium, 205
Berlin, 48, 60
Bolivia, 56
Bombing, variable in aircraft fleet studies, 175–179
Brazil, 216, 240
Brodie, Bernard, on NATO, 50
"Brush-fire" concept, 2–3
Budapest, 21
Budget, military: *see* Defense expenditures

Bureau of the Budget, 112, 117
Burke, Admiral Arleigh, on noninterference principle, 246–247

C-130 *Hercules,* 162–163
*Caribou,* 162
Castro, Fidel, 17, 22, 25, 54, 211, 240
Casualties Korean War, 2; in nuclear battle, 94
Central Intelligence Agency, 112
Central Treaty Organization, 56, 57n
China, Communist: 227; civil war, 16, 20, 24, 27; India and, 17, 23, 26, 60; in Korean War, 16, 20, 24, 30–31; in limited-war matrix, 104–106; manpower factor in limited war, 58–59; nuclear war views, 33; Quemoy-Matsu, 16, 21, 25, 27; Tibet and, 17, 25, 27; U.S. alliances against, 56, 57n; "wars of national liberation" view, 33
China, Nationalist: 217; civil war, 16, 20, 24, 27; *see also* Taiwan, Quemoy, Matsu
Civil defense, in guerrilla war, 212, 215, 223
Civil Reserve Air Fleet, 70
Civilians, *see* Popular support, Populations, indigenous
Climate, *see* Environment
Colombia, 17, 23, 26
COMET, 250
Command control, airfleet composition, 182–183; communication structure, 184–191; of local units, 188–191, 214; in nuclear battle, 47, 188; SSM and, 151; structure for limited war, 73
Commander in field, communication and control re, 188–191; nuclear weapons use, 47
Communication, and command control, 184–191; in command structure, 72–73; and force structure, 188–191
Composite Air Strike Force, 193
Concentration, "FEBA", 92–93; "hugging", 91–93, 95; U.S.S.R. on, 97n
Congo Rebellion, issues and scope, 17, 23; "Third Power" involvement, 25
Conventional war, air-mobile battle groups for, 169–170; budget emphasis on, 134–136; characteristics of, 18; force ratios in, 209–214; illustrations of, 27–31; map of threat distribution, 61; military-technological and geographical matrix for, 103–107; nuclear weapons use, 43–52, 90–97; U.S. force structure outline for, 67–74; weaponry for, 97–101
Cost analysis, in defense planning process, 119–121
Costa Rica, 56
Counterguerrilla warfare, *see* Guerrilla tactics, Special Forces, Unconventional war

Country Teams, divided responsibilities in, 230–233
Cuba, 211; Bay of Pigs, 27, 239–240; Castro rebellion, 17, 22–23, 25, 35; quarantine, 17, 19, 23, 26–27, 41
Cyprus, 17, 21, 27, 35, 40
Czechoslovakia, 29

Dahomey, 56
*Dakota* (C-47), 76, 99
DAVY CROCKETT, 95
Decentralization, 214; "parallel" communications, 188–191
Decision making, *see* Command control, Defense planning
Declaration of Rights and Duties of States, 243
Decoys, 98
Defense expenditures, U.S.: 2, 8–9; airmobile battle group costs, 171–172; budget breakdown (1963–1964), 128; Bureau of the Budget, 112, 117; cost ranges of limited-war systems, 133–136; decision levels, 111ff; operations and maintenance costs, 124–128; procurement decisions, 128–131, 134–136; research and development costs, 127–128, 134–136; SSM vs. tactical aircraft costs, 152–154; tactical aircraft cost variables, 176–178; technological plateau problem, 136–139; technological redevelopment problem, 142–144; *see also* Defense planning, Systems analysis
Defense Intelligence Agency, role in defense planning, 112
Defense planning, U.S.: aircraft fleet composition determinants, 175–183; current commitments, 53–56, 57n, 249–254; decision levels, 111–118, 122–124, 253; force size, modernization, R&D decisions, 124–131; geographical and military-technological matrix for, 103–107; inter-Service cooperation, 233–235; Kennedy on limited-war forces, 4–5 MAP, 217–221; military resistance to change, 139–142; for nuclear limited war, 43–52; proximity, logistics, and internal stability as determinants, 58–62; systems analysis problem, 136–139; technological plateau problem, 136–139; technological priorities in, 134–136; for types of limited war, 5–9; *see also* Military assistance
de Gaulle, Charles, 51, 206
Department of Defense, inter-Service cooperation, 233–235; planning and review structure, 111–121; resource allocation decision levels, 122–131
Department of Defense Research and Engineering, 115
Department of State, 232
Deployment, *see* Response, strategic

Deterred wars, characteristics of, 18–19; examples of, 27
Deterrence, 19, 51
Dienbienphu, 24, 39
"Digging-in", 94
Dispersion, in guerrilla war, 102, 211; in nuclear battle, 91–92; U.S.S.R. on, 97n
Dominican Republic, 226
Draper Report, on assistance against overt attack, 203–204; on specialized weapons development, 220; on subversion, 3
Duration, of post-World War II limited wars, 16–17

Econometrics, *see* Systems analysis
Egypt, Arab League, 59; Sinai Campaign, 16, 21, 24, 29–30; Suez Intervention, 16, 21, 24, 29–30; *see also* Arab-Israeli conflict
Eisenhower Doctrine, 56, 57n, 245
Eisenhower, Dwight D., 199
Elite groups, as human factor in limited war, 87–89, 208, 215–216, 227
El Salvador, 56
ELAS Rebels, 16, 20, 207
Environment, effect on limited-war operations: basic types, 81–83; man-made features, 82, 84–86; matrix of enemy and locale, 103–107; natural features, 79–86; political and economic, 208
Escalation, communications and risks of, 188, 190–191; in conventional war, 41–42; in deterred wars, 19; nuclear weapons use and, 46–48, 51
Expenditures, *see* Defense expenditures
Europe, *see* NATO

F-105, 174
F4C, 174
Far East, U.S. military commitment in, 56, 57n
"Fire brigades", 2
Food processing, for unconventional war, 219
Force ratios, in conventional war, 209–210; in unconventional war, 210–214
Force structure, air-mobile units affect, 163–172; communications and control, 188–191; for conventional war, 67–74; Kennedy reorganization, 4–5; for limited war, 67–77, 122–131; nuclear, 91–97; post-Korean, 3; strategic response and, 196–199; technological innovation affects, 77–78, 98–99, 139–142, 148–149; for unconventional war, 214–216, 233–235
France, Algeria and, 17, 22, 37–38, 205–206, 211; Arab-Israeli conflict role, 30; Indochina and, 16, 20, 24, 34; NATO and, 51; Suez Intervention, 16, 21, 24; unconventional war role, 205–207

Gaza, 21, 29
Geography, limited-war determinant, 7, 58, 79–86; post-World War II limited-war areas, 20–23; *see also* Environment
Goa, 17, 22, 25
Great Britain, Arab-Israeli conflict role, 30; Cyprus and, 25, 40–41; India and, 26, 60; Kuwait and, 19, 22; Malaya and, 16, 20, 24, 40–41, 210–211, 214; post-World War II belligerent activities, 16–17, 20–22, 24–25; Suez Intervention, 16, 21, 24, 171; unconventional war role, 206
Greece, 2, 16, 20, 24, 27, 35, 40, 48, 207, 214
Ground forces, *see* Army, Special Forces
Guatemala, 56, 237–238
Guerrilla battle, Air Force role, 234, 253; air-mobile battle group use, 169, 171; counterguerrilla activities, 74–76, 211–216; evolutionary stages in, 36–39; force ratios in, 210–214; intelligence in, 34, 101–102, 223–225; limited-war matrix for, 104–106; "nuclear guerrillas", 95–96; supply problem, 101; tactics of, 100–102; weaponry, 101; *see also* Popular support, Special Forces, Unconventional war

Helicopters, 8, 137; for air-mobile battle groups, 161ff; in guerrilla war, 101, 169
Hitch, Charles, 120
Honduras, 56
Howze, Hamilton, 250
"Hugging", *see* Concentration
Hukbalahap, 16, 20, 34, 214, 226
Human factors, *see* Elite groups, Popular support, Populations, indigenous
Hungary, 16, 19, 21, 25, 39, 244

India, China border war, 17, 23, 26; Goan occupation, 17, 22, 25, 60; Kashmir dispute, 16, 22, 24
Indochinese war, 16, 20, 24, 27, 35, 38, 205–206
Indonesian War for Independence, 2, 27; issues and resolution, 16, 20; "Third Power" involvement, 24
Intelligence, 187; in guerrilla battle, 34, 101–102, 223–225; in nuclear battle, 92
Internal stability, limited-war determinant, 59
Internal wars of subversion, *see* Guerrilla battle, Unconventional war
Iran, 56, 59
Iraq, 16–17, 20, 22, 59
Israel, 56, 59, 87; Sinai campaign, 16, 21, 29–30; *see also* Arab-Israeli conflict

Japan, 56, 87, 227
Jordan, 16, 29, 56

Kashmir Dispute, 16, 20, 24
Katanga, 23, 25
Kennedy, John F., 249; 1962 speech on Cuba, 54; limited-war reassessment, 4–5; NATO policy, 48; on nature of military training, 252–253
Kenya, 16, 21, 24, 35
Khrushchev, Nikita, on unconventional war, 33
Kikuyu, *see* Mau Mau
Kissinger, Henry, on NATO, 50
Korean War, 41, 60; birth of limited-war concept, 2–3; changing objectives in, 30–31; scope and resolution, 16, 20
Kuwait, 17, 19, 22, 25

Laos, civil war, 16, 22, 35, 37–38, 60, 206; U.S. military commitment to, 56, 57n
Larson, Arthur, on unconventional war, 245
Latin America, 204, 207, 216, 227
Lebanon, Marine landing, 16–17, 21, 25, 245; U.S. military commitment to, 56, 57n
Legality, and unconventional war, 242–248
LeMay, General Curtis, 76
Lemnitzer, General Lyman, 50
Lenin, Nicolai, on unconventional war, 32
Limitation of conflict, in Arab-Israeli war, 29; in developed areas, 86; in Korean War, 30–31; and nuclear weapons use, 46–48, 51; *see also* Escalation; Limited war
Limited war, characteristics of, 28; classes of, 6–7, 18–19, 27; command and communications in, 184–191; elite groups and, 87–89, 208, 215–216, 227, 233; environmental determinants in, 79–86; force structure for use in, 67–77, 122–131; geographical and military-technological matrix for, 103–107; human factor in, 87–89; Kennedy reassessment of, 3–5; map of threat distribution, 61; NATO and, 48–52; nuclear weapons use in, 43–52; outline of post-World War II, 16–27; proximity, logistics, and internal stability as determinants of, 58–59; theory, 2–3, 13–15; U.S. military commitment to, 53, 56, 57n, 58; *see also* Conventional war; Defense planning, Force structure; Guerrilla battle; Unconventional war
Lippmann, Walter, on unconventional war, 245
Logistics, air-mobile battle groups and, 166–168; air supply, 161–166; in conventional war, 169–170; environmental features affect, 82; ground supply, 159–161, 162; human factor and, 87; indigenous forces and, 218; limited-war determinant, 58–59; seaborne supply, 96; strategic lift, 192–199; in unconventional war, 169–171, 213

Magsaysay, Ramon, 20, 226
Maintenance, of air-mobile force, 124–125, 166–167; of close-support aircraft, 181; of communications, 185; by indigenous population, 87–89, 219; in nuclear battle, 93
Malaya, 3, 16, 20, 24, 27, 34–35, 40, 210, 214
Manpower, nuclear weapons use, 43–45; in post-World War II limited wars, 16–17; in unconventional war, 209–214; *see also* Force ratios
Mao Tse-tung, on unconventional war, 32
Marine Corps, Kennedy on limited-war duties, 5; limited-war role, 71, 251
Massive retaliation, 3
Matsu, 16, 21, 25, 27
Mau Mau, 16, 21
MAULER, 134
McNamara, Robert, on NATO, 48; on unconventional war, 251–252
Merchant Marine, 196
Mexico, 240
Middle East, conventional war possibilities in, 59; U.S. military commitment in, 56, 57n
Military, indigenous: military assistance problems, 87–89, 215–221, 225, 227; *see also* Elite groups, Special Forces
Military assistance, for conventional wars, 3, 56, 57n; Country Teams, 230–233; Draper Report, 203–204; inter-Service responsibility for, 233–235; professional training for, 228–229; for unconventional war, 39, 56, 57n, 215; *see also* Military Assistance Advisory Groups, Military Assistance Program
Military Assistance Advisory Groups, nature and mission, 76–77, 228–229
Military Assistance Program, organization of, 217; specialized equipment for, 217–221
Military Sea Transport Service, 70
Missiles, surface to surface: DAVY CROCKETT, 95; nuclear escalation and use of, 156–157; PERSHING, 3, 134; tactical aircraft comparison with, 151–157
Mobility, of air-mobile battle groups, 167–169; air resupply and, 161–166; in conventional war, 6, 169–170; ground resupply and, 158–161, 163; in guerrilla war, 169; in nuclear battle, 91–95; *see also* Logistics
*Mohawk*, 251
Morality, and unconventional war, 242–248

Morgenthau, Hans; on elite groups, 208
Morocco, 56
Moslem Army of National Liberation (ALN), 37; *see also* Algerian Rebellion
Motivation, in unconventional war, 219
Mozambique, 205

National Guard, and strategic response, 196–197, 249
National resources, *see* Defense expenditures
National Security Council, role in defense planning, 112, 123
Navy, combat aircraft for, 250–251; inter-Service cooperation, 234–235; limited-war force structure, 68ff; limited-war role, 106, 149; planning responsibilities, 111ff; sealift capabilities, 72, 194, 196, 250; specialized aircraft belief, 175
Negotiation, weapon in unconventional war, 37–38, 49–50
Netherlands, Indonesia and, 16–17, 20, 24; West New Guinea and, 17, 23, 26, 205
Niger, 56
*Nike Zeus,* 3
Noninterference, principle of, 246–248
Norstad, General Lauris, 50
North Atlantic Treaty Organization, 6; force ratios, 209–210; MAP for, 217–218; nuclear forces issue, 44, 48–52; U.S. commitment to, 54, 56; unconventional war role, 204–207.
North Vietnam, *see* Viet Cong, Vietnamese Rebellion
Nuclear war, communications and command in, 188, 190; Communist China on, 33; non-European, 7; SSM and tactical aircraft for, 154–156; tactics, 46, 90–97
Nuclear weapons, limited-war use, 6, 19, 43–52; NATO and, 48–52; theory on tactical use, 90–97
Numerical superiority, *see* Force ratios, Manpower

Operation "Crusader," 95, 159
Operations research, *see* Systems analysis
Overseas bases, *see* Bases, U.S.

Pakistan, Kashmir issue, 16, 20, 56
Panama, 56
Paramilitary units, for unconventional war, 36
Paratroops, 99–100
Participation, issue in unconventional war, 41–42
Pathet Lao, belligerent in Laos, 17, 22, 25
Patton, General George, 161

Peace Corps, 232
PERSHING, 3, 134
Phantom II (F4C), 174, 250
Philippines, 3, 16, 20, 24, 27, 34, 35, 40, 56, 214, 226
Planning, *see* Defense planning
Police, in guerrilla situation, 36, 211–212, 215, 224–226
Policy planning, *see* Defense planning
Popular support, for counterguerrilla activity, 40, 47, 76, 101–102, 215, 224–227; guerrilla need for, 35–37, 101–102, 213; nuclear weapons use and, 45
Populations, indigenous: elite groups, 87–89, 208, 215–216, 227; military, 87–89, 215–221, 225, 227; Special Forces training of, 74–76; technical competence of, 87–89
Port Said, 21
Portugal, 205; Angola and, 17, 23; Goa and, 17, 22
Power plants, control in unconventional war of, 36
President, role in defense planning, 112, 117, 123
Prisoners, in guerilla war, 100
Proximity, limited-war determinant, 58
Public opinion, post-Korean, 2–3; *see also* Popular support
Pusan, 31

Quemoy, 16, 21, 25, 27

Radar, 8, 98, 104, 140
Rainfall, limited-war determinant, 80–83; *see also* Environment
RAND Corporation, 121
Reconnaissance, Air Force, 70, 155–156, 173ff
Research and development, *see* Technology
Reserve Merchant Marine, 70
Reserves, 70, 196–197, *see also* National Guard
Resource allocation, *see* Defense expenditures, Defense planning
Response, strategic: airlift, 194–195, 249–250; force structure changes for, 196–199; overseas bases for, 197–198; reserve readiness, 196–197; sealift, 72, 194–196, 250; turnaround time, 193–196
Rio Pact, 56
"Roles and missions" question, vii
Rostow, W. W., on unconventional war, 243–244, 246–247, 252
Rusk, Dean, 56

Sanctuary, 95
Satellites, U.S.S.R, 50

Saudi Arabia, 56
Science, *see* Defense planning, Technology
Sea warfare, limited-war matrix for, 106; nuclear, 96–97; *see also* Navy sealift, for strategic response, 72, 194, 196, 250
Secret Army Organization, and Algerian rebellion, 22, 25, 37–38
Secretary of Defense, role in defense planning, 112, 115–117, 123
Senegal, U.S. commitment to, 56, 57n
Sinai Campaign, 16, 21, 24, 29–30
Southeast Asia Treaty Organization, 56, 57n, 206
South Vietnam, *see* Vietnam, Republic of
Special Forces, expansion, 253; nature and mission, 74, 76–77, 228–229
Stalin, Josef, 207
Strategy, Korean, 30–31; NATO, 6, 48–52; for nuclear limited war, 43–52; for unconventional war, 33–34, 208
Submarines, 71, 198–199
Subversion, initial tactic in unconventional war, 36–37; U.S. commitments, 56; *see also* Guerrilla battle, Unconventional war
Suez Canal, 16, 21, 24, 29–30, 171
Supply, by air, 99–100, 161–163; for air-mobile battle groups, 166–168; by ground, 159–161, 163; in nuclear battle, 91, 93; by sea, 71, 96; *see also* Airlift, Logistics, Sealift
Surprise, limited-war tactic, 14–15, 100, 193, 219
Surveillance, *see* Intelligence, Reconnaissance
Syria, 16, 29, 59
Systems analysis, operational definition, 118–121; Program Evaluation and Review Technique, 120–121

Tactics, in air warfare, 152–156, 173–183; in guerrilla battle, 100–102; in nuclear battle, 46, 91–97; technological innovations affect, 97–100
Taiwan, 16, 21, 27, 44–45, 60
Targets, in air warfare, 98, 152ff; in nuclear battle, 45–46
Taylor, General Maxwell, 3, 50
Technology, communication and command affected by, 186; cost factor in defense planning, 5–8, 129–131, 134–136, 142–144; force structure and changing, 77–78; 139–142; military assistance and sophisticated, 87–89, 218–221; plateau problem, 136–139; systems analysis, 118–121
Terrain, *see* Environment, Geography
Terror, unconventional war tactic, 36
TFX, 250
*The Uncertain Trumpet*, 3
"Third Powers", outline of limited-war involvements, 24–26

Tibet, 17, 19, 21
Timor, 205
Tito, Josef Broz, 207
Training, military: of air-mobile battle groups, 168–169; limited-war career specialization, 228–229
Transportation, *see* Logistics
Treaty obligations, U.S.: outline of, 56, 57n; *see also* Military assistance, NATO
Tripartite Declaration, 56
Tunisia, 59
Turkey, 56
Turnaround times, of planes, 193–194; of ships, 193–194

Uncertainty, limited-war factor, 14–15; in nuclear exchange, 47; *see also* Escalation
Unconventional war, Aron on, 32; characteristics of, 18; Chinese statement on, 33; counteroffensive problems, 236–241; evolutionary stages of, 35–39; force ratios for, 209–214; force structure reorganization for, 214–216, 233–235; illustrations of, 28; Kennedy on, 4–5, 252–253; Khrushchev on, 33; legality and morality in, 242–248; map of threat distribution, 61; matrix of factors in, 103–107; McNamara on, 251–252; negotiation in, 37–38, 49–50; NATO powers and, 204–206; Rostow on, 252; U.S. commitments to, 56, 57n; U.S. current planning for, 249–254; *see also* Guerrilla battle, Limited war, Special Forces
Union of Soviet Socialist Republics, Arab-Israeli conflict role, 29–30; Cuba and, 17, 23, 26, Hungary and, 16, 19, 21, 25; Khrushchev on unconventional war, 33; Korean War role, 20, 24, 31; limited-war determinants of, 58–59; in limited-war matrix, 104–106; nuclear battle concepts, 45–46, 49, 51, 97n; unconventional war involvements, 16–19, 21, 23–24, 26
United Arab Republic, *see* Egypt
United Nations, Africa and, 205; Arab-Israeli conflict and, 29–30; Declaration of Rights and Duties of States, 243; Korean War involvement, 16, 20, 31; limited-war role, 14, 16–17, 20–23; regional defense arrangements, 57n–58n
United States, Korean War objectives, 30–31; limited-war commitments, 56, 57n; NATO nuclear issue, 44ff; post-World War II limited-war engagements, 16–26; Vietnamese war objectives, 41–42; *see also* Defense planning
United States Information Agency, 232
United States Strike Command, 70, 249–250

Venezuela, 216, 227

Viet Cong, 17, 23, 26

Vietnamese Rebellion, 17, 23, 35, 37–39, 60; force ratios in, 211; U.S. military commitment to, 26, 39, 41–42, 56, 57n, 226

Village self-defense, *see* Civil defense, counterguerrilla tactic


War, *see* Conventional war, Deterred war, Guerrilla battle, Nuclear war, Unconventional war

Wars of National liberation, *see* Unconventional war

Warsaw Pact, 50

Weaponry, cost factor in defense planning, 125–126; force structure and, 4–5; technological innovations in, 77–78, 98–99; in unconventional war, 218–221

Weather, effect on air warfare, 168, 176

West New Guinea, 17, 21, 26, 205


Yemen, 17, 22, 25, 59

Yugoslavia, 48 207